D0375551

Polling and the Public

What Every Citizen Should Know

Fifth Edition

Herbert Asher
Ohio State University

CQ PRESS

A Division of Congressional Quarterly Inc.
Washington, D.C.

CQ Press
A Division of Congressional Quarterly Inc.
1414 22nd Street, N.W.
Washington, D.C. 20037

(202) 822-1475; (800) 638-1710

www.cqpress.com

Printed and bound in the United States of America

05   04   03   02   01   5   4   3   2   1

Cover design: Dennis Anderson

♾ The paper used in this publication meets the minimum requirements of the American National Standard for Information Sciences—Permanence of Paper for Printed Library Materials, ANSI Z39.48-1992.

Library of Congress Cataloging-in-Publication Data

Asher, Herbert B.
    Polling and the public : what every citizen should know / Herbert Asher.—
5th ed.
        p. cm.
    Includes bibliographical references and index.
    ISBN 1-56802-582-3 (alk. paper)
    1. Public opinion polls.   2. Public opinion—United States.   I. Title.

HM1236 .A75   2001
303.3′8′0973—dc21
                                                                    2001023140

To the memory of my parents,
Joseph and Betty Asher

Contents

Preface

Since the last edition of this book was published, the prominence and pervasiveness of public opinion polling in the United States has grown. Citizens are presented with the results of public opinion polls on a wide variety of topics, be it presidential misbehavior, the elections of 2000, the Elián Gonzáles saga, the Middle East peace process, welfare reform, election reform, consumer confidence, or sexual behavior in America. Because polls are closely followed by political leaders and media elites as well as by many citizens, polls—and the reporting of poll results—are having a growing influence on discourse and decision making in every part of society and at all levels of government.

Despite their prominence, polls are still not well understood. My central objective in first writing this book was to help citizens become wiser consumers of public opinion polls. In revising the book for a fourth time, I have maintained that objective. The prevalence of public opinion polls and their frequent misuse make it imperative that citizens be able to evaluate critically the various assertions made on the basis of the polls. Candidates for public office, incumbents, and many different public and private groups sponsor public opinion surveys to advance their own objectives. As polling data become more central to political and civic discourse, it is more important that citizens understand the factors that can influence poll results.

Chapter 1 explains the types of polls, their importance, and Americans' varying attitudes toward public opinion research. Chapters 2–5 address the methodological aspects of polling, such as nonattitude assessment, the wording and ordering of questions, sampling techniques, and interviewing procedures. These topics are treated in a nontechnical fashion with numerous examples that illustrate major points. Chapters 6–8 are more analytical, focusing on how the media cover polls, the role of polls in campaigns and elections, and the interpretation of polls. The last chapter considers the place of polls in a democratic polity.

This book should be readily understandable to a diverse audience—college students taking courses in American politics, public opinion, communications, and journalism, as well as practitioners in the fields of journalism and campaign management. In addition, the general public should find it a helpful guide to evaluating the methods and merits of public opinion polls. As with earlier editions, no statistical expertise is assumed or required.

I appreciate the assistance of Charles Smith in the preparation of this fifth edition. And I am grateful to Jay A. DeSart, Paul Freedman, and Thom Yantek, who offered helpful revision suggestions as I planned this new edition. The staff of CQ Press did its usual fine job of editing and getting the book into print in a timely fashion. Finally, I express my deep appreciation to the various polling organizations and newspapers that are so generous in sharing their surveys with the broader public. They provided many of the substantive examples I used here. In particular, the CBS News/*New York Times* polls and the ABC News/*Washington Post* surveys have been invaluable resources in the preparation of this and previous editions, as have many of the newspaper articles about these polls, particularly those by Richard Morin.

Herb Asher

☑ 1 Polling and the Public

Americans today are being bombarded with the results of public opinion polls sponsored by the news media, candidates for public office, incumbent officeholders, and many different public and private organizations. As a result, Americans are learning more than ever about their own attitudes as well as the views of citizens of other nations. In recent years, the demise of the Soviet Union and its empire and of totalitarian regimes in other parts of the world have produced a flourishing polling industry that regularly assesses citizens' views in the new democracies about issues of public policy and election preferences. For example, public opinion polls conducted in March 1997 in Poland, Hungary, and the Czech Republic queried citizens about whether their country should join the North Atlantic Treaty Organization (NATO). Poles were the most supportive of joining NATO and Czechs the least enthusiastic (Spolar 1997). And in older democracies throughout the world, American-style campaign techniques, including the widespread use of public opinion polling, have become commonplace. For example, in the 1999 Israeli elections the victorious Barak campaign employed the services of various Democratic Party operatives from the United States. One was polling practitioner Stanley Greenberg, who had served as President Bill Clinton's pollster in the 1992 presidential election and in the early years of his administration (Nagourney 2000).

In the United States, polls are increasingly being used not only to inform Americans about what their compatriots and citizens of other nations believe, but also to convince and even manipulate Americans in ways advantageous to the polls' sponsors. Therefore the aim of this book is to help citizens become more astute judges of polls so they will not be misled or deceived by assertions made on the basis of polling data. This objective will be accomplished by explaining in nontechnical language the various factors that can affect poll results—such as question wording, sampling techniques, and interviewing procedures—and by critiquing various types and uses of polls.

The Importance of Polls

Why should citizens become more astute consumers of polls? One reason is simply to avoid being manipulated by those who use polls inappropriately to promote their own ends. Other reasons are more positive. Some people make major economic and career decisions on the basis of public opinion polling. For example, the businessperson who commissions a survey on customer preferences or the television station manager who underwrites a survey on audience demographics will use the information obtained to make important decisions about service or programming. Likewise, potential candidates for public office may commission a poll to assess their electoral prospects before deciding whether to run. In these examples the polling is likely to be conducted by a commercial polling organization. But the more knowledgeable the businessperson and the would-be candidate are about polls, the better able they are to communicate their objectives and requirements to the survey organization and to apply the results of the survey to their own decision making.

Polls also are important for the average citizen. Through the substantial coverage the media give polls, citizens can compare their own beliefs with their compatriots' and determine whether others share their views. As citizens use the polls in this manner, they need to be aware of the factors that affect the poll results so they do not accept or reject them too quickly or uncritically.

Polling plays an integral role in political events at the national, state, and local levels. In any major event or decision, poll results are sure to be a part of the news media's coverage and the decision makers' deliberations. How should an international crisis, such as the Iraqi invasion of Kuwait, be resolved? How should the United States respond to events in Bosnia or the Middle East or the Ivory Coast? Should President Clinton be removed from office because of the Monica Lewinsky scandal? Should Elián González be reunited with his father? Should state taxes be raised? What is the best location for a new library in the community? Polls may influence how politicians respond to such issues, and citizens need to understand the essentials of public opinion polling to follow all aspects of the polls.

Finally, public opinion polls are playing an ever-larger role in political discourse in the United States because of the improved technology of polling, the introduction of courses in polling methodology in journalism curricula, the widespread assumption (challenged by Benjamin Ginsberg—see Chapter 9) that polls are the best way to measure public opinion, and the belief that public opinion polls are instruments of democracy because they allow everyone's views to be represented. All of these factors ensure that future political debate on issues will be characterized by even greater reliance on the polls. To participate in a political debate in an informed and analytical fashion, Americans will have to come to grips with public opinion polls—a useful tool of government and a valuable source of information to citizens and leaders alike.

The Pervasiveness of Polls

That public opinion polling is a growth industry in the United States is undeniable. The polls most familiar to Americans are those conducted for and reported by the major communications media. For example, each of the three major television networks sponsors polls in collaboration with a print medium: CBS News with the *New York Times,* ABC News with the *Washington Post,* and NBC News with the *Wall Street Journal.* Likewise, the major news magazines often commission polls on national issues. Thus *Newsweek* regularly employs Princeton Survey Research Associates, *Time* (often in conjunction with CNN) uses Yankelovich Partners Inc., and *U.S. News and World Report* hires the Tarrance Group and Lake Sosin Snell and Associates.

The pervasiveness of polls is clearly demonstrated by their widespread use in major news stories. An examination of the stories featured on the covers of the three leading U.S. news magazines—*Time, Newsweek,* and *U.S. News and World Report*—between 1995 and 2000 reveals that public opinion polls played a big role in about one-third of all the cover stories. Moreover, many of the other stories incorporated polling data. Readers of these magazines, then, would be more astute judges of the reporting if they were knowledgeable about the strengths and weaknesses of public opinion polls.

The proliferation of polls also is evident in television and newspaper coverage. Typically, these polls survey citizens about their views on political issues, candidates, and incumbents (especially the president); their preferences about possible courses of government action; and their general attitudes toward politics and the political process. Major national polls also cover topics such as tax reform, social values, hostage crises, abortion, foreign policy, the budget deficit, Supreme Court nominations, and countless other political and nonpolitical matters. In 1994 one of the prime topics of the polls was health care reform, with all sides on the issue trying to use poll results to advance their respective positions. In 1996 and 1997 polling on welfare reform was widespread, and in 1998 and early 1999 polling on the impeachment of President Clinton was commonplace.

Sometimes survey questions seem to violate standards of good taste. After President Ronald Reagan's surgery for what turned out to be colon cancer, a survey commissioned by *Time* asked respondents how serious they thought the president's health problems were, and both *Time* and an ABC News/*Washington Post* poll asked Americans whether they thought the president was likely to complete his term. A *Newsweek* poll inquired whether citizens were concerned that the president might not "be able to meet the demands of a second term." Many citizens undoubtedly had questions in their own minds about the president's health, and therefore the media thought their readers and viewers would be interested in reading about public opinions on the matter. Ghoulish speculation was the result.

Indeed, when an issue or event becomes visible and especially controversial, the public is usually surveyed to assess its reaction. For example, in 1994 when it became clear that the criminal trial of O. J. Simpson fascinated Americans, many polls were conducted to assess citizens' reactions to the trial. Particularly intriguing to reporters were the sharp racial differences in beliefs about Simpson's guilt or innocence. More recently, when a doctor assisted a woman diagnosed with Alzheimer's disease to commit suicide, many polls were conducted on topics such as euthanasia, living wills, and death with dignity. Likewise, when cloning and adultery became major news stories in 1997 and 1998, public opinion polls about these topics soon followed.

Almost any topic seems amenable to polling. For example, the January 31, 2000, issue of *U.S. News and World Report* featured a story on "hell" that described a public opinion poll in which a sample of Americans was asked whether there was a hell (64 percent said yes) and what they thought hell was like. Some poll topics may seem more frivolous. As the final episode of the television show *Cheers* neared in 1993, the *Times Mirror* Center for the People and the Press queried Americans about such weighty topics as whether Sam should have stayed single, married Diane, or married Rebecca. The survey also asked Americans who their favorite *Cheers* character was and which character they would like to see continue in his or her own series (Mills 1993). Clearly, polling has become pervasive.

The prominent national polls are complemented by the visible and reputable state and local polls that focus on specific state and local matters, and on national affairs as well. For example, the *Daily News* (New York) and "Eyewitness News" (produced by the ABC-TV affiliate in New York City) have polled New Yorkers over the years on their views of the New York police, New York mayors, the likelihood of the Yankees and Mets baseball teams making the World Series, and other matters of local concern. Likewise, the *New York Times,* in conjunction with WCBS-TV, has conducted extensive studies of race relations in New York City. Many states have first-rate polling organizations, often affiliated with a university or a major news medium. For example, the Eagleton Institute at Rutgers University, working with the *Newark Star-Ledger,* surveys New Jersey residents about their state government and about New Jersey as a place to live. Publications such as *Public Opinion Quarterly* and *Public Perspective* provide summaries of state and local (as well as national) poll results.

The polls described thus far are certainly the most prominent and probably the most credible to the American public. Their prominence stems from the often-substantial media coverage their results receive; their credibility derives from the public's perception that they are conducted scientifically and that the media and other entities that sponsor the polls are themselves legitimate and objective. The most critical factor in making these polls scientific (and thus valid) is a carefully selected sample of respondents (most often 1,000 to 1,500 persons); after all, no polling organization can interview the entire adult American population of more than 200 million. From such a sample, the public and media can generalize (within certain limits to be discussed later) from the specific sample to the larger population from which the sample was drawn.

Commissioned Polls

Although polls by the major news media seem the most prominent, they are only a tiny fraction of the public opinion polling done in the United States. Many other organizations commission polls for purposes other than informing citizens. For example, many companies may hire a polling firm to gauge the pubic response to their products, and academic investigators may use surveys in their research. Some of such polls are of high quality; others are not. The results of these polls may not attract much public notice, but they still can affect the lives of individual citizens.

Examples of Commissioned Polls

An excellent example of a commissioned poll was the one paid for by the Internal Revenue Service (IRS) in 1984 to study the problem of tax cheating. Among the items in the survey were these statements with which the respondent was supposed to agree or disagree:

It's not so wrong to hold back a little bit on taxes since the government spends too much anyway.

The present tax system benefits the rich and is unfair to the ordinary working man or woman.

Since a lot of rich people pay no taxes at all, if someone like me under-pays a little, it's no big deal. (Sussman 1984b)

In the survey 19 percent of respondents admitted cheating on their re-turns; young, upwardly mobile professionals were the most likely to cheat. The IRS study also investigated ways to reduce cheating and found that Americans strongly rejected the use of paid informants to catch cheaters (Sussman 1985c). Although the honesty of tax cheaters' responses to questions about tax cheating is questionable, the IRS probably gained from this survey some useful insights into the magnitude of the cheating problem and the feasibility of alternative solutions.

The IRS study is typical of thousands commissioned by public and private bodies to address specific concerns. Some of these surveys are based on national samples; others are based on specialized samples that are more appropriate to the research questions being addressed. For example, a promotional brochure of the Gallup Social Science Research Group, a division of the Gallup Organization, lists some of the social research surveys it has conducted. These include:

American College of Surgeons. A national personal interview survey of the general public and members of Congress to measure opinions related to surgeons and surgical care.

New Jersey State Lottery Commission. A marketing survey using telephone interviews to . . . aid policymakers in reaching decisions regarding future growth of the New Jersey State Lottery. . . .

Catholic Press Association. A television survey of readers of local diocesan newspapers and religious magazines on attitudes toward religious media.

American Jewish Committee. Semiannual surveys of the national general public on attitudes related to Israel.

Japan Embassy. An annual national personal interview survey of the general public and mail survey of opinion leaders on attitudes toward Japan.

Commissioned surveys of this type are likely to be high-quality enterprises mainly because the sponsors have a genuine need for accurate information to address some organizational goal or problem. To that end, the sponsors employ a reputable firm, such as the Gallup Organization, to design and conduct the survey and perhaps to analyze the data and interpret the results. Many other groups, however, conduct surveys for a different reason—not to address a public concern scientifically and objectively, but instead to promote a certain position and to convince the public of the wisdom of that stand. To that end, the sponsors design the survey to yield desired results. This is most often accomplished by the use of highly loaded questions, although more subtle methods also are used. Sometimes in such surveys the samples of people interviewed are skewed to ensure a predetermined outcome. In many cases, the poll itself is secondary to the real aim of the group: to raise money to support its objectives.

With the advent of computerized mailings, many organizations have entered the business of raising funds and conducting polls through direct mail. Most often the polling becomes a device to generate donations—that is, the sponsoring organization encourages recipients of the mailings to make their views known *and* to contribute to a good cause. Many of these appeals come from political groups, some of them broad in scope, such as the Democratic and Republican Parties, and others narrower in focus, such as the Wilderness Society, the Union of Concerned Scientists, the National Right to Work Committee, the Religious Coalition for Abortion Rights, and many, many others. For example, in 1998 the Republican National Committee mailed a "Critical Issues Advisory Survey" to thousands of potential contributors on the GOP's mailing lists. The survey included a few questions as well as a direct appeal for funds (see page 8). Until the early 1990s, the Democrats lagged behind the GOP in the use of computerized mailings. But the "2000 Campaign Strategy Survey" sponsored by the Democratic Congressional Campaign Committee demonstrates that they too had learned the advantages of attaching a poll to a fund-raising effort (see page 9).

Indeed, many groups mail extremely biased literature and then ask respondents for their opinions. Consider these examples. The Committee Against Government Waste has asked, "Before you received this letter, were you aware of the gross mismanagement and waste of funds in the U.S. Department of Defense's purchase of parts?" The American Farmland Trust has asked, "Were you aware of the gravity of the problem of our vanishing farmland before receiving this mailing?" In case the literature accompanying the poll does not convince respondents of the correctness of the group's position, a carefully constructed question or statement may achieve the same end, as illustrated by the following questionnaire items and their sponsoring organizations:

> Are you in favor of allowing construction union czars the power to shut down an entire construction site because of a dispute with a single contractor, thus forcing even more workers to knuckle under to union agents? *National Right to Work Committee*

> Were you aware that a good part of why America has been leaning toward nuclear weapons is due to inflated prices of conventional weapons parts? *Committee Against Government Waste*

Dear Republican Supporter,

Your name was selected to receive this ELECTION YEAR CRITICAL ISSUES ADVISORY SURVEY due to your long-standing commitment to the principles of the Republican Party. As the Chairman of the Republican National Committee, I need your opinions and advice as I and my advisors plan strategy for this year's all-important mid-term elections.

Your answers to this ELECTION YEAR CRITICAL ISSUES ADVISORY SURVEY will be tabulated with the answers of other grassroots Republicans across our nation. The confidential results are vital and will give me invaluable information. Your participation is crucial for valid results. Thank you.

---

1. Republicans in Congress believe that Americans pay too much of their hard-earned money in taxes. They want to lower taxes to allow Americans to keep more of what they earn and to help the economy grow. Liberal Democrats and their allies think taxes should be raised. Do you agree with the Republicans who want to cut taxes?

○ AGREE   ○ DISAGREE   ○ UNDECIDED

2. Republicans believe that government has grown too big and too intrusive into our lives. They want to scale government back, getting it off our backs and out of our wallets. Liberal Democrats want bigger and ever-more-intrusive government. Do you agree with Republicans that government should be smaller and less intrusive?

○ AGREE   ○ DISAGREE   ○ UNDECIDED

3. Republicans believe that the American family is the building block of our nation. They want to make certain that no government action harms the family and want to make every effort to strengthen the family unit. Liberal Democrats believe that government is more important than the family and is better able to take care of basic needs than the family. Do you agree with Republican efforts to strengthen the family?

registration number [   ]

○ AGREE   ○ DISAGREE   ○ UNDECIDED

👉 **Don't forget to validate your survey on reverse**

The upcoming mid-term elections are crucial to the future of our nation. The liberal Democrat Party will go all-out to retake the Congress. Your support of the Republican National Committee and its Chairman, Jim Nicholson, is critical. Your completed ELECTION YEAR CRITICAL ISSUES ADVISORY SURVEY will give Chairman Nicholson an important, confidential view of the opinions of grassroots Republican supporters like you.

SURVEY VALIDATION
Please initial here to validate your answers.

With your completed ELECTION YEAR CRITICAL ISSUES ADVISORY SURVEY, please enclose a contribution in acceptance of your Sustaining Membership to the Republican National Committee. Both your advice as given on your completed SURVEY and your financial assistance of the RNC are critical. Please reply today.

Thank you for your support.

○ Yes, I have completed my ELECTION YEAR CRITICAL ISSUES ADVISORY SURVEY and initialed in the box above to validate my answers.

○ I accept your invitation to become a Sustaining Member of the Republican National Committee. Enclosed is my contribution in acceptance of my Sustaining Membership in the amount of:

○ No, despite the importance of this project, I cannot lend my financial support at this time. (Please try to send at least $5 to cover the cost of processing and tabulating your SURVEY.)

☐ $500   ☐ $250   ☐ $100   ☐ $50   ☐ $25   ☐ $15   ☐ other $_____

Please make check payable to: Republican National Committee. You may make your gift in acceptance of your Sustaining Membership by credit card if you choose by filling out the following information: Type of Credit Card: ☐ Personal ☐ Corporate   ☐ Visa ☐ Mastercard ☐ American Express ☐ Discover

Credit Card Number: _____ Expiration Date: _____ Amount of Gift: _____

Name as it appears on card: _____ Signature: _____

Contributions and gifts to the Republican National Committee are not deductible as charitable contributions for federal income tax purposes.

Paid for by the Republican National Committee. Funds received in response to this solicitation will be deposited in the RNC's federal account unless otherwise prohibited. Contributions from foreign nationals are prohibited.

Federal election law requires us to report the following information: Employer: _____

Occupation: _____ Please check if self-employed ☐   Phone Number (optional): _____

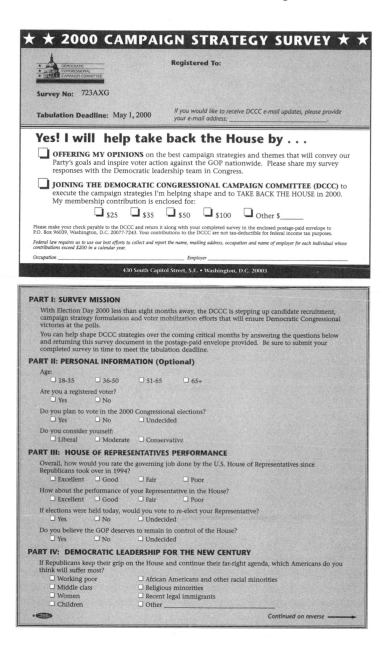

★ ★ **2000 CAMPAIGN STRATEGY SURVEY** ★ ★

DEMOCRATIC
CONGRESSIONAL
CAMPAIGN COMMITTEE

Registered To:

Survey No: 723AXG

Tabulation Deadline: May 1, 2000

If you would like to receive DCCC e-mail updates, please provide your e-mail address: _____

Yes! I will help take back the House by . . .

☐ **OFFERING MY OPINIONS** on the best campaign strategies and themes that will convey our Party's goals and inspire voter action against the GOP nationwide. Please share my survey responses with the Democratic leadership team in Congress.

☐ **JOINING THE DEMOCRATIC CONGRESSIONAL CAMPAIGN COMMITTEE (DCCC)** to execute the campaign strategies I'm helping shape and to TAKE BACK THE HOUSE in 2000. My membership contribution is enclosed for:

☐ $25   ☐ $35   ☐ $50   ☐ $100   ☐ Other $____

Please make your check payable to the DCCC and return it along with your completed survey in the enclosed postage-paid envelope to P.O. Box 96039, Washington, D.C. 20077-7243. Your contributions to the DCCC are not tax-deductible for federal income tax purposes.

Federal law requires us to use our best efforts to collect and report the name, mailing address, occupation and name of employer for each individual whose contributions exceed $200 in a calendar year.

Occupation _____   Employer _____

430 South Capitol Street, S.E. • Washington, D.C. 20003

PART I: SURVEY MISSION

With Election Day 2000 less than eight months away, the DCCC is stepping up candidate recruitment, campaign strategy formulation and voter mobilization efforts that will ensure Democratic Congressional victories at the polls.

You can help shape DCCC strategies over the coming critical months by answering the questions below and returning this survey document in the postage-paid envelope provided. Be sure to submit your completed survey in time to meet the tabulation deadline.

PART II: PERSONAL INFORMATION (Optional)

Age:
☐ 18-35   ☐ 36-50   ☐ 51-65   ☐ 65+

Are you a registered voter?
☐ Yes   ☐ No

Do you plan to vote in the 2000 Congressional elections?
☐ Yes   ☐ No   ☐ Undecided

Do you consider yourself:
☐ Liberal   ☐ Moderate   ☐ Conservative

PART III: HOUSE OF REPRESENTATIVES PERFORMANCE

Overall, how would you rate the governing job done by the U.S. House of Representatives since Republicans took over in 1994?
☐ Excellent   ☐ Good   ☐ Fair   ☐ Poor

How about the performance of your Representative in the House?
☐ Excellent   ☐ Good   ☐ Fair   ☐ Poor

If elections were held today, would you vote to re-elect your Representative?
☐ Yes   ☐ No   ☐ Undecided

Do you believe the GOP deserves to remain in control of the House?
☐ Yes   ☐ No   ☐ Undecided

PART IV: DEMOCRATIC LEADERSHIP FOR THE NEW CENTURY

If Republicans keep their grip on the House and continue their far-right agenda, which Americans do you think will suffer most?
☐ Working poor   ☐ African Americans and other racial minorities
☐ Middle class   ☐ Religious minorities
☐ Women   ☐ Recent legal immigrants
☐ Children   ☐ Other _____

Continued on reverse ⟶

Do you endorse the idea that a greater number of smaller farms should be encouraged to relieve the growing burden being placed on large farms to fulfill our agricultural needs?   *American Farmland Trust*

Our nation is still blessed with millions of acres of public lands, including roadless wilderness areas, forests and range lands. Land developers, loggers, and mining and oil companies want to increase their operations on these public lands. Do you think these remaining pristine areas of your public lands should be protected from such exploitation?   *Sierra Club*

Do you feel that all of the TV networks are in serious danger of losing the public's confidence and trust because they hire so many liberal Democratic activists as top corporate executives who formerly worked for Ted Kennedy, Walter Mondale, Gary Hart, George McGovern, Mario Cuomo, Jimmy Carter and the National Democratic Party?   *Fairness in Media*

As a result of our efforts to save dolphins from getting caught in the nets of tuna fishermen, legislation was introduced in the U.S. that led to "dolphin safe tuna" labels. Do you support the kind of direct action that brought about this labeling to force companies to operate in more responsible ways?   *Greenpeace Update Survey*

Chief lobbyist for the NRA, Tanya Metaksa, announced recently, "We have the assurance of the Speaker [Newt Gingrich] that there will be repeal" of the assault weapons ban. Do you agree that concern for public safety and the will of the people should matter more to Congress than the dangerous agenda of the National Rifle Association?
Handgun Control

Our Founding Fathers built America on the principle of a United States, a united people. Our country's motto, "e pluribus unum" (from many into one) reflects that, as does our historic vision of America as a "melting pot," where people from diverse cultures come here to adopt new ways . . . and become Americans. But record-high levels of immigration are making assimilation impossible. So we are moving away from this principle of unity toward an ethic of diversity, as reflected in growing acceptance of "hyphenated-Americans"—such as "Latino-Americans," "African-Americans," and "Asian-Americans." Do you think the move from America as a "united people" toward America as a collection of "separate diverse peoples" is healthy or unhealthy for our nation?
American Immigration Council

Although tobacco is estimated to kill at least 418,000 people each year, and to cost you and me and every American taxpayer more than $100 billion, our federal government continues to spend millions to encourage the growing of tobacco and to subsidize the tobacco industry. Therefore, do you think the government should: immediately discontinue all aid to tobacco, phase out all aid for tobacco over a longer period of

time, or continue to aid tobacco growers and the tobacco industry at
present levels?   *Action on Smoking and Health*

All of the preceding items were carefully constructed to generate responses sympathetic to the sponsors' objectives. In fact, for several reasons
these enterprises should not be called "polling." First, in most cases the
sample is not scientifically selected; instead, the surveys and fund-raising
requests are mailed out to lists of citizens who are thought to be likely supporters. Whether the people who actually respond are at all representative
of a larger population is of little concern. Second, the questions are often
poorly formulated and fundamentally flawed (deliberately so). Third, if the
survey data collected are tabulated at all (and many times they are not), little
analysis can be conducted, because the original survey was very short and
omitted key questions about the demographic and political characteristics
of the respondents. In other words, collecting opinions is not necessarily
polling.

Pseudo-polls

Orton (1982) has identified similar examples of what he calls *pseudo-
polls*. In such polls the representativeness of the respondents is highly
questionable. For example, the print and electronic media often encourage
members of their audiences to write or phone to express their views. But
even with hundreds or thousands of replies, these "straw polls" are usually
not representative simply because the people who volunteer to participate
are likely to differ in important ways from the overall population. They may
be more interested, informed, and concerned about the topic at hand and
thus hold views different from those of the overall population. A prominent
example of a pseudo-poll occurred in 1980 when ABC News encouraged
viewers to call (at a cost of fifty cents) to indicate whether they thought
Jimmy Carter or Ronald Reagan had won the presidential debate.

In 1992, shortly after President George Bush's State of the Union address, the CBS television program "America on the Line" featured telephone call-in surveys. At the same time, CBS also conducted a scientific
poll that included questions identical to those on the call-in survey. The
results of the two surveys differed. Unfortunately, the results of the call-in
responses received the greater attention, despite the major differences
between the two sets of results. For example, in response to the question
of whether they were better or worse off than they were four years ago,
54 percent of the callers in the phone-in poll said they were worse off
compared with only 32 percent of the respondents in the scientific survey
(Morin 1992a).

Radio talk shows and call-in polls became more prominent in the 1990s. A 1993 *Times Mirror* poll (Kohut 1993) revealed that citizens who listened to and called radio talk shows were not representative of the overall citizenry; instead, they tended to be more Republican, more conservative, more male, and slightly more wealthy and educated. Thus it is not surprising that the radio phone-in polls often generate results more conservative and pro-Republican than the outcomes obtained through scientific polling.

Other examples of pseudo-polls are the questionnaires that members of Congress send to households within their congressional districts. Typically, these are addressed to "Postal Customer," with no sure way of knowing just who in the household actually completed the survey. Although thousands of these questionnaires may be returned to a congressional office, it is difficult to ascertain whether the respondents' demographic characteristics and actual opinions on the issues are truly representative of the broader constituency. In some instances the questions themselves are loaded to guarantee responses compatible with a legislator's own predisposition and record. This is not to say that completed questionnaires are ignored or discarded; in most cases the results are tabulated and later reported to the constituency in a newsletter. But, as Sussman (1985g) argues, these questionnaires are mainly "a public relations gimmick, aimed at convincing voters that officeholders care about the folks back home." And as Morin (1987) observes, "Too many of these polls reek from a kind of self-serving flatulence that insults the average voter while exposing the unctuous pomposity of the elected official."

Other examples of pseudo-polls are the highly publicized surveys on marital relations once conducted by feminist author Shere Hite and Abigail Van Buren, otherwise known as "Dear Abby" (Squires and Morin 1987; Smith 1988). Hite distributed 100,000 extensive open-ended questionnaires to women's groups and to individual women who requested a questionnaire. She received about 4,500 replies, a response rate of only 4.5 percent. In one of her columns, Abby wrote: "Readers, I need your cooperation for an important survey. Questions: Have you ever cheated on your mate? How long have you been together? You need not sign your name, but please state your age and indicate whether you are male or female." She received more than 200,000 responses (Smith 1988).

In both the Hite and Abby surveys, the sampling method and the questions generated unrepresentative and misleading results, despite the large number of respondents to Abby's poll. (Reputable, scientific national polls typically have a sample of about 1,500 respondents.) Hite found that 70 percent of women married five or more years were having extramarital affairs; 15 percent of Abby's married female respondents claimed to have been unfaithful. As Smith (1988) argues, both surveys could not be correct and, indeed, both were overwhelmingly likely to be wrong because of the pitfalls inherent in the sample selection and the actual questionnaire. Allowing citizens to select themselves into a survey guarantees biased results because of the motivations that lead people to participate in such surveys in the first place.

Since the 1970s, magazines have regularly published the results of sex surveys of their readers. Typically, they conduct these surveys by including the questionnaire in the magazine and encouraging readers to complete the survey and mail it back. *Redbook* and *Cosmopolitan* in the 1970s, *Playboy* in the 1980s and *The Advocate* in the 1990s are among the magazines that have sponsored such surveys. In some cases the response rate was low, but the number of completed questionnaires very large simply because of the size of the magazine's readership. For example, the *Playboy* response rate was about 2 percent, but this translated into 100,000 replies. By contrast, *The Advocate* response rate was 18 percent with almost 13,000 questionnaires returned (Lever 1994, 18). Despite the large number of replies to a typical magazine survey, one must be very careful when generalizing the results to any broader population, whether it be to straight males based on the *Playboy* survey or to gay males based on *The Advocate* poll. The reason: self-selection presents a double problem. First, the readers and subscribers to various magazines may not be representative of the broader population of which they are members. Second, the people who actually complete the questionnaires may not be representative of the magazines' readers and subscribers in the first place. Nevertheless, the results of these surveys typically receive a lot of media coverage (and probably enhance magazine sales).

The latest example of a pseudo-poll is the online survey on the Internet. Many businesses, media outlets, and other organizations invite visitors to their Web sites to participate in online surveys. Like other pseudo-polls, the online survey may generate thousands of responses, but it is not a valid survey because respondents self-selected themselves to participate in the survey rather than being part of a scientifically selected sample. Indeed, they are not likely to be a representative sample, because only those people who are sufficiently interested in the topic of the survey are likely to participate, and, more fundamental, many citizens do not have access to the Internet in the first place. Online surveys are discussed in greater detail in Chapter 5, including conditions under which they might provide useful information.

The key point, of course, is that pseudo-polls are highly flawed and may give misleading portraits of public opinion because of loaded and unfair question wording, self-selection biases in the respondents, outright efforts to stack the results, or other deficiencies. Despite their deficiencies, however, these unscientific enterprises are included here under the rubric of polling because they are becoming more prevalent in the United States. Citizens are subjected to many different kinds of polls, all of which may later affect them in some way through the decisions that are based on the results. For this reason it is important that citizens be aware of the gamut of polls and be able to evaluate them. If they are able to recognize unscientific polls and their associated deficiencies (as well as the shortcomings of scientific polls), then they are less likely to be misled by the results of such surveys. This leads to the central concern of this book—the citizen as a potential consumer of public opinion polls.

The Citizen as a Consumer of Polls

As noted earlier in this chapter, opinion polling is pervasive in the United States. Whatever the quality of these polls, they can affect the attitudes and behavior of citizens. Even media-sponsored polls designed to simply report citizens' attitudes (and perhaps to keep up with the competition and improve ratings) also may help to *shape* preferences, particularly during a presidential primary season. Then, polling is frequent and the linkages among a candidate's poll standing, media coverage, and primary election fate are pronounced. (The role of polls in elections is considered in Chapter 7.)

Americans are major consumers of the results of public opinion research conducted on a wide variety of topics. But are they smart consumers? Americans should be aware of the problems and limitations of polls before they "buy" anything from them. Just as customers in a supermarket often inspect the list of ingredients in a product, so too should consumers of public opinion question what went into a poll before accepting its results. Citizens who are simply passive consumers of poll results need to recognize that often someone is actively promoting the poll results to generate support for his or her objectives. It might be the president citing polls to argue that the American people support administration policies. It might be a local builder waving the results of a neighborhood poll purporting to show local support for a rezoning ordinance to permit commercial construction in an area. It might be a regional transportation commission citing poll results to justify the establishment of bus lanes on freeways. Or it might be a friend or neighbor selectively using poll results to win an argument.

In the course of becoming better consumers of public opinion research, citizens need not become experts at drawing samples, constructing questionnaires, and analyzing data. Instead, they can develop an intuitive awareness of the steps involved in conducting a survey and the possible consequences of these steps so that as consumers of polls they are better able to reject bad "merchandise" and to appreciate good buys. Thus, the major aim of this book is to sensitize citizens to the problems and limitations of opinion polling. Readers should note that this book should in no way be construed as a condemnation of public opinion research; most of the highly publicized polls as well as many private polls reflect high standards of polling. Indeed, public opinion polling has improved dramatically over the past fifty years in areas such as sample design, question wording and format, interviewing techniques, and methods of data analysis. See the fiftieth anniversary issue of *Public Opinion Quarterly* (1987) for discussions of how polling practices have changed over time. An appreciation of the art of conducting and analyzing surveys will leave citizens less susceptible to the intellectual tyranny that can occur when a public opinion poll is deemed by its sponsor to be scientific and its results therefore beyond question or challenge.

Citizens' Views of Polls

Ordinary citizens' reactions to public opinion polling are often positive, although their views of pollsters themselves may be more skeptical. One study rated the credibility of forty-four different professional groups who spoke out on public issues; pollsters finished thirty-forth in the ranking (Morin 1999b). In 1985 both the Gallup and Roper organizations conducted national surveys that assessed popular awareness of and reactions to public opinion polls (Clymer 1985; Sussman 1985e). The Gallup Organization conducted a similar survey in 1996 (Morin 1996b). Twenty-five percent of the respondents in the 1996 Gallup survey said they regularly followed the results of a public opinion poll in a newspaper or magazine; an additional 16 percent said they did so occasionally. Fifty-nine percent of respondents said they did not follow a poll regularly in the print medium; of course, they might sporadically read about polls, or they might be aware of the polls through the electronic media.

Both the Gallup polls and Roper surveys indicated that Americans held fairly positive views about the accuracy of polls. More than two-thirds of the Gallup sample said the polls were right most of the time, and 56 percent of respondents to the Roper survey said the polls were almost always or usually accurate. Finally, 76 percent of the people interviewed in the first Gallup survey thought polls were a good thing; 12 percent thought they were a bad thing. By 1996 support for polls as "a good thing" had increased to 87 percent.

Despite these indications of positive attitudes toward polls, other evidence, often anecdotal in nature, suggests the public takes a more skeptical view. Most teachers and practitioners of public opinion polling have encountered citizens who have expressed utter distrust of polling. Some citizens complain that they and their friends and relatives have never been interviewed and therefore wonder just how representative samples can be. This kind of skepticism is widespread. Koch (1985) finds that people who have never participated in a poll are dubious about the accuracy of survey results.

Others base their doubts on the size of the samples selected. In talking about polling with diverse audiences, I repeatedly hear people ask how a sample of 1,500 respondents can possibly represent 200 million adult Americans. And despite my brilliant answer by analogy—a doctor takes only a sample of a person's blood (fortunately) and a chef need taste only a spoonful of soup (assuming the soup is stirred properly) to test its seasoning—much skepticism about polls remains. Indeed, one question posed in the 1985 Roper survey showed that only 28 percent of Americans believed that national polls with sample sizes of 1,500–2,000 could be accurate, while 56 percent said they could not be (Sussman 1985e). Similar results were obtained in the 1996 Gallup survey. Another study (Dran and Hildreth 1995) found that citizens who questioned the accuracy of polls attributed their skepticism to characteristics of the respondents as well as aspects of the polling enterprise itself. Skeptics worried whether pollsters talked to the right people, and whether sample sizes were adequate. Other concerns focused on pollster manipulation of surveys and media misuse of polls.

Indeed, one substantive area in which the polls have received much criticism is their growing role in elections and election coverage by the media. The argument is often made that polls have contributed to the packaging of candidates; aspiring leaders are accused of first consulting the polls and then staking out their positions, thereby abdicating their leadership responsibilities on issues. Similarly, the use of polls in reporting elections is seen as encouraging a horse-race mentality among the media; instead of focusing on issues and the candidates' qualifications, the dominant theme becomes who's ahead and who's behind, who's gaining and who's falling back, as measured by the polls. Candidates themselves have complained about the role of polls. For example, former Tennessee governor Lamar Alexander, an unsuccessful candidate for the GOP presidential nomination in 1996 and 2000, worries that the polls have too much influence on media coverage of candidates and on campaign contributions in the early stages of the presidential selection process. Alexander asserts that "if the polls are combined with the $1000 limit on contributions, or other factors, to weed out people based on these premature [surveys], then that's unfortunate for the process because it deprives voters of having the widest range of choices"(Rivlin 1999). A Gallup poll conducted for *Newsweek* in October 1988 found that 52 percent of respondents believed that news or-

Reprinted by permission of the *Detroit Free Press.*

DON'T FORGET THAT ELECTION YEAR IS
ALSO LIE-TO-THE-POLLSTERS YEAR.

ganizations' polls on the presidential contest should not be reported in the final weeks of the general election campaign. An NBC News/*Wall Street Journal* poll in November 1988 showed that 63 percent of Americans believed that voters were influenced too much by the polls.

Exit polls—interviews with citizens just after they have voted—enable the television networks to project election outcomes even before the polls have closed. This practice has angered many citizens and political elites. Newspaper columnist Mike Royko has encouraged voters to lie to exit pollsters, while others (such as Munro and Gans 1988) have simply encouraged a public boycott of exit polls. Congress has conducted hearings in an effort to get the networks to alter voluntarily the ways they report exit polls and election projections. Other observers have condemned the impact of polls on American politics, none more harshly than Daniel Greenberg, who wrote:

> Given the devastation that opinion surveys have brought to the American political process, we shouldn't be asking how polls can be sharpened but rather why they are endured and how they can be banished.
>
> Polls are the life-support system for the finger-to-the-wind, quick-change politics of our time and, as such, are the indispensable tools for the ideologically hollow men who work politics like a soap-marketing campaign. . . .
>
> The effect of this—on campaigns, as well as on administrations between campaigns—is an obsession with salesmanship rather than with governance. (Greenberg 1980)

The nation's political cartoonists, many of whom are syndicated in newspapers that themselves conduct polls, have had a field day attacking the polls, particularly their frequency, duration, and intrusiveness in the presidential selection process. Smith (1987, 209) found that polls were treated negatively in 61 percent of the comics and cartoons he analyzed and worried how this would affect citizens' reactions to the polls. And political satirists such as Art Buchwald (1987) and Russell Baker (1988, 1990) also have lampooned the polls. More recently, political commentator and writer Arianna Huffington has established a Web site called "Partnership for a Poll-Free America." Huffington has been particularly critical of the polling enterprise because of low response rates, a topic discussed in Chapter 4.

Various practitioners of polling and survey research have become concerned about what they see as increased disinterest, skepticism, cynicism, or even hostility toward the polls. Prominent pollsters such as Harry O'Neill of the Roper organization and Kathy Frankovic, director of polling at CBS News, have called on their industry colleagues to be more reflective about their enterprise and more sensitive to its shortcomings (O'Neill 1997; Morin 1998a). Black (1991) advocates greater sensitivity to the needs of respondents by (1) making the interview itself a more interesting and rewarding experience for respondents; (2) keeping promises made to respondents in such areas as the length of the interview and the provision of final reports if requested by the respondent; and (3) maintaining high quality throughout the polling enterprise. Lang and Lang worry that some of the more recent entrants into the polling business may have weaker ties to the profession and a lesser commitment to the high standards that should characterize public opinion polling (Morin 1992c). They urge careful self-policing by the polling industry to protect the profession and ultimately its reputation among the public. Others (such as Tanur 1994) recommend better education of citizens as consumers of polls (which is indeed the main purpose of this book). The point is that there is growing unease among many practitioners of polling, because the lofty status that public opinion assessment has enjoyed may be in some jeopardy.

The American Association for Public Opinion Research (AAPOR), the major professional association of public opinion researchers, recently acted to protect the integrity and reputation of the polling enterprise. In May 1997 AAPOR issued a publication detailing the "best practices" that should characterize public opinion research. The last recommendation called for the disclosure of "all methods of the survey to permit evaluation and replication" and presented a comprehensive list of items that exceeded the standards for minimum disclosure laid out in the AAPOR code (see Chapter 6 for a fuller discussion of disclosure standards). AAPOR also condemned a number of survey practices, such as presenting the results of any self-selected poll as if they were the product of genuine scientific survey research. "Push polling" also drew sharp criticism from AAPOR. Basically, push polls are an election campaign tactic disguised as legitimate polling. A campaign contacts voters, presents some negative information about another candidate, and then asks some questions about that candidate. The aim of push polls is not to acquire legitimate information about the election contest; rather, they are designed to push potential voters away from a particular candidate by providing them with negative information about the candidate. (Push polling is discussed in greater detail in Chapter 7.)

The Luntz case illustrates how politicians, or a political party, may use polls to promote their own agenda. In April 1997 the executive council of AAPOR formally chastised pollster Frank Luntz for violating AAPOR's Code of Professional Ethics and Practices. Prior to the 1994 congressional elections, Luntz claimed that his research showed that sizable majorities of Americans supported all parts of the GOP's Contract with America. But when asked to make public the wording of his poll and other information, Luntz refused and AAPOR rebuked him for failing to meet the standards of disclosure. Later it was revealed that Luntz's evidence of support for the Contract with America was highly suspect and misleading. Nevertheless, the alleged poll results were used by the House Republican leadership to build legislative support for the items in the contract. In general, political leaders who use the polls to "prove" that the public supports their positions have an advantage in the public debate and discussion of issues.

Although they are sometimes angry or skeptical about poll results, Americans generally think polls are accurate and fair. They often resent the intrusiveness and presumed power of the polls, but they eagerly consume the latest public opinion findings about a myriad of topics. This love-hate relationship is probably inevitable in the U.S. political system. Americans want their voices to be heard, and therefore they attack the polls when they think such devices are undermining genuine citizen involvement and influence. Yet in a large and heterogeneous nation such as the United States, the polls may be the best mechanism for reflecting the diversity of public opinion. The simple fact that polls generally count all respondents equally bestows on polls a democratic character that enhances their appeal in a democratic society.

Polling and Democracy

The role of polling in a democratic society has not been without controversy, however. Advocates of polls emphasize that polling is an opportunity for citizens to participate in a democracy and that it permits quick and repeated assessments of public opinion. Polling is particularly valued by those who prefer a democracy in which the people govern directly rather than through intermediaries such as elected representatives. Proponents advocate polling citizens on their policy preferences and enacting these preferences, thereby circumventing the "middleman"—the elected representative—and possibly ignoring many important features of the governing process such as dialogue, bargaining, and compromise. Many in this group are fascinated with the possibility that technological innovations such as interactive cable television might facilitate direct governance by the citizenry. Until its demise in the early 1980s, the QUBE system in Columbus, Ohio, was seen as the wave of the future; Columbus residents on the QUBE system were able to vote from their homes on issues of the day and have their choices tabulated instantly. Indeed, NBC News used the QUBE facilities to conduct an instant survey of viewers' reactions to President Carter's 1979 speech in which he said that reducing America's dependence on foreign oil was the moral equivalent of war. Since then, the communications infrastructure has advanced to such an extent that the virtues and feasibility of direct democracy through technology are being extolled even more.

Some proponents of the more traditional, representative notion of democratic theory also welcome public opinion polls, because they provide systematic information on the preferences of the citizenry. They argue that citizens' opinions should influence the behavior of their elected representatives and that any mechanism, such as polls, that can provide information on citizens' opinions is bound to foster democracy. But the empirical evidence is mixed on the extent to which popular preferences are actually translated into public policy. On the one hand, examples of the government's seeming unresponsiveness to public opinion are numerous. For example, polls have regularly shown that overwhelming majorities of Americans favor some form of gun control, such as handgun registration or waiting periods, yet not until late 1993 did Congress pass the Brady bill, first introduced in 1987. Moreover, the Brady bill was the first major federal gun control legislation since 1968. On the other hand, some empirical studies have found substantial congruence between the attitudes of the public and the actions of government on certain issues (Erikson 1976; Page and Shapiro 1983, 1992). Although these studies are careful not to hastily attribute government decisions to popular preferences, they do suggest conditions under which citizen influence is likely to be significant.

Another benefit of polls, according to polling proponents, is the opportunity for citizens to learn about their compatriots and to dispel myths and stereotypes that might otherwise mislead public discourse. For example, poll results reported by Morin challenge the stereotype of evangelical and fundamentalist Christians as monolithic, homogeneous supporters of the religious right (Morin 1993a, 1993c). A *USA Today*/CNN/Gallup poll conducted in December 1993 showed that classic stereotypes on the gun control issue were misleading. For example, the attitudes of gun owners on various aspects of gun control did not differ substantially from the attitudes of nonowners, particularly for less-sweeping forms of gun regulation. Other public opinion polls can provide insights, sometimes surprising and unexpected, on the issue of race, ethnicity, and prejudice in the United States. A Louis Harris poll conducted in 1993 showed that the traditional victims of bigotry—blacks, Asians, and Latinos—often express intolerant views of other minority groups. And a study by Sniderman et al. (1993) debunked the simplistic notion that conservatives were prejudiced toward blacks and liberals were not. Although on many items conservatives were less tolerant than liberals toward blacks, the key point for Sniderman and his colleagues was that these differences were often very small.

In contrast to the favorable arguments of proponents, many critics of polling worry about the harmful consequences of polls for a democratic political system. They agree that citizen influence is a key component of a democracy and that public opinion, properly measured, can be useful in governing. But they argue that polls give a misleading impression of how a democracy actually operates. Public opinion is not synonymous with the results of public opinion polls, yet today the two are treated as though they are identical. A focus solely on poll results ignores the dynamics of how opinions are formed and how they change and often overlooks factors that may shape (and manipulate) public opinion, such as the behavior of leaders and

interest groups. Polls may present an overall picture of the distribution of opinion, but the reporting and use of polls often ignore important differences in preferences among subgroups. The result is a misleading picture of similar attitudes across different segments of the American population. Margolis (1984) claims that polls may not be the optimal way to measure public opinion on politically and socially sensitive topics. He argues that in some instances actual behavior provides a more valid expression of public opinion than verbal responses to survey questions.

A more radical criticism of polls is that they are simply a sop to the citizenry, that they give people a false sense of being influential when in reality political power is held and exercised by a few elites who may or may not act in the public interest. Social scientist Johan Galtung (1969) makes the point most effectively when he argues that surveys are too democratic: they generally count all respondents equally, whereas people are tremendously disparate in the resources and skills they bring to bear on political decisions. To the extent that a survey is seen as a quasi-referendum on issues, it is misleading; the participants in the referendum have different opportunities to shape government outcomes.

Another major criticism of polls concerns their consequences for leadership in the United States. The simplistic version of this argument says that leaders blindly follow the polls rather than work to educate and persuade the public. This argument is exemplified by an editorial in the *Akron Beacon Journal* (May 8, 1994) entitled "Foreign Poll-icy." It begins by asserting, "The name of Stanley Greenberg may not be familiar to most Americans. It should be. He is Bill Clinton's pollster, and for all intents and purposes, he conducts the country's foreign policy." Indeed, other observers such as Barnes (1993) have described the critical role Greenberg played in the Clinton administration just as he did in the presidential campaign itself. Likewise, polling results in 1998 and 1999 on health care, patients' rights, and prescription drugs showed that Americans cared about these issues. These polls prompted the GOP congressional leadership to offer its own health care proposals to head off any political backlash on these issues (Alvarez 1998).

Other critics of polling argue that leaders have been weakened by the polls, because the widespread awareness of public preferences generated by the polls limits the ability of leaders to make unpopular choices. Still others complain that leaders can easily manipulate the polls (perhaps by giving a major televised address that can influence opinions in polls taken right after the address) and therefore generate poll results unfairly supportive of their policies. Some make the fundamental point that polls (and the media) have altered the style and substance of governance, particularly by emphasizing immediate consequences for the next election. The result is a short-sighted approach to problem solving. Compare this with the proponents' defense of the impact of polls on leadership, which argues that officials should have information about citizens' attitudes before they make major decisions and that the polls, whatever their limitations, are the best way to acquire that information.

What, then, is the verdict on opinion polls in the United States? They are now an integral part of the political and social landscape, and they are likely to become even more prominent in the future. Polls can provide useful information to citizens and leaders; they also can be highly misleading and inaccurate. Polls may enhance the opportunities for citizen influence; they also can serve to manipulate the public. In 1965 George Gallup wrote optimistically about the future of the polls:

> As students, scholars, and the general public gain a better understanding of polls, they will have a greater appreciation of the service polls can perform in a democracy. In my opinion, modern polls are the chief hope of lifting government to a higher level, by showing that the public supports the reforms that will make this possible, by providing a *modus operandi* for testing new ideas. . . . Polls can help make government more efficient and responsive; they can improve the quality of candidates for public office; they can make this a truer democracy. (Gallup 1965–1966, 549)

More than three decades have passed since these claims were made, and current discourse about the polls has become much more critical. Nevertheless, as citizens become wiser consumers of polls, Gallup's lofty aspirations for the polls are more likely to be realized.

The chapters that follow consider polls in detail and raise some methodological points, often in the context of important substantive examples. Chapter 2 addresses the problem of nonattitudes—that is, when citizens do not have genuine opinions on a topic and yet they answer the questions. In such cases, the topic is inappropriate for the sample, because despite pollsters' best efforts citizens often do respond to questions on which they have no real opinions, thereby yielding misleading results.

Chapter 3 discusses the wording of questions and their order and context. Examples of poorly worded questions likely to produce skewed results have already been cited, but the wording of a question is not the only important consideration. A survey is, after all, a series of questions, and the placement and context of those questions can greatly affect the results.

Chapter 4 focuses on various sampling techniques and their advantages and disadvantages. It also deals with sample size and error. Chapter 5 explains in detail how different interviewing procedures can affect results.

Chapter 6 examines how the media report the polls, and Chapter 7 analyzes the role of polls in elections. Because Americans learn about polls primarily through the mass media, media coverage of polls greatly influences public opinion. This influence is particularly interesting in the case of high-visibility national polls, because the medium that reports the polls also is responsible for conducting them. Chapter 7 argues that the polls have come to play an intrusive role in elections and that the use of polls by candidates and the reporting of polls by the media often do a disservice to citizens and to the electoral process. Elections are the most visible opportunity for citizens to influence their government, and to the extent that polls affect that opportunity, citizens should be sensitive to the role of polls in elections.

Chapter 8 explains that the analysis of poll results is more an art than a science, affording many opportunities for manipulative interpretation and dissemination of poll results in order to sway public opinion. Chapter 9 ties together the various themes, offers suggestions about better utilization of polls, and discusses the effects of polls on the American polity.

2 The Problem of Nonattitudes

To produce an informative and accurate public opinion poll, a researcher must perform several tasks successfully. These include constructing a questionnaire with properly worded and ordered questions, selecting a representative sample, correctly interviewing the respondents in that sample, analyzing the data appropriately, and, finally, drawing the correct conclusions. But before any of these tasks can be performed, a researcher must ask a fundamental question. Is the proposed topic of the poll one on which citizens have genuine opinions? If it is, then the topic is suitable for a public opinion survey. But if the topic is so remote from citizens' concerns that they do not hold real views on it, then any poll on the topic will measure *nonattitudes* rather than attitudes. Any information obtained will be suspect—even if the questions are properly worded, the sample scientifically selected, and the data appropriately analyzed.

The presence of nonattitudes is one of the simplest yet most perplexing problems in public opinion polling. Too often in a survey context, people will respond to questions about which they have no genuine attitudes or opinions.[1] Even worse, the analyst treats the nonattitude responses as if they represent actual public opinions. Under these circumstances, a misleading portrait of public opinion can emerge—that is, no distinction is

---

1. The terms *attitude* and *opinion* are used interchangeably. Many social scientists differentiate between attitudes and opinions by treating opinions as more transitory, as verbal manifestations of some underlying attitude, words elicited by the public opinion survey. For the purposes of this chapter, this distinction is by no means critical, although the reader should recognize that public opinion data at times may simply be verbal responses (opinions) that pollsters hope accurately reflect some underlying attitudes.

made between people with real views on an issue and those whose responses simply reflect their desire to appear in an interview situation as
informed citizens. Unfortunately, pollsters often find it difficult to differentiate between genuine attitude holders and persons merely expressing
nonattitudes.

It is tempting to assume that citizens are interested in and informed
about the issues widely discussed by public officials and the media. Indeed,
researchers often take for granted that citizens know the basic facts about
their government and political system. Sometimes these assumptions lead
pollsters to include questions on topics that people know very little about
even though the topics are prominent. As a result, the responses to such
questions might reflect nonattitudes rather than genuine opinions. For example, an obvious topic for public opinion polling is the state of the economy. Although citizens can certainly express valid opinions about their
own and the nation's economic situation, an extended inquiry might be hindered by citizens' ignorance about key facts of economics. Morin (1993b)
cites studies demonstrating the public's deficiencies in economic knowledge. Those studies showed that only one in five respondents came reasonably close to knowing the national unemployment rate, and that only about
half of citizens could identify the correct definition of the federal budget deficit in the four choices presented to them. The public also has major gaps
in its knowledge of the American political system. A study that compared
citizens' levels of knowledge in the 1940s and 1950s with contemporary
ones found that, after controlling for educational levels, Americans today
at each level of education are less informed about many aspects of politics
than their counterparts in the earlier decades (Delli Carpini and Keeter
1991). The study speculated that today people are simply less interested in
politics. Because respondents with low interest are more likely to express
nonattitudes, these results suggest that pollsters must exercise great care to
avoid measuring nonattitudes.

The presence of nonattitudes in survey responses has been well docu-
mented (Converse 1970; Taylor 1983; Norpoth and Lodge 1985). A particularly intriguing study by Bishop, Oldendick, and Tuchfarber (1980)
included a fictitious item in surveys conducted in the Greater Cincinnati
area. Respondents were presented with the following statement and question about a nonexistent Public Affairs Act: "Some people say that the 1975
Public Affairs Act should be repealed. Do you agree or disagree with this
idea?" One-third of respondents offered an opinion. After an effort to filter out nonattitude responses on this fictitious question, researchers found
that 10 percent of the sample still offered an opinion. (The use of screening
or filter questions will be discussed later in this chapter.) When the *Washington Post* included a question on the nonexistent Public Affairs Act in a

1995 national survey, 43 percent of respondents offered an opinion: 24 percent supported repeal of the act and 19 percent were opposed (Morin 1995a).] The *Post* also administered slightly modified versions of the question to two other samples of respondents. One sample was asked: "President Clinton said that the 1975 Public Affairs Act should be repealed. Do you agree or disagree?" The other sample was asked: "The Republicans in Congress said that the 1975 Public Affairs Act should be repealed. Do you agree or disagree?" The responses changed when references to Clinton and the Republicans were included; 53 percent of respondents now offered an opinion. And, as expected, the Clinton version of the question found Democrats more favorable than Republicans to repeal of the act by a 36 to 18 percent margin. But in the Republican version of the question the results were reversed, with 36 percent of Republicans favoring repeal compared with only 19 percent of Democrats. Clearly, respondents were seeking cues and guidance from the wording of the question itself, something more likely to happen when people are confronted with topics they have no meaningful attitudes about in the first place.

The existence of nonattitudes is not surprising; after all, an interview is a social situation in which a respondent interacts in person or by telephone with an interviewer the respondent does not know. Few people in such circumstances want to admit they are uninformed, particularly on a popular or timely issue. So most people answer the questions, and the interviewer duly records their responses. At this point, an illustration of how a public opinion survey based on nonattitudes can go astray and mislead the public might be useful.

An Example of Nonattitudes

Some years ago I was part of a sample of Ohioans queried about their views on land use problems. The interview was conducted over the phone, and the sample was probably picked from the telephone book. (I surmised this since the interviewer knew my name.) After the interviewer identified herself and the sponsor of the poll, she asked, "Tell me, Mr. Asher, what comes to your mind when you hear the term *land use?*" As a social scientist familiar with public opinion polling, I recognized this as a screening question aimed at determining whether it was worthwhile for the interviewer to proceed with the interview. Surely, if I did not have the vaguest idea what *land use* meant, there would be little point in continuing the interview. In any event I responded, "Hmmm. Land use. How you use the land!" This response must have been sufficiently brilliant for the interviewer to continue with the survey, for she then asked me, "Mr. Asher, what do you think is the most important land use problem facing Ohio?" I mentally squirmed and silently gave thanks that the telephone interviewer could not see my difficulty in thinking up a land use problem. After a delay of about ten seconds, I responded with something like "planned growth and development." She then asked, "Which level of government—state, county, or local—do you think should have primary responsibility for addressing the problem of planned growth?" I responded, although to this day I cannot recall which level of government I mentioned.

The interview continued, and about three minutes later the interviewer asked me, "Mr. Asher, what do you think is the second most important land use problem facing Ohio?" This time I really had to struggle for an answer. Finally I uttered triumphantly, "Sufficient parks and green space." And, of course, the interviewer then asked me which level of government—state, county, or local—should have primary responsibility for rectifying this problem. I gave an answer (which I cannot recall) and said to myself that if the interviewer asked me about the third most important land use problem facing Ohio, I was going to blast her and the entire research project on the grounds that it was measuring nonattitudes. Fortunately for the interviewer, she never asked that question, and the interview was completed.

Some months later, a government report based on this survey described which land use problems Ohioans ranked as most important and which levels of government Ohioans wanted to take the lead in addressing these problems. The report also contained policy recommendations and cited scientific evidence to support its conclusions. As I read the report I grew angrier and angrier; it used survey results derived from what I assume were nonattitudes, opinions from respondents like me who gave answers in response to the questions but had little information about or interest in land use.

As sponsors of public opinion polls should recognize, not every issue of central importance to them will be an appropriate topic of inquiry for the citizenry at large. Different people have different concerns, and those who conduct public opinion polls must incorporate that fact into their plans and proceed accordingly.

The Use of Screening Questions

Researchers can take steps in opinion polls to minimize the problem of nonattitudes. The simplest strategy is to make it socially acceptable for respondents to say they are unfamiliar with the topic of a question. This response would result in that question being skipped. Another strategy is to employ screening or filter questions to separate likely attitude holders from nonattitude respondents. With both strategies the intent is to minimize the number of responses that are superficial reactions to the interview stimulus. The study by Bishop and his colleagues (1980) on the fictitious Public Affairs Act employed a variety of screening questions to reduce the frequency of nonattitudes. Examples are: "Do you have an opinion on this or not?" "Have you thought much about this issue?" Respondents who could not pass the screening questions were not asked about the Public Affairs Act.

The 1984 American National Election Study (ANES) conducted by the Center for Political Studies (CPS) at the University of Michigan also used a variety of means to lessen the problem of nonattitudes. One item on this survey asked respondents whether they thought the federal government had become too powerful. The exact wording of the question was: "Some people are afraid the government in Washington is getting too powerful for the good of the country and the individual person. Others feel that the government in Washington is not getting too strong. Do you have an opinion on this or not?"

Of the 973 citizens in the sample who were asked whether they had an opinion, 550 (57 percent) said yes and 423 (43 percent) said no. The sizable number with no opinion may surprise readers who are aware that the recurring theme of Ronald Reagan's presidential victories in 1980 and 1984 was the need to reduce the scope and power of the federal government. Thus this example suggests that topics hotly discussed by political elites may not be of great importance to the average citizen. In this example, asking people whether or not they had an opinion was an effective screening question that eliminated nearly half of the respondents. But how many of the eliminated respondents would have answered the entire survey if the screening question had not been used and if instead people simply had been asked whether they thought the government was becoming too powerful or not? As it was, among the 550 citizens with an opinion on the issue, 311 thought government had grown too powerful, 218 thought it had not, 10 said it depended, and 11 said they did not know (even though they had stated in response to the screening question that they had an opinion on the issue).

Another screening question used in the 1984 CPS election study allowed respondents to say that they had not thought much about the issue. These respondents were not asked their opinions, thereby reducing the measurement of nonattitudes. The item read:

> Some people think the government should provide fewer services, even in areas such as health and education, in order to reduce spending. Suppose these people are at one end of the scale at point number 1. Other people feel it is important for the government to provide many more services even if it means an increase in spending. Suppose these people are at the other end, at point 7. And, of course, some other people have

opinions somewhere in between at points 2, 3, 4, 5, or 6. Where would you place yourself on this scale or haven't you thought much about this?

Of the 971 persons who were asked this question, 150 (about 15 percent) said they had not thought much about the matter. This does not mean, however, that the other 85 percent had thought a lot about the issue and had genuine opinions. The following pattern of their responses to this item raises questions about their answers ($N = 821$):

N	Response
48	1. Provide many fewer services; reduce spending a lot.
82	2.
141	3.
293	4.
138	5.
58	6.
48	7. Provide many more services; increase spending a lot.
13	Don't know.

Note that the largest number of responses ($N = 293$) fell in the middle, in category 4. This distribution may reflect large numbers of citizens who are satisfied with the status quo or who genuinely take a neutral position on the issue. Or it may reflect the tendency of some citizens with genuine, nonneutral preferences on the issue to hide their preferences by opting for the safe middle category. Many such responses can be moved out of the middle category by using a branching format question, in which citizens who opt for the middle category are then asked whether they favor one side or the other more (Aldrich et al. 1982).

It is also possible that the presence of a large number of people in the middle category may signal problems of nonattitudes in the measurement. Perhaps some proportion of people in the middle category place themselves there because they do not want to admit to the interviewer that they have not thought much about the issue or are unable to place themselves along the scale. For them, the middle category may appear to be a safe position that makes them seem informed without having to take sides on the issue. If so, then some of the category 4 responses may be nonattitudes rather than genuinely neutral opinions, and the portrait of American public opinion on this issue may be misleading.

The pattern of responses on the spending question was not evident in citizens' replies to the following item on racial integration from the same study:

Some people think achieving racial integration of schools is so important that it justifies busing children to schools out of their own neighborhoods.

Others think letting children go to their own schools is so important that they oppose busing. Where would you place yourself on this scale or haven't you thought much about this?

Here only 69 of 968 respondents (7 percent) said they had not thought much about the issue, as opposed to the 15 percent who had not given much thought to the question of government spending. That more people said they had thought about the busing issue seems intuitively correct, because busing is the kind of issue that hits home and captures citizens' attention. Moreover, the distribution of the busing responses reveals relatively few in the middle category; most responses (93 percent) are bunched in the two most antibusing, pro-neighborhood schools categories:

N	Response
33	1. Bus to achieve integration.
15	2.
25	3.
70	4.
91	5.
186	6.
462	7. Keep children in neighborhood schools.
17	Don't know.

This skewed pattern of responses demonstrates that few Americans are neutral about busing and that the middle category is not the choice for large numbers of citizens with nonattitudes on the issue. Or perhaps the meaning of a middle position on the busing item is less clear than it is on the question of providing services, with the result that fewer people opt for the middle position.

The 1996 American National Election Study utilized thermometer questions to assess citizens' feelings toward various political figures. But before the respondents answered, they were given the option of skipping over names that they did not recognize, thereby lessening the measurement of nonattitudes. This measurement tool is based on the ability of people to relate points on a thermometer to figurative degrees of warmth and coldness toward objects. Survey respondents were given the following instructions:

I'd like to get your feelings toward some of our political leaders and other people who are in the news these days. I'll read the name of a person and I'd like you to rate that person using something we call the feeling thermometer. Ratings between 50 degrees and 100 degrees mean that you feel favorable and warm toward that person. Ratings between 0 degrees and 50 degrees mean that you don't feel favorable toward the person and that you don't care too much for that person. You would rate the

Table 2-1   Thermometer Ratings of Five Political Figures (percent)

	Evaluation				
Candidate	Rating other than 50	Rating of 50	Does not recognize	Cannot evaluate	Rating (N)
Dole	82	16	0	2	100 (1,712)
Clinton	93	7	0	0	100 (1,711)
Perot	68	29	1	2	100 (1,712)
Buchanan	65	25	5	5	100 (1,712)
Gramm	40	26	27	7	100 (1,711)

Source: 1996 American National Election Study conducted by the Center for Political Studies, Institute for Social Research, University of Michigan.

Note: Table entries are the percentage of respondents ranking each political figure in each category.

person at the 50 degree mark if you don't feel particularly warm or cold toward the person. If we come to a person whose name you don't recognize, you don't need to rate that person. Just tell me and we'll move on to the next one.

Ideally, respondents who do not recognize a name or feel they are unable to evaluate the person named would indicate that to the interviewer. However, the instructions may encourage some respondents to place the subjects of the survey at the 50-degree mark, including those whose names the respondents do not recognize.

Table 2-1 indicates how respondents rated various political figures. (Keep in mind that Republican Bob Dole, Democrat Bill Clinton, and independent Ross Perot were the major presidential candidates in 1996; Pat Buchanan had unsuccessfully sought the GOP nomination that year and in 1992; and Phil Gramm was new to presidential politics in 1996 with a short-lived candidacy for the GOP nomination.)

The percentage of respondents who did not recognize Bob Dole, Bill Clinton, Ross Perot, or Pat Buchanan or who could not evaluate them was very small; the comparable percentage for Phil Gramm was much higher— 34 percent. It appears, then, that the screening questions worked well, because more than a third of the respondents did not rate the less-prominent Phil Gramm. However, it is disquieting that among the citizens who did assign a thermometer score to these political leaders, more citizens gave a rating of 50 to Buchanan, Perot, and Gramm than to Dole and Clinton. Of those citizens evaluating Dole on the thermometer, only 16.3 percent [16/(82 + 16)] gave him a score of 50; the comparable percentage for Clinton was 7.0 [7/(93 + 7)]. But for Perot, Buchanan, and Gramm, the proportion of citizens using the thermometer who placed them at the mid-point was 29.9 percent [29/(68 + 29)], 27.8 percent [25/(65 + 25)], and 39.4 percent [26/(40 + 26)], respectively.

In one sense it is not surprising that more people placed Gramm at 50; he was less well known than the other political figures in 1996 and therefore may have been more likely to evoke neutral responses. But the problem of measuring nonattitudes also may be at work here. The greater frequency of ratings of 50 for Gramm may indicate that the screening questions did not eliminate all those persons who had no genuine attitudes about him.

An indirect test of this notion is presented in Tables 2-2 and 2-3, which show how educational levels and degree of interest in the campaign were related to assigning political figures a thermometer score of 50. One might expect citizens with higher levels of education to make more discriminating evaluations and therefore be less likely to assign thermometer scores of 50. As Table 2-2 indicates, this expectation holds reasonably well, although the grade school entries break the pattern, perhaps because of the very small number of respondents in this category.

Table 2-3 relates the frequency of ratings of 50 to the respondents' level of interest in the campaign. As expected, the more interested the re-

Table 2-2 Frequency of Ratings of 50 for Five Political Figures by Respondents' Education (percent)

Candidate	Grade school	High school	Some college	College graduate	Post-college
Dole	24	25	14	10	5
Clinton	9	10	6	2	4
Perot	30	34	30	29	24
Buchanan	31	40	29	18	13
Gramm	34	45	40	38	34

Source: 1996 American National Election Study conducted by the Center for Political Studies, Institute for Social Research, University of Michigan.

Note: Table entries are the percentage of respondents assigning a thermometer score who gave the candidate in question a score of 50. For example, the 40 in the "high school/Buchanan" category means that 40 percent of respondents with a high school education gave Buchanan a score of 50; the other 60 percent of high school respondents assigned Buchanan a numerical score other than 50.

Table 2-3 Frequency of Ratings of 50 for Five Political Figures by Respondents' Interest in the Campaign (percent)

Candidate	Very much interested	Somewhat interested	Not very interested
Dole	8	17	27
Clinton	3	6	14
Perot	23	33	33
Buchanan	18	29	39
Gramm	24	46	51

Source: 1996 American National Election Study conducted by the Center for Political Studies, Institute for Social Research, University of Michigan.

Note: Table entries are the percentage of respondents assigning a thermometer score who gave the candidate in question a score of 50. For example, the 39 in the "Buchanan/not very interested" category means that 39 percent of the not very interested respondents who were able to rate Buchanan gave him a 50, while the other 61 percent gave him a score other than 50.

spondents, the less likely they were to assign a score of 50 because of their greater awareness of and involvement in the campaign. This pattern held for all five political leaders. But note that less than 30 percent of the low-interest respondents rated Dole and Clinton at 50, but 51 percent rated Gramm at that midpoint. These numbers may suggest that little information went into the evaluations of Gramm and raise the question of what a score of 50 represents: was it a genuinely neutral point or simply a convenient and safe home for the expression of nonattitudes that were not filtered out by the screening questions?

A study by Herrmann et al. (1998) on public attitudes toward food safety issues (for example, salmonella and listeria) found that the use of filter or screening questions that measured citizens' concern about and awareness of food safety issues affected the distribution of responses. More specifically, questions that began with "How concerned are you about . . . ?" elicited higher levels of concern than those that began with "Are you concerned . . . ?" and, if concerned, followed by "How concerned are you . . . ?" The use of screening questions measuring awareness of food safety issues in conjunction with the "concern" screen resulted in a portrayal of the American public as less worried about food safety issues than when no filters or screens were used. The authors suggest that if public opinion is translated into policy decisions, it makes a difference which portrayal of the American public is presented. The various filter questions were appropriate, the authors argued, because they generated responses from citizens who were more informed and concerned about the issues and therefore more likely to express genuine attitudes.

Pay Respondents in BitCoin

Nonattitudes and the Middle Position in Survey Questions

The preceding examples illustrate how difficult it is to assess the magnitude of the nonattitude problem. They also raise another problem in attitude and opinion measurement: What does it mean when a person replies to a survey question, "I don't know" or "I can't decide" or "It depends"? Do these responses represent a genuine neutral stance or something else? Should the responses of holders of nonattitudes be included at the neutral or middle point, or should they be at a distinct point off the measurement scale in order not to create a misleading image of large numbers of citizens thoughtfully adopting the middle position?

The response alternatives included in an item affect the extent of nonattitudes. For example, a CBS News/*New York Times* poll conducted in November 1985 asked a national sample of Americans, "Who should have the most say about what cuts should be made to balance the budget—the President or Congress?" Note that the question did not give respondents the option of stating that the president and Congress should have an equal say. About 4 percent of the sample volunteered this response, but what percentage of Americans would have opted for this alternative had it been explicitly presented? In marked contrast is the following question in a November 1985 ABC News/*Washington Post* poll: "As things presently stand, who do you think is ahead in military power, the United States or the Soviet Union, or do you think they are about the same in military strength?" Twenty-four percent said the United States was ahead, 26 percent said the Soviets were, 4 percent had no opinion, and 46 percent said that both nations were about the same in military strength. In fact, in the eight times between 1979 and 1991 that this question was asked of samples of Americans by ABC News/*Washington Post* pollsters, the percentage of respondents citing "the same" ranged from 34 to 55 with an average of 44. One can only speculate what the responses would have looked like if the middle choice had not been provided.

Research on the effects of including a middle choice in the response alternatives shows that such an option typically generates about 25 percent more noncommittal responses (Schuman and Presser 1977; Bishop et al. 1980; Presser and Schuman 1980). This finding suggests that the omission of such a choice will result in many substantive responses that are not very meaningful from citizens who have weak or nonexistent attitudes on a subject. In one study, Presser and Schuman (1980) administered two forms of survey items to random subsamples. The only difference between the two forms was that one offered a middle alternative and the other did not. For example, one item asked about the penalties for using marijuana: "In your opinion, should the penalties for using marijuana be more strict, less strict, or about the same as they are now?" The other version read: "In your opinion, should the penalties for using marijuana be more strict or less strict than they are now?" On average, about 23 percent of respondents answered "about the same as they are now" when that choice was included in the question, compared with only about 8 percent who volunteered that response when it was not included.

Research by Bishop (1987) further demonstrates how the presence or absence of a middle response alternative can affect survey responses. Based on a series of experiments, Bishop's work confirmed earlier research in finding that citizens are much more likely to choose the middle alternative when it is included in the question than when it is omitted. Moreover, simply mentioning the middle category in the preface of a survey question will encourage respondents to select that option even when it is not listed among the response alternatives. More important, Bishop presents evidence (p. 227) that suggests that "people who select a middle alternative when it is offered would not necessarily answer the question in the same way as other respondents if forced to choose between the polar alternatives" when the middle option is not provided.

The interpretation of a "don't know" response can be especially problematic, because "don't know" can mean many different things (Coombs and Coombs 1976–1977; Faulkenberry and Mason 1978). For some people, "don't know" simply reflects the absence of a real attitude on the topic, but for other people it may represent an inability to choose among contending positions. Smith (1984, 229) points out other ways in which "don't know" responses might arise. Respondents may be too insecure to take a stance, or they may decline to state their opinions out of a strong sense of privacy or because they do not want to offend anybody. Some respondents may want to hasten the completion of the interview by saying "don't know," thereby avoiding follow-up questions. Finally, just as respondents' nonattitudes may be disguised as attitudes, so too their middle responses (including "don't know") may mask genuine attitudes. Gilljam and Granberg (1993) found that poll respondents who were induced to respond to a survey item after they had initially given a "don't know" response to that item expressed attitudes that were predictive of behavior. They concluded that, indeed, some poll respondents who had genuine attitudes kept them concealed by opting for the "don't know" response.

Converse (1976–1977) investigated the characteristics of respondents as well as the properties of survey questions that might affect the frequency of "no opinion" and "don't know" answers. She found, as expected, that the higher the level of education of respondents, the less likely they were to give "no opinion" replies. For question characteristics, she found that

"I'm undecided, but that doesn't mean I'm apathetic or uninformed."

the most important feature was the content of the item. As the subject matter of the question became remoter from the concerns and interests of citizens, the frequency of "don't know" responses increased.

Other research sheds further light on how survey responses are affected by response alternatives and their ordering. Krosnick and Alwin (1987) found that respondents with less cognitive sophistication—less formal education and limited vocabularies—were more likely to be influenced by the order of responses. Bishop (1990) also found that the effects on responses of using or not using a middle alternative are most pronounced among citizens who are less involved with the particular topic of the survey question. In general, the implications of the Converse, Bishop, and Krosnick and Alwin studies are that the consequences of response alternatives and their ordering are genuine but complex. Therefore pollsters must be sensitive to the potential distortion and even manipulation of responses that might occur because of how the response choices are presented.

Is it a good idea to force responses into polar categories and minimize middle or neutral answers? Or is it better to encourage people to choose the middle position? The answer, of course, is that it depends. If people have genuine attitudes, then the public opinion researcher wants those attitudes clearly expressed. The inclusion of a middle category in such a situation might result in cautious citizens opting for the middle position, particularly on controversial issues where they might not want to reveal their true opinions to the interviewer. Yet the omission of a middle category might lead people with weak or nonexistent opinions on an issue to choose one of the genuine response options, thereby creating false impressions of genuine attitudes. A similar dilemma occurs with screening questions. The researcher wants to screen out nonattitudes, but does not want to make it too easy for people to avoid answering questions on which they have real views, or too difficult for them to answer questions when they have real, although weak, attitudes.

This is a problem without a simple, neat solution. The public opinion pollster and the consumer of the research must simply be sensitive to whether and in what form screening questions are used on a survey. They must also be aware of the response alternatives provided to the respondents. Finally, the appropriateness of particular substantive questions to particular samples of citizens should always be a central concern of the political analyst and the public opinion consumer. In the political realm, issues of great concern to political elites may be of little interest to the rank and file.

Response Instability and Nonattitudes

If a survey is measuring genuine attitudes, the responses should show some degree of stability over time. Yet often survey responses fluctuate wildly over a relatively short period. This type of fluctuation raises questions about how real the measured opinions were in the first place. Instability of responses to identical polling questions asked over time may be an indicator of nonattitudes. Zaller and Feldman (1992) offer a different explanation, however, for unstable attitudes. They argue that citizens do not have highly specific, fixed attitudes about many topics; instead, people often have multiple and sometimes conflicting opinions on issues. How people respond to a particular survey question on a topic may be a function of what they happen to have on their minds at the time of the survey. And what is on their minds will be influenced by both their most recent life experiences as well as the cues provided by the actual survey question. Thus it is possible for citizens to respond differently on issues over a short period of time without that instability necessarily indicating nonattitudes, because it may be that the real world or the survey context within which people respond to polling questions has changed. Assessment of the magnitude of the non-attitudes problem then becomes even more difficult.

The work of Zaller and Feldman has many implications. First, it serves as a reminder that the responses to survey questions can be affected by characteristics of the survey instrument itself, including question wording, question order, and response alternatives—topics discussed in Chapter 3. Second, it also serves as a warning that opinions on complex topics should always be assessed using multiple items—not just one or two survey items. Unfortunately, in many omnibus public opinion surveys in which the investigators are trying to cover a wide variety of topics, it may be impossible to include multiple items on a single topic because of time and space considerations. Thus the results one gets are a function of which particular item was used. (This problem is discussed in greater depth in Chapter 8.) Finally, Zaller and Feldman's notion that the considerations that citizens utilize in the survey context affect their responses to specific questions provides a rationale for giving respondents new information to ascertain whether their responses change. For example, suppose a sample of senior citizens are asked about their views of Medicare-provided prescription drug benefits and that their responses are overwhelmingly supportive of such a program. Now suppose a follow-up question that asks respondents whether they would support such a program if it means higher Medicare premiums produces much lower support for the program. Is this change in the distribution of opinions an indication of nonattitudes? The answer, of course, is no. The different distribution reflects the different considerations that come into play in the responses to the two questions. The first question evokes a health concern; the second question introduces the cost factor and changes how respondents think about the issue. (This example of introducing new information to the respondent should not be confused, however, with the illegitimate push polls discussed in Chapter 7. Study of whether respondents' views on an issue change when new information is presented to them is appropriate.)

One strategy that uses multiple items to determine how genuine measured opinions really are is the "mushiness index" developed by the polling firm of Yankelovich, Skelly, and White. The index was designed to assess the volatility of the public's views on issues, particularly the ones on which citizens provide answers even though they have little information and understanding about them. The mushiness index has four components in addition to a person's position on a particular issue: how much the issue affects the respondent personally, how well informed the respondent feels he or she is on the issue, how much the respondent discusses the issue with family and friends, and the respondent's own assessment of how likely it is that his or her views on the issue will change (Keene and Sackett 1981).

On the basis of these criteria, Yankelovich, Skelly, and White placed issues into three categories ranging from very volatile or "mushy" to firm. They found that, in general, attitudes on domestic policy were less mushy than those on foreign policy.

The usefulness of the mushiness index is illustrated by the following example (Keene and Sackett 1981, 51). A sample of Americans was asked: "Do you favor or oppose restricting imports of foreign goods such as Japanese cars, textiles, and steel, which are less expensive than American products?" Fifty-four percent favored restricting imports, 41 percent opposed restrictions, and only 5 percent were unsure. But when the sample was broken down into three groups according to responses to the four mushiness criteria, the patterns of response were quite different. Among the mushiest group, 39 percent favored restrictions, 37 percent opposed them, and 24 percent were unsure; among the firmest group, 62 percent favored restrictions, 37 percent opposed them, and 1 percent was unsure.

How much respondents know about an issue (one component of the mushiness index) clearly affects their attitudes, as an April 1986 CBS News/New York Times poll made clear. The poll queried Americans about their support for the Nicaraguan contras, rebels who were fighting against the Marxist Sandinista government. Overall, 25 percent of the sample was willing to aid the contras; 62 percent opposed such an action. But when the sample was divided according to whether the respondents knew which side the United States supported in Nicaragua, major differences were observed (Shipler 1986). Among those respondents who knew which side the United States favored, 40 percent supported aid to the contras, and 52 percent opposed it. But of those who were not aware of American policy, only 16 percent favored aid to the contras, and 59 percent opposed such assistance.

When expansion of NATO became a prominent political issue in 1997, pollsters began asking questions on the issue. Because Americans are likely to have low levels of information and substantial nonattitudes about NATO and NATO expansion, a "mushiness" approach to ascertaining attitudes about the future of NATO would be appropriate. One poll conducted in early 1997 found that about 70 percent of respondents had heard little about NATO expansion (Morin 1997b). Almost one-fourth of respondents incorrectly believed that Russia already was a member of NATO, and about 60 percent were predisposed toward NATO enlargement, a level of support that dropped substantially when NATO expansion was linked to the financial and other costs associated with bringing new members into the alliance. In general, surveys dealing with foreign affairs are more susceptible to the measurement of nonattitudes, because such topics tend not to be as salient and interesting to many Americans.

The mushiness index is not used widely in surveys, in part because it is too costly and time-consuming to ask all the questions needed to construct the index, particularly when the survey covers multiple substantive issues. Nevertheless, the concept of mushiness is of interest analytically, because it helps to explain a number of apparent anomalies in American public opinion. One puzzle is the rapid swings in public opinion often observed after the president of the United States delivers a speech devoted to a single issue, particularly foreign policy. Public opinion is most volatile on issues that seem distant in terms of their likely effects on people and their susceptibility to citizen influence. Americans often praise presidents for their ability to move public opinion, not recognizing that on some issues a somewhat mindless "follow the leader" mentality is at work; a president would be successful in moving public opinion in any direction, assuming the White House is able to present the issue in ways beneficial to both presidential and citizens' objectives.

The rationale underlying the mushiness index did not originate with Yankelovich, Skelly, and White; more than fifty years ago George Gallup (1947) espoused survey designs that measured multiple aspects of a person's opinion. Indeed, Schuman and Presser (1981) and other investigators have emphasized the need to measure the importance of an issue to a person as well as his or her opinion on that issue in order to better understand the dynamics of attitude change. Yankelovich, Skelly, and White did, however, have the public relations acumen to coin a catchy phrase for their finding, which built on the results of earlier public opinion studies.

Many survey questions seem to be prime candidates for high mushiness scores, yet unfortunately these scores will not be calculated because, faced with insufficient time and space on the survey, researchers will not ask the necessary follow-up question. Thus poll users need to ask themselves whether the topic of a survey is likely to be of concern to respondents or whether they will see the topic as an abstraction with little immediate and practical relevance. If the former, mushiness and nonattitudes are not likely to be a serious problem. The complicating factor is that the topic of the survey is likely to be of varying importance to different segments of the American population. Unemployed steel and auto workers are more likely to be concerned about foreign imports and thus to have more stable attitudes on that issue than, say, college students. Likewise, senior citizens are more likely to have well-developed views on Social Security and Medicare than a youthful population group. Consequently, American public opinion on a particular issue includes the rather divergent views of various subgroups of the population, some of whom have genuine attitudes on the issue while others do not. Moreover, for those seeking to relate public opinion to the processes and decisions of government, the whole of public opinion may be less important than the opinion of a particular subset of people. On certain issues the views of a few people with genuine attitudes may have the greatest impact on government policy and policy makers.

Conclusion

The problem of nonattitudes remains one of the least-considered aspects of public opinion polling. Other facets of public opinion research, such as question wording and sampling, receive much more attention, even to the point of being mentioned in television and newspaper reports of public opinion polls. But very few people raise the fundamental questions: Was the topic of the survey of interest to the respondents? Did the poll query people on topics about which they held genuine views? Did the survey questions adequately capture the complexity of the issue being studied?

Assessing the size of the problem of nonattitudes is a difficult task made even more problematic by the tendency of people to respond to questions not in terms of the questions' actual purpose and content, but in terms of the cues provided by the questions and whatever meaning (often idiosyncratic) respondents read into them. For example, a person asked whether she favors selling military equipment to Saudi Arabia might answer the question not on the basis of any information about Saudi Arabia, but on the basis of a predisposition toward the weapons industry in general (she might be a stockholder in a firm that manufactures weapons). Likewise, citizens asked whether they favor joint U.S.-Russian space ventures might respond on the basis of their underlying view of Russia rather than on the basis of opinions about the best way to explore outer space.

Although nonattitudes can be a polling problem, Americans should not disregard polls, because on many issues the general public has genuine attitudes and is willing and able to express them. On other issues only a small subset of the public may have real opinions, but even then events may transform such an issue into one that engages the serious attention of the mass public. Moreover, sometimes the public may even seem fickle on the issues it cares about and on its positions on these issues. Oreskes (1990) observed that in 1989, 64 percent of Americans said the drug problem was the most important one facing the nation. Yet a year later only 10 percent cited drugs as the most serious problem. Certainly it was not victory in the drug war that led citizens to downgrade the importance of the drug problem. Instead, it was more a matter of media and presidential emphasis on issues; when the media and the president focused on the drug menace, then many Americans saw the issue as the critical one facing the nation. But as new issues arose and media and political attention shifted, Americans' views of which issues were critical also changed. Public opinion polls do provide valid assessments of what Americans are thinking, but keep in mind that not all issues are appropriate topics for public opinion surveys.

Nonattitudes are more a problem of the respondent than of the measuring instrument—that is, nonattitudes can arise even when a question is carefully constructed without any loaded words or implied alternatives. Nevertheless, deficiencies in the questions themselves can contribute to the problem of nonattitudes, as well as to many other difficulties encountered in public opinion polling. Chapter 3 takes a closer look at how question wording, question order, and question context can affect the results of public opinion polls.

3 Wording and Context of Questions

Of all the pitfalls associated with public opinion polling, question wording is probably the one most familiar to consumers of public opinion research. The use of a loaded word or an inflammatory phrase can affect the pattern of responses to a survey question. For example, for a poll to show weak support for federal assistance to financially beleaguered entities (such as the savings and loan industry in the 1990s), the pollster need only ask Americans whether they favor a federal "bailout" of these entities. Few people favor a bailout, but many more support federal loans with proper safeguards that the moneys will be repaid. A poll likely to indicate scant support for providing foreign aid will ask an argumentative and leading question such as: Do you favor giving foreign aid to other nations when there are children in the United States who are suffering from hunger? To demonstrate support for foreign aid, a pollster could "load" the question differently: Do you favor giving foreign aid to other nations in order to help them resist communist subversion and thereby enhance our national security?

Individuals and groups with an ax to grind can easily construct questions that will generate desired responses. The response alternatives they provide the interviewees also can help them achieve the intended result. As noted in Chapter 2, if a middle alternative is not listed as one of the choices, fewer citizens will opt for that choice, which can alter the interpretation of a poll. For example, if a mayor wants a poll to indicate support for a city's spending policies on garbage collection, he or she might ask this question: Do you think the city is spending too much, too little, or about the right amount on garbage collection? Clearly, the response "about the right amount" is an endorsement of the mayor's current policies. But if "about the right amount" were not included as an explicit response alternative, respondents would provide fewer such replies because they would have to volunteer that response. A high response to either of the other two alternatives, of course, would create an impression of citizen dissatisfaction with the mayor's spending on garbage collection.

If advocacy groups want to demonstrate through public opinion surveys that their issues are at the forefront of citizens' concerns, they might simply commission polls that ask citizens to select from a list of problems the most important one facing the nation. The key to obtaining the desired result would be to place the advocacy group's issue on a list of relatively minor problems. For example, if an environmental group wanted to demonstrate the importance of the environment, it might ask Americans which of the following is the most important problem facing the nation—environmental quality, excessive telemarketing, traffic congestion, and ticket scalping at entertainment events. Undoubtedly, this survey would discover that environmental quality was the number one issue cited. But what if the environmental group presented the results of this rather silly example without providing the actual question wording and response alternatives? Citizens might mistakenly assume that education, national defense, Social Security, health care, and other prominent issues were on the list and that environmental quality came out on top in competition with all of those other major issues.

Bad question wording also may occur when polls are conducted by entities that are trying to generate specific responses. Even so, most professional polls are not blatantly manipulated; instead, questions are typically worded in a nonbiased, fair, and straightforward fashion. But as we shall see, even when the sponsor has no obvious ax to grind, question wording choices greatly influence the results obtained. In many instances highly reputable polling organizations have arrived at divergent conclusions simply because they employed different (although well-constructed) questions on a particular topic.

Less obvious than the impact of question wording is the effect on responses of the order and context in which specific questions are placed. A typical public opinion survey includes many questions, and the placement of a particular question can affect the responses to it. Yet most consumers of public opinion research know little about item order and therefore have little sense of how the context has helped to shape the responses.

Consider the following hypothetical example—a survey assessing popular attitudes toward economic relations with China. The key question measuring support for most-favored-nation trade status for China is preceded by a battery of items about Chinese human rights violations. Obviously, the early questions on Chinese human rights violations will predispose respondents to be more hostile toward granting China favorable trade conditions. Or imagine a survey in which the popularity of the president is measured after a series of questions dealing with administration scandals and difficulties with the economy and Congress. Certainly, reactions to the president will be more negative when respondents are first reminded of these problems. The point of both examples is that the context in which a particular survey item is embedded can help to shape responses to that item.

This chapter presents numerous examples of questions from a variety of real-world settings. It will become clear, if it is not so already, that some "question effects" are obvious and therefore less likely to mislead people, and others are subtle and more problematic and may indeed manipulate and mislead unsuspecting consumers of public opinion research.

Question Wording

Five decades ago Stanley Payne wrote *The Art of Asking Questions,* a fundamental work on interviewing techniques. In the final chapter he presented a checklist of one hundred considerations, organized around themes such as the topic being studied, the structure of the question and the response alternatives, the treatment of the respondents, the words themselves, sources of bias, and the readability of the questions. Most of what Payne said then still holds true today and demonstrates that constructing good questions is largely a matter of common sense (Payne 1951).

Some problems with the wording of questions are obvious and may even be intentional, particularly in pseudo-polls whose sponsors are seeking specific results (see Chapter 1). Clearly, the use of loaded words will affect the results. For example, referring to labor union officials as union czars or union bosses rather than union leaders will certainly affect opinions about union officials. Likewise, questions can be argumentative, pushing respondents in a particular direction. For example, the American Foundation for AIDS Research asked the following question in 1994:

> The AIDS epidemic is a national emergency. It has already claimed over 180,000 lives in the U.S. alone. Over one and a half million Americans now carry the AIDS virus. Do you think the majority of Americans realize how widespread this tragedy has become, and that the worst is still ahead?

Note that this is a compound question. It asks about two topics—the extent of the epidemic and its future—yet the respondent is not allowed to distinguish between the two. Sometimes compound questions are more disguised in that the duality of the item is not evident until one interprets responses to the question. Classic examples of such questions are: Do you still beat your spouse? Have you stopped using illegal drugs? Yes and no answers to both of these questions leave the impression that at some point respondents beat their spouses and used illegal drugs. Obviously, the solution here is to use two questions: Did you ever use illegal drugs in the past? Are you currently using illegal drugs?

Compound
Best Practices

Survey questions are also flawed when they provide false or misleading information in order to influence responses. A 1994 pseudo-poll for the National Republican Senatorial Committee included the following item: "Do you support President Clinton's tax increase on Americans who earn more than $30,000 a year? (The top tax rate increased from 31% to 36%.)" Among the many things wrong with this question is the possibility that it might leave the citizen who earned more than $30,000 with the incorrect impression that his or her tax rate increased from 31 percent to 36 percent.

Wording problems also can arise on routine topics included in legitimate surveys. Seemingly straightforward questions that employ relatively simple language can seem ambiguous to respondents. Even basic questions about the number of persons in a household or the number of children in a family can present difficulties. For example, in surveys in which the wife and husband were interviewed independently, their responses did not agree perfectly about such factual items as the number of children they had (Asher 1974b). Perhaps errors were made in transcribing their responses. Or perhaps the question was ambiguous. One spouse might have responded in terms of children living at home, the other in terms of the total number. Or one spouse might have included children from a previous marriage, and the other might not have. Martin (1999) finds that respondents' reports of who lived in a household are generally accurate except when members of a respondent's household are not continually present, such as students, or are away periodically, perhaps because of work-related reasons. Indeed, he estimates that up to four million people nationally might be overlooked because of problems in reporting household members. Measurement of a respondent's age also has proven to be surprisingly problematic. Peterson (1984) shows that four different ways of measuring age in a survey yield substantially different refusal rates (that is, the percentage of respondents refusing to answer the question), although the age data obtained are very similar across the four formats. By contrast, Harker (1998) finds that two different ways of measuring a person's income do not affect the response rates, but do yield different reports of income levels. Finally, the simple way in which older surveys categorized race—white, black, and other—may no longer suffice as the United States becomes more racially and ethnically diverse and more and more citizens have multiracial backgrounds.

Fowler (1992) argues that survey questions, even apparently straightforward ones, must be adequately pretested before they are included in an actual poll. He discusses seven questions—used in national health surveys—that were subjected to extensive pretesting and found to have a number of ambiguous terms. For example, the very simple question "Do you exercise or play sports regularly?" was found to be ambiguous, because different respondents had different views on what constituted exercise. The question was then modified to read: "Do you do any sports or hobbies involving physical activities, or any exercise, including walking, on a regular basis?"

Imagine the ambiguity that can arise from the simple question "Have you taken a vacation in the last few years?" Does "last few years" mean one or two years, or could it mean three, four, or five years to some respondents? And what constitutes a vacation—going somewhere or does staying at home by the swimming pool count?

If question wording can affect measurement of objective matters such as a person's age and the number of children in a family, then how much might wording affect more subjective phenomena? The answer is that wording can make a great difference as shown in the following examples. In 1982 the Advisory Commission on Intergovernmental Relations sponsored three surveys asking Americans which services they would cut if funds were short (Herbers 1982). One question asked: "Suppose the budgets of your state and local governments have to be curtailed, which of these parts would you limit most severely?" About 8 percent of the respondents cited "aid to the needy" when that response was listed as one of the service areas that could be cut. But when the term "public welfare programs" was used in place of "aid to the needy" and the other choices remained the same, many more respondents (39 percent) opted to cut welfare. Obviously, aid to the needy is much more popular than public welfare, and the program label used in the survey strongly influenced the results. In fact, Americans tend to complain about welfare in general but be highly supportive of specific programs that could justifiably be included under the rubric of welfare.

One general rule in constructing survey questions is to avoid double negatives. Yet such a mistake was made in a 1992 Roper poll conducted for the American Jewish Committee on the Holocaust. The results of this poll and the subsequent media coverage generated a lot of controversy and consternation (Kifner 1994; Ladd 1994; Moore and Newport 1994; Morin 1994c, 1994d). The Roper question asked: "Does it seem possible or does it seem impossible to you that the Nazi extermination of the Jews never happened?" Fully 22 percent of respondents said that it seemed possible that the Holocaust never occurred, and another 12 percent did not know. When these results became known, many people expressed their shock and concern about American ignorance of the Holocaust and fears about the success of anti-Semitic revisionist historians. But it turned out that these results largely stemmed from a convoluted question. The Roper organization itself was so dismayed that such a poorly worded question had seen the light of day that it redid the survey for the American Jewish Congress. This time the question was: "Does it seem possible to you that the Nazi

Best
Practices

extermination of the Jews never happened, or do you feel certain that it happened?" With this wording, only 1 percent of respondents said it seemed possible that the Holocaust had never occurred. The Gallup Organization also tested the impact of alternative question wording and got results similar to those of Roper (Ladd 1994). The pain and confusion caused by the first Roper question show how careful one must be in wording questions.

Often in providing respondents with some background to a question, a pollster may go too far. In a June 17, 1985, editorial entitled "A Grain of Salt, Please," the *Washington Post* complained about the increasingly common practice of informing respondents about a topic in order to ascertain their opinion on it. Obviously, the kind of information provided to respondents will have a lot to do with the views they express later on the issue. The *Post* editorial cited a statement in a Harris poll as an example of how ludicrous matters can become. The following agree/disagree statement was presented to a sample of Americans in January 1985: "When [Bernard] Goetz said in his confession that he used dum-dum bullets, that he was sorry he didn't gouge out the eyes of the four [young men] he shot, and that if he could have reloaded his gun fast enough, he would have taken out after them, he looks more like a *Death Wish* gunman out stalking to kill criminals, not an innocent victim just trying to defend himself [from a mugging]." As the *Post* opined, "The wonder is not that a majority agreed with the statement, but that 38 percent of the respondents had the gumption to disagree."

My favorite example of an argumentative question purporting to inform respondents comes from the 1982 Democratic primary race for governor in Ohio. Three major candidates were running: the former lieutenant governor, Richard Celeste; the incumbent attorney general, William Brown; and the former mayor of Cincinnati, Jerry Springer. The pollster for the attorney general (Pat Caddell's Cambridge Survey Research) included the following question in a statewide survey:

> As you may know, in 1974, Jerry Springer, who had gotten married six months earlier, was arrested on a morals charge with three women in a hotel room. He also used a bad check to pay for the women's services, and subsequently resigned as mayor of his city. Does this make you much more likely, somewhat more likely, somewhat less likely, or much less likely to support Jerry Springer for governor this year?

In addition to being factually incorrect on a number of points, this question was a blatant effort by the pollster first to feed consumers information that would generate negative responses about a candidate and then to use the replies in a highly selective way for political purposes (see the discussion of push polling in Chapter 7). In the context of the discussion of nonattitudes

FRANK AND ERNEST by Bob Thaves

IT SEEMS TO ME THAT "HOW MANY IN YOUR HOUSEHOLD?" WOULD BE A SIMPLE QUESTION TO ANSWER, DR. JEKYLL.

THAVES 12-3

FRANK & ERNEST reprinted by permission of Newspaper Enterprise Association, Inc.

in Chapter 2, this question was an attempt to create attitudes on the basis of the interview situation—something that can be done in a variety of ways. One technique is to present hypothetical situations to citizens and then ask them to react to these situations. More often than not, the information obtained is of dubious use, because the hypothetical situations have forced the respondents into a world that has little real meaning for them.

Sometimes the response alternatives that a question provides also can affect survey results. For example, Kagay and Elder (1992) examined attitudes toward Clinton and Bush as measured in two July 1992 polls, one conducted by Gallup and the other by CBS News/*New York Times*. The Gallup poll asked voters if their opinions of a candidate were favorable or unfavorable; respondents could volunteer that they did not know enough to offer an opinion. By contrast, the CBS News/*New York Times* poll presented respondents four choices: favorable, not favorable, undecided, or haven't heard enough about a candidate to have an opinion. Needless to say, compared with the Gallup poll, the CBS News/*New York Times* poll found fewer Americans offering an opinion, because it provided two opportunities for citizens to refuse to rate the candidates, and the Gallup poll provided no such opportunity. Thus the CBS News/*New York Times* poll found 36 percent of Americans favorable to Clinton, 24 percent unfavorable, 31 percent undecided, and 9 percent stating that they had not heard enough. The Gallup poll, by contrast, found 63 percent favorable toward Clinton, 25 percent unfavorable, and only 12 percent volunteering "don't know."

Morin (1993d) has shown that slight modifications in the choices presented in the standard presidential approval question can alter the results. The standard question reads: "Do you approve or disapprove of the job [   ] is doing as president?" Respondents are next asked whether they strongly or somewhat approve or disapprove. Another way of asking the question is to combine opinion and intensity in one item: "Do you strongly approve, somewhat approve, somewhat disapprove or strongly disapprove of the job [   ] is doing as president?" In Morin's study, conducted during the Clinton administration, these different wordings affected the results. The half of the sample that received the first wording gave Clinton a 53 percent approval rating and a 38 percent disapproval rating. But the other half of the sample, responding to the second version of the question, gave Clinton a 62 percent approval rating (the two approval responses combined) and a 32 percent disapproval rating (the two disapproval responses combined). A *Time*/CNN poll conducted in August 1994 asked Americans, "Who is more responsible for today's gridlock in government?" Respondents, though, were offered only two choices—Clinton or Republicans in Congress. "Democrats in Congress" was not an option, yet it was a logical possibility. The results revealed that 48 percent of respondents blamed the Republicans, 32 percent blamed Clinton, and 12 percent volunteered that both were equally at fault. Democrats in Congress might have been tempted to trumpet these results, but it was clear that the results were partially a product of the choices provided to respondents.

As the Republican Congress and President Clinton went through their budget battles in 1995 and 1996, both sides tried to spin poll results to their advantage, and both complained about how the media were reporting the polls. For example, in late 1995 the *New York Times* published poll results showing that Americans, by a 67 to 27 percent margin, preferred not to cut Medicare in order to balance the budget, a result described as a setback for the GOP budget plan (Budiansky 1995). The Republicans cried foul, claiming that the polling question was unfair and inaccurate and that their plan did not cut Medicare but simply slowed its rate of growth. A subsequent *Newsweek* poll that talked about "limits" on Medicare rather than "cuts"—and incorporated the GOP tax cut plan—found less opposition to the Republican budget plan; Americans opposed it by only a 51 to 41 percent margin. Americans were swayed, then, by whether the focus was on cuts to Medicare or limits to Medicare.

Two other surveys tapping opinions about Medicare found the same thing (Morin 1995c). One survey asked Americans, "Would you favor or oppose major reductions in the rate of increase in Medicare spending to balance the federal budget?" Forty-four percent of respondents supported such reductions in Medicare to achieve a balanced budget. But in another national survey conducted a week later, only 22 percent of respondents agreed with the notion of "cutting Medicare benefits to reduce the budget deficit." It is no wonder, then, that throughout the budget debate the GOP spin doctors were encouraging Republican members of Congress to talk about reducing the rate of growth in Medicare, while their Democratic counterparts were telling Democrats to talk loudly and often about cuts in Medicare (Kolbert 1995).

Americans' opinions about U.S. troops in Bosnia provide another ex-

ample of how relatively modest differences in question wording can dramatically affect citizens' responses to polls (Morin 1995e). On the night that President Clinton delivered a televised address announcing that U.S. troops would be sent to Bosnia, many survey organizations queried Americans about their views on U.S. involvement in that country. For example, an ABC News poll stated, "Clinton said now that a Bosnia peace treaty has been signed, he's sending 20,000 U.S. troops to Bosnia as part of an international peacekeeping force." When asked whether they favored or opposed this action, 39 percent of Americans supported the president's proposal and 57 percent opposed it. A Gallup poll, however, found 46 percent in favor of the president's plan and only 40 percent opposed after asking Americans, "Now that a peace agreement has been reached by all the groups currently fighting in Bosnia, the Clinton administration plans to contribute U.S. troops to an international peace-keeping force. Do you favor or oppose that?" Clearly many Americans did not have strong views or much information about Bosnia and, as discussed in Chapter 2, undoubtedly relied on the question wording to provide cues and information about how to respond. The ABC News question refers to Clinton; the Gallup question refers to the Clinton administration. The ABC News question refers to

"Clinton . . . sending troops"; the Gallup question mentions that the "Clinton administration planned to contribute U.S. troops." Thus the ABC News question ties the decision more directly and personally to the president than does the Gallup question. Moreover, the Gallup question is more explicit about the fighting that had occurred in Bosnia, thereby providing Americans who wanted the fighting to stop with a stronger argument to support the president. But, unlike the ABC News item, the Gallup question does not inform respondents about how many troops will be sent to Bosnia. Overall, then, the intent of both survey items is the same—to assess Americans' support for this foreign policy initiative. The slight differences in question wording, however, make it difficult to determine just where American public opinion stands.

As the political parties jockeyed in 2000–2001 for advantage in using the federal budget surplus, poll results again indicated that Americans' preferences looked different depending on how the question was asked. Stevenson (2000) asked citizens what they preferred "the leaders in Washington . . . do with the remainder of the surplus." Two alternatives were presented:

> Should the money be used for a tax cut, or should it be used to fund new government programs?

> Should the money be used for a tax cut, or should it be spent on programs for education, the environment, health care, crime-fighting and military defense?

For the first alternative, 60 percent of Americans favored a tax cut, and 25 percent preferred spending on new programs. But for the second alternative, only 22 percent favored a tax cut, and 69 percent supported spending for the mentioned programs. There is nothing necessarily inconsistent about this pattern of responses, because Americans may have felt that the "new programs" mentioned in the first alternative would be frivolous and not include the important, current programs mentioned in the second alternative. Whatever the case, the wording makes a major difference; support for tax cuts drops when the alternative is additional spending for specific policy areas that Americans like.

The final example of the impact of question wording is taken from the impeachment of President Clinton, presumably a topic about which Americans were informed and felt strongly (whatever their preferences), and therefore one on which question wording was likely to have fewer effects. But even here the wording effects were dramatic, as summarized by Morin (1999a) who reviewed several polls. A *Washington Post*/ABC News poll asked half of a sample of Americans whether Clinton should resign if he were impeached or whether he should "fight the charges in the Senate." The other half of the sample was asked whether Clinton should resign if impeached or whether he should "remain in office and face trial in the Senate?" Fifty-nine percent said Clinton should resign rather than fight the charges, but only 43 percent said he should resign rather than face a Senate trial. Morin speculates that the key factor here is the word "fight" in the first alternative; Americans do not like political combat. The second alternative—face trial—is less threatening to Americans. An even more surprising result occurred when Americans were asked the following two very similar questions in a *New York Times*/CBS News poll:

> If the full House votes to send impeachment articles to the Senate for a trial, then do you think it would be better for the country if Bill Clinton resigned from office, or not?

> If the full House votes to impeach Bill Clinton, then do you think it would be better for the country if Bill Clinton resigned from office, or not?

In response to the first question, 43 percent of the sample favored a presidential resignation; in response to the second, more than 60 percent favored resignation. Morin speculates that because the second question did not mention a trial, respondents may have thought that impeachment was equivalent to being found guilty and thus the president should resign. But the first question explicitly mentions a trial, which suggested that the process was not yet complete.

Branching and labeling can have a big effect on the apparent stability of attitudes (Krosnick and Berent 1993). *Branching* refers to the follow-up questions asked after an initial query is presented to respondents. For example, political scientists typically measure political party identification by a series of questions. The first simply ascertains whether a person is a Democrat, a Republican, or an independent. If respondents say Democrat or Republican, they are then asked whether they are strong or not very strong Democrats or Republicans. If respondents say they are independents, they are then asked whether they lean toward the Democrats or the Republicans. Note that at each stage of the questioning, the response alternatives are *labeled*—that is, each response option is specified in words. <u>Unlabeled</u> options are said to be used when, for example, respondents are asked to place themselves on a scale that ranges from one to seven where only the endpoints are labeled with words; this type of scale is often used to measure citizens' policy attitudes and positions. Social scientists have shown that political party loyalties seem to be more stable than citizens' policy attitudes. But Krosnick and Berent (1993) argue that this finding may simply stem from measuring party identification by a labeled branching technique and assessing policy attitudes by an unlabeled procedure.

Sometimes poll respondents are asked comparative questions: "Do you prefer X to Y?" or "Do you favor A over B?" Research indicates that the order in which the alternatives are presented may affect the results— that is, asking respondents whether they prefer X to Y versus asking them whether they prefer Y to X may generate different results (Wanke et al. 1995; Wanke 1996). For example, Wanke et al. asked samples the following questions:

> Would you say that traffic contributes more or less to air pollution than industry?

> Would you say the industry contributes more or less to air pollution than traffic?

When traffic was mentioned first and industry was mentioned second, 45 percent of respondents said that "traffic contributes more" and 32 percent said that "industry contributes more." But when industry was mentioned first and traffic second, 57 percent of respondents stated that "industry contributes more" compared with 24 percent citing traffic. Evidently, in these kinds of comparison questions people focus on the first item. In other words, asking people to compare X and Y essentially becomes a judgment on X with many aspects of Y ignored. If so, then the responses to the pollution questions are not that surprising. For the consumer of polls, the order of the items being compared becomes one more consideration in assessing the accuracy of poll results.

Often no single questionnaire item can adequately measure the multifaceted construct a public opinion analyst is studying. The researcher therefore may ask a series of questions and combine the results into an index. For example, *political efficacy* is a concept that has long been of great interest to political scientists (Asher 1974a). It refers to a citizen's feelings of effectiveness in dealing with government. Early measures (since modified) of political efficacy generally relied on four statements:

1. I don't think public officials care much what people like me think.
2. Voting is the only way that people like me can have any say about how the government runs things.
3. Sometimes politics and government seem so complicated that a person like me can't really understand what's going on.
4. People like me don't have any say about what the government does.

These items are usually included in surveys in an agree/disagree format, with a disagree response representing the efficacious position on all four

Doonesbury   BY GARRY TRUDEAU

items. A researcher could construct an efficacy index by simply counting the number of items to which the respondent gave an efficacious answer. For the four statements just listed, three or four efficacious responses might be classified as high in efficacy, two efficacious answers as medium, and one or zero as low.

The use of an index is justified on both substantive and methodological grounds (Asher 1974c). Substantively, the index does a better job of representing the complexity of the concept being studied than any single item could. Methodologically, the use of a multiple-item index can lessen the harmful effects of the random measurement error that is present in survey data. Whenever a researcher measures opinions, the very process of measurement may yield results that are not perfectly accurate. If the measurement error is random, the obtained results are just as likely to be above or below the true value. Thus combining a number of items in an index will tend to cancel out some of the random measurement error. However, consumers of public opinion polls are often not provided sufficient information about the components of an index, including the actual wording of the questions. Moreover, consumers are not informed about the ways in which separate items relate to each other and how they are combined into an index; they often must accept on faith that the index has been constructed properly from individual items that themselves were appropriately worded. Chapter 8 presents some substantive examples of situations in which multiple items on a topic were available for analysis.

Question Order and Context

Question order can dramatically affect responses to survey items by altering the framework and context within which a question is answered. An excellent example of the effect of question order occurred in 1980 when the Harris organization employed a "double vote" question to measure citizens' candidate preferences in the presidential primaries. Respondents were asked at the beginning of the interview whether they intended to vote for President Jimmy Carter or Sen. Edward Kennedy in the hotly contested Democratic nomination battle. Next followed questions about domestic and foreign policy, including items about inflation and the economy, American hostages in Iran, and the Soviet invasion of Afghanistan. Toward the end of the interview, the respondents were again asked how they intended to vote. Surprisingly, over the course of the interview support for President Carter declined sharply. The only explanation for this drop was that as respondents thought about Carter's record, their views of him became more negative.

A similar phenomenon occurred in an ABC News/*Washington Post* study of the placement of a presidential popularity question in a survey (Sussman 1984a). In November 1983 a sample of Americans was asked about presidential popularity twice, once at the beginning of the interview and again at the end, with a variety of issue questions in between. Unlike in the preceding example of Kennedy versus Carter, there was very little difference in the overall distribution of the responses at the two time points. Initially, 59 percent approved of the president's performance, 37 percent disapproved, and 4 percent had no opinion. Later, 59 percent approved, 39 percent disapproved, and 2 percent had no opinion. Not obvious from these figures, however, is the fact that more than 15 percent of those sampled changed their opinion about the president over the course of the twenty-minute interview; 8 percent moved from approval to disapproval and 7 percent moved the opposite way.

Many researchers have studied the effects of question order and context. Schuman and Presser (1981) demonstrate that effects of question order are important, particularly when the questions are general, somewhat amorphous, and have little direct relevance to respondents. They strongly suggest that anyone examining the distribution of responses to identical questions asked at multiple points in time take into account whether the context in which the questions were asked also was identical. The significance of this point is supported by the work of Bishop, Oldendick, and Tuchfarber (1982). They argue that the decline in Americans' level of political interest uncovered in a 1978 survey was partly attributable to changes in the context and order in which questions were asked; the real decline in political interest was not nearly as worrisome as originally thought.

A 1984 study by Bishop, Oldendick, and Tuchfarber found that respondents' reports of how much they follow government and politics depended on the context in which the question was asked. For example, if respondents were asked how much they follow government and public affairs after they were asked some difficult questions about their knowledge of their representative's record, they were likely to lower their estimate of their attentiveness to politics. But if respondents were first asked about their attentiveness to politics, they tended to assert a higher level of interest.

The works of Eubank and Gow (1983) and Gow and Eubank (1984) further illustrate the effects of question order and context. They examined the 1978, 1980, and 1982 American National Election Studies (national sample surveys of Americans), which political scientists have used extensively to study the effects of incumbency on citizens' vote choices in U.S. House elections. Political scientists have found that incumbency is a very strong factor in voting, but Eubank and Gow argue that this finding is somewhat artificial because of the placement of questions in the American National Election Studies. They point out that before respondents were questioned about their vote for Congress, they were asked a series of questions about their incumbent U.S. representative. This sequence of questions made it more likely that respondents would claim to have voted for the incumbent when in fact they had not, a tendency especially pronounced among less-knowledgeable citizens, who are generally more susceptible to the effects of question order.

The ability of one question to affect responses to another has been demonstrated by Hyman and Sheatsley (1950), Schuman and Presser (1981), and Schuman, Kalton, and Ludwig (1983). Their studies examined responses to the following two items:

> Do you think the United States should let Communist newspaper reporters from other countries come in here and send back to their papers the news as they see it?

> Do you think a Communist country like Russia should let American newspaper reporters come in and send back to America the news as they see it?

When these two questions were asked in the order just given, support for letting communist reporters come to the United States was much lower than when the questions were asked in the reverse order. The explanation for this pattern seems clear: it was difficult for respondents to deny communist reporters the opportunity to come to the United States if they had already said that American reporters should be allowed to go to the Soviet Union. This effect of context is strong when the questions are contiguous in a survey, but the effect remains strong even when the items are separated by many other questions.

Another example of context effects is provided by Schuman, Presser, and Ludwig (1981), who studied the consequences of different orderings of a general and a specific question on abortion. The items read:

> Do you think it should be possible for a pregnant woman to obtain a legal abortion if she is married and does not want any more children? [general]

> Do you think it should be possible for a pregnant woman to obtain a legal abortion if there is a strong chance of serious defect in the baby? [specific]

The authors found that responses to the general item were very much influenced by whether the item came first or second—that is, support for abortion in general was much higher when the general item came first. Responses to the specific question were not affected by item order. Their explanation for this finding, although speculative, suggests the kinds of cognitive calculations that may shape a response:

> One plausible explanation for the effect turns on the fact that there are a number of different reasons for supporting legalized abortion. A possible defect in an unborn child is a specific reason that appeals to a large part of the population. When the more general item is asked first, some respondents may say yes but mainly with such a specific reason in mind. When the item on abortion because of a defective child is asked first, however, this indicates to respondents that the general item that follows does not refer to that specific case. Thus respondents who are reluctant to favor abortion except within narrow limits should find it easier to oppose the general rationale after having favored (and "subtracted") the more specific rationale about the defective child. (Schuman, Presser, and Ludwig 1981, 220)

In contrast to the example about communist reporters, in which a particular question order promoted consistency, here a particular ordering generated divergence, because some respondents favored abortion in the specific case but opposed it more generally.

A final example of the effects of question order is taken from an analysis by Abramson and colleagues (1987). The authors were puzzled to find that between 1980 and 1984 the percentage of citizens disagreeing with the statement "If a person doesn't care how an election comes out then that person shouldn't vote in it" dropped from 58.7 percent to 42.8 percent. This statement was one of four items that had traditionally been used to measure feelings of citizen duty. In surveys before 1984 this item had been preceded by two related statements with which Americans typically expressed high levels of disagreement. But in 1984, this item, although identical to earlier versions, was not preceded by the other two questions. Abramson and his colleagues provide convincing evidence that the apparent decline in citizens' feelings of duty between 1980 and 1984 was not

real, but was instead a consequence of the different questions that preceded this item in the survey. The general lesson here is that before the
users of polls conclude on the basis of survey data that an attitude change
has occurred over time, they must be able to rule out other explanations
for change, such as differences in question wording and question order.

Assessments of question order and context effects are more problematic for self-administered mail questionnaires than for telephone and personal surveys. In telephone and personal surveys, the interviewer controls
the order in which respondents are given the questions and this order is consistent across respondents. But for self-administered mail questionnaires (as
well as many self-administered Internet surveys), respondents can answer
the questions sequentially, they can read the entire questionnaire first, they
can jump around and answer questions out of order, and they can go back
and change answers after responding to other questions. There is evidence
that in some instances question order is less consequential in self-
administered mail surveys, because respondents are likely to read all the
questions before responding or respondents can change answers after
reading later questions (Schwarz and Hippler 1995). Thus perhaps in the
earlier example about American and Russian reporters the order of the two
questions would be less important in a mail survey because respondents
may have read both questions, whatever their order, before answering the
questions. Or respondents could have changed their responses when they
realized they were being inconsistent by supporting freedom for American reporters in Russia but opposing freedom for Russian reporters in the
United States.

Although the ordering of specific survey items among other questions is considered context, context also refers to the substantive framework within which questions are placed. Pollsters can choose the framework
within which they ask questions, and this choice can be very consequential. A survey about the U.S. military buildup posed in the context of the
successful bombing of Iraq would probably elicit more supportive attitudes
toward defense spending than a similar survey framed in the context of the
huge national debt. In their work on white Americans' attitudes toward affirmative action, Kinder and Sanders (1986) found clear differences in the
factors that affect opinion, depending on whether the questions were presented in the context of reverse discrimination (affirmative action discrimi-
nates against whites) or in the context of undeserved advantage (affirmative
action gives blacks advantages they have not earned). For example, whites'
opinions were more racially motivated when affirmative action was placed
in the context of undeserved advantage.

Finally, context can refer to the broader environment in which an interview is occurring. Personal circumstances, recent societal events, and

the content of media coverage can alter the meaning of a survey question for respondents. An identically worded question can mean dramatically different things to respondents depending on the frame of reference they bring to the interview situation. And one part of that frame of reference will be the social and political context at the time of the interview. For example, in their review of surveys on sexual behavior Michaels and Giami (1999) found evidence of major changes in how sexual activity and sexual relationships have been conceptualized and studied over time. Whereas surveys prior to the 1970s often linked heterosexual intercourse to marriage, more recently questions on sexual behavior have been changed to accommodate other kinds of relationships and other sexual behaviors as societal mores and practices have changed.

Conclusion

Citizens are in a better position to evaluate the effects of question wording than they are to assess the consequences of question order for several reasons. First, much of what is involved in question wording is common sense; people often recognize easily that a question is worded in a misleading and loaded fashion. More important, because the media, when reporting survey results, often provide the wording of the survey questions, citizens are able to form their own judgments about the quality of the question wording. Newspaper and television reports give consumers no information about the overall structure and content of the survey, however (although the major news organizations are very willing to mail the complete report of a poll to interested citizens who request it). Because information is limited, then, citizens normally do not have any basis to form independent judgments about whether their responses to a particular item have been affected by its placement within the questionnaire. Moreover, the effects of question order and context are likely to be subtle, further hampering any attempts to assess these effects even when the text of the complete survey instrument is provided.

Fortunately, polling organizations are becoming more sensitive to the consequences of question order, and survey research textbooks are at last addressing the problem in more detail. Today reputable pollsters give more attention to effects of context and are more likely to inform the consumers of their polls about the potential consequences of question order. Nevertheless, it remains quite easy for the unscrupulous pollster, intent on generating a preferred response to a particular question, to mislead and manipulate the public by embedding that question in the survey in order to yield the desired answer.

☑️ 4 Sampling Techniques

Of the many aspects of public opinion polling, sampling arouses the greatest skepticism among Americans. One source of this skepticism is the actual composition of the sample, as reflected in the plaintive question "How come no one has asked me about my opinion on that issue?"

An experience I had in October 1984 exemplifies Americans' suspicion of polls. I was to speak about the 1984 presidential election before a group of about seventy labor union leaders. As he introduced me, the president of the Ohio AFL-CIO, who was obviously disturbed by national polls showing Democratic nominee Walter Mondale badly trailing President Ronald Reagan, conducted his own two-part poll. He first asked the audience how many were for Mondale and how many supported Reagan. Everyone was for Mondale. He next asked how many people in the audience had been interviewed by national pollsters about their presidential preference. None had. He concluded by expressing disdain for the entire enterprise of polling. After that inauspicious introduction, he turned the platform over to me so that I might give my poll-based analysis of the 1984 campaign.

Sampling is the selection of a subset of respondents from a broader population. When the sampling process is conducted properly, this subset will be representative of the broader population. This chapter covers several aspects of sampling so that consumers of public opinion research can better understand how and why samples are selected. A nontechnical review of various sampling designs is followed by a brief discussion of some factors that affect sample size. Sampling error and confidence levels in relation to the interpretation of poll results are covered as well. The chapter then discusses *total* sample size versus *actual* sample size. Too often reports of poll results pay little attention to the actual number of cases on which a conclusion is based—a number that can be substantially smaller than the total sample size. The chapter concludes with a discussion of response rates and sample weighting.

Sampling Designs

The aim of a good sampling design is to select a sample that is appropriate for the research topic and within the investigator's budget. Because it is impossible to interview an entire population—whether that of the United States, of New York, of all doctors, or of all senior citizens—a researcher selects a sample of that population. From that sample, the researcher will generalize to the broader population from which the sample was drawn. Typically, the sample is of interest because of what it reveals about the overall population and not because of the actual sample characteristics themselves. Thus researchers seek to select samples that accurately reflect the broader population from which they are drawn. This selection process can be carried out in a variety of ways, depending on the nature of the respondents, the objectives of the research, and the resources available to the investigator.

All of the designs discussed here are examples of *probability sampling,* the dominant and preferred mode of sampling public opinion. Probability samples have several advantages. Foremost, they tend to be more representative than other kinds of samples, because they generally avoid the selection biases inherent in nonprobability samples in which the investigator has discretion over who should be included in the sample.

Another advantage of probability samples is that they allow researchers to use statistical theory to ascertain the properties of the survey sample. One such property is the *sampling error* (discussed later in this chapter), which enables the investigator to estimate, with a certain level of confidence, how discrepant the sample results are from the true population values. The defining characteristic of a probability sample is that it permits the researcher to determine the probability of any single person being selected for the sample.

Nonprobability sampling does not enable one to determine the sampling error. For example, the television reporter who stands at a street corner and interviews people passing by in order to assess public opinion on an issue has actually selected a nonprobability sample. The reporter has no way of telling how representative these interviewees are or how accurate the sample results are. Radio call-in surveys also are based on nonprobability samples, because the callers may or may not be representative of the larger community. Likewise, the questionnaires mailed by members of the U.S. House of Representatives to households in their districts exemplify a nonprobability sampling procedure. Thousands of questionnaires may be returned, but there is no assurance that they constitute an accurate sample of the district. In these examples, selection biases affect who is included in the sample.

Simple Random and Systematic Sampling

In one method of probability sampling, simple random sampling, every element in the population has an equal chance of being selected for the sample. Moreover, every configuration of elements has the same chance of composing the sample. The chief requirement for simple random sampling is a list or an enumeration of the persons in the overall population. With such a list, the actual process of sampling is straightforward. The researcher assigns a unique number to each person and then selects a sample of these numbers. A primitive way of selecting the sample would be to put all the numbers in a hat, mix them up, and then draw the sample. A more likely method today is use of a table of computer-generated random numbers to select the sample. Simple random sampling is appropriate when a reasonably complete and current listing of the population is available.

Simple random sampling of individuals is not a feasible way to select a national sample of Americans. For one thing, no complete and up-to-date list of all Americans (not even the census list) exists. But even if there were a good list, random sampling would not be useful, particularly if a researcher planned to interview respondents personally rather than on the telephone. Sending interviewers all over the country would make the cost of the poll prohibitive (see the discussion later in this chapter of cluster sampling techniques, which do allow the selection of samples from large geographical areas when personal interviewing is to be used).

Systematic sampling is a variant of random sampling: the researcher picks every Nth name from the list after picking the first name at random. For example, to select a sample of 500 students from a student directory of 25,000 names (a 2 percent or one-fiftieth sample), the researcher might first pick at random a number between one and fifty. If that number is twelve, the sample would consist of the twelfth name in the directory, the sixty-second name, and every fiftieth name thereafter.

Systematic sampling is conducted easily. The only caution is that the listing of the names should have no cycle or periodicity to it lest the skip interval coincide with the periodicity. Normally, names listed in alphabetical order present no problems of periodicity, as opposed to, say, a list in which male and female names alternate. In the latter case, if the skip interval were an even number, the sample would be composed entirely of either males or females, thus introducing a bias to the study. A less obvious example of a periodicity problem might be a list of homes in a major housing development. Anyone picking a sample of homes in order to interview the owners would want to ensure that there is no special pattern in the listing of homes—that is, if every tenth house on the list is on a corner lot, the researcher might inadvertently select a sample that includes only corner homes. This selection could introduce a serious bias to the study because corner-lot houses tend to be larger and more expensive, and thus owned by wealthier people, than houses on the rest of the block. In systematic sampling, every element in the population has an equal chance of being in the sample, as is the case in random sampling. But unlike in random sampling, every configuration of elements does *not* have the same chance of composing the sample.

Stratified Sampling

The key characteristic of stratified sampling is that the population is divided into subsets, or strata, according to some characteristics of interest to the investigator. After stratifying the population, researchers may sample randomly or systematically within the strata. For example, to interview a sample of members of the U.S. House of Representatives, one might first stratify the members according to political party affiliation (Democratic versus Republican) and seniority (for simplicity, high versus low), two characteristics of relevance to the research, rather than pick a random sample. This stratification creates four categories: high-seniority Democrats, low-seniority Democrats, high-seniority Republicans, and low-seniority Republicans. One would then sample within each of the strata.

Stratification guarantees that a sample will include a sufficient number of cases with characteristics of interest to the researcher, because he or she can determine the size of the sample within each stratum. The major advantages of stratified sampling are a reduction in sampling error and a guarantee of representativeness with respect to the variables used in stratifying. The reduction in sampling error occurs when the strata differ from each other but internally are relatively homogeneous. For example, anyone seeking to compare the attitudes of northern and southern Republicans in Congress would find it more efficient to set up these strata and sample within them than to pick a sample from among all Republicans.

Cluster and Multistage Sampling

Cluster sampling entails multiple interviews within the same geographical area, typically a neighborhood. The advantage of cluster sampling is economic. It is expensive to support an interviewer in the field and to send that interviewer to a particular site to conduct an interview. The overall cost of a field survey is lower if the interviewer conducts multiple interviews at one site.

Cluster sampling is often part of a multistage sampling scheme employed by organizations that wish to interview personally a national sample of Americans. The Survey Research Center (SRC) of the University of Michigan is one such organization; it utilizes multistage sampling in which geographical areas, not individuals, are sampled at all stages except the last. Typically, the SRC's sample design selects a sample of counties; then within the sample of counties a sample of cities, townships, and unincorporated areas; then from the sample of cities, townships, and unincorporated areas a sample of city blocks and land tracts; and then a sample of residential dwellings located on the sampled blocks and land tracts. For example, Cook County, Illinois, might be included in the sample of counties; the city of Chicago might be selected within Cook County; a number of blocks would be selected from within Chicago; some dwelling units would be chosen from the selected blocks.

Note that up to this stage in the example geographical units and not individuals have been sampled. Sampling geographical units is relatively straightforward. It is easy to pick a sample of counties and a sample of localities within the counties because lists of counties and municipalities are readily available. Likewise, it is fairly easy to pick samples of blocks and dwelling units because local governments keep such information for the purpose of tax assessment. At each step in the typical multistage design, the probability of a geographical unit being included in the sample is proportional to its population. Thus Cook County and Los Angeles County are almost certain to be included in a sample of counties, whereas sparsely populated rural counties will have very little chance of being included. A sample concentrated in the major metropolitan areas of the country helps to control the cost of supporting and transporting interview staff.

In cluster sampling, once interviewers arrive at selected dwelling units they consult the instructions given them to determine whom to interview; it is not left to their discretion. These instructions are usually couched in terms of the age and gender composition of the households in the dwelling unit. For example, an interviewer might be instructed to survey the oldest male or the second oldest female in a household. Note that this information about the characteristics of individuals within the household does not have to be known to researchers earlier in the sampling process; indeed, this kind of sampling scheme requires no prior knowledge about individuals—information that can be difficult to acquire—but only knowledge about geographical entities, which is easily obtained.

Sampling Techniques for Telephone Interviewing

The sampling designs just described are the classic ones covered in most textbooks on survey research. They do not, however, include the dominant technique used by major polling organizations: telephone interviews. Telephone surveys offer several advantages. The first is speed: often pollsters want to assess as quickly as possible the public's reaction to a major event, such as the presidential debates in 2000. In such situations, personal interviews and mailed questionnaires take too much time. Another advantage is that telephone interviews are substantially cheaper to conduct than personal interviews, yet they still enable the interviewer to collect detailed and pertinent information from respondents. Although respondents tend to become fatigued more quickly in a telephone interview than in a personal interview, there usually is enough time to collect a reasonably extensive set of responses. Third, in many instances a telephone interview has the virtue of being less threatening and intrusive to private citizens; they do not have to let a stranger into their home in order to participate in the interview.

At one time telephone-based samples were considered suspect because of the obvious class bias in the use of telephones; poor families were less likely to have phones. Today, almost all Americans have home phones, which makes telephone samples more appropriate even though some class bias still exists. According to Lavrakas (1987, 14–15), most estimates in dicate that at least 95 percent of households in the United States have telephones, although across the fifty states there are variations in telephone ownership. People without telephones are more likely than telephone owners to be uneducated, poor, in a minority group, of low occupational status, and living in a single-adult household.

In earlier years, telephone directories served as the basis for picking samples. Directories are still used today, particularly for local samples, but several problems are associated with their use. One is that telephone directories are always out of date because of the high level of mobility of the U.S. population. Moreover, picking a national sample from telephone directories is a logistical nightmare—one would have to consult almost 5,000 directories. The most serious problem, however, is the popularity of unlisted telephone numbers. In 1996, an estimated 29.6 percent of American households had unlisted phone numbers compared with only 21.8 percent in 1984 (Survey Sampling Inc. 1997). In some metropolitan areas, particularly in California, the percentage of households with unlisted phone numbers exceeded 60 percent.

Both Lavrakas (1987) and Piekarski (1989) refute the common assumption that upper-income white households are more likely to have unlisted telephone numbers. Instead, they find that unlisted households are more likely to be younger, unmarried, lower income, minority, less educated, and more mobile. National data confirm these patterns (*Genesys News* 1996). For example, households headed by people eighteen to thirty-four years old had an unlisted rate of 51 percent compared with 18.9 percent for those headed by persons over sixty-five. Black and Hispanic households had unlisted rates of 55.2 and 58 percent, respectively, compared with 31.2 percent for whites. Only 29.6 percent of homeowners had unlisted numbers compared with 54.3 percent of renters. Lavrakas (1987, 33) cites a general rule: the farther a pollster samples from the central city, the more the proportion of households with unlisted phone numbers drops. He cites the Chicago area as an example, noting that within the city about 50 percent of households have unlisted numbers. By contrast, inner-ring suburbs have an unlisted number rate of about 20–30 percent, outer-ring suburbs a rate of 10–20 percent, and rural areas a rate of about 5 percent.

Households with unlisted numbers fall into two major categories: those that chose not to be listed and those that are unlisted because a change of residence resulted in a new telephone number unavailable to callers until publication of a new edition of the telephone book (telephone directories typically are published annually). There are differences between citizens who are unlisted through choice and those unlisted because of mobility. The "mobility unlisted" tend to be younger, more urban, lower income, and renters; the "choice unlisted" tend to be better off financially (Survey Sampling Inc. 1997). The third and smaller category of unlisted citizens is made up of subscribers who sporadically lose their telephone service because of financial problems and regain it later when their problems are resolved. In general, mobility increases the percentage of unlisted telephone numbers among all demographic groups (*Genesys News* 1996). For example, among households headed by persons eighteen to thirty-four years old the 51 percent unlisted rate increased to 69.9 percent among households that had moved in the past year. Likewise, the 18.9 percent unlisted rate for households headed by persons over age sixty-five soared to 54.2 percent for households that had moved in the past year.

One way around the problems inherent in the use of telephone directories is *random-digit dialing*—random numbers are generated to produce the telephone numbers to be called. With random-digit dialing, it is critical to know the area codes and exchanges (the first three digits in the seven-digit telephone number) in an area. Once this information has been collected, a computer random-number generator or a table of random numbers can be used to provide the last four digits of telephone numbers to be dialed. This procedure does result in unlisted numbers being reached, as evidenced by the surprised reactions of respondents who ask, "How did you get my number? It's unlisted!" When a residential household is reached through random-digit dialing, the interviewer does not automatically interview whoever answered the phone. Instead, interviewers typically first collect information about the number of adults in the household and the number of males and females. Then the interviewers must follow a set of instructions that tells them, for example, to interview the oldest male in the first household or the youngest female in the second household or the second oldest male in the third household. The combination of random-digit dialing and the instructions about respondent selection generates a sample highly representative of American households.

Random-digit dialing has become more complicated with the technological revolution in communications. For example, more area codes are being added because of the proliferation of new telephone numbers (discussed later in this chapter). Typically, telephone service providers divide an existing area code region into two new regions, each with its own area code. Thus people may find themselves with a new area code but with the same seven-digit telephone number. Pollsters and samplers, then, need to update their area codes.

The more than 40,000 phone numbers added daily in the United States (Survey Sampling Inc. 1997) often are for cellular phones, faxes, pagers, and modems as well as for the extra phone lines needed to accommodate talkative family members. Thus an increasing number of households in the United States have multiple phone numbers—and a greater chance of being selected for the sample. Today reputable pollsters correct their samples for this problem lest they introduce an affluence bias.

Another development on the horizon that may lessen some of the advantages of random-digit dialing is number portability (*Genesys Q & A* 1997). Currently, the three-digit exchange in a telephone number represents well-defined geographical areas within a community that can be useful information to pollsters and other researchers. For example, the geographical information provided by the three-digit exchange may enable researchers to incorporate contextual data—information about the properties of the geographical region—into their analyses. With number portability, citizens will be able to keep their telephone numbers when they move. But if number portability becomes commonplace, it will be difficult to use random-digit dialing to contact households in specific geographic areas.

Piekarski et al. (1999) argue that random-digit dialing has become a less efficient method of sampling residential households in recent years because of the huge increase in the volume of telephone numbers. They note that while the estimated number of households with telephones increased about 11 percent from 1988 to 1998 (from about 85 million to 95 million), the total volume of telephone numbers soared 89 percent (from 400 million in 1988 to almost 719 million in May 1999). This huge increase stemmed from the proliferation of fax machines, pagers, modems, and cellular phones. Thus, in today's random-digit samples, a smaller proportion of the phone numbers may actually come from a residential household.

Sample Size

Sample size is a major puzzle for Americans who wonder how a national sample of 1,500 respondents can accurately represent the views of 200 million adult Americans. Contributing to the confusion is the fact that an equally accurate statewide survey requires a sample similar in size, even though any state's population is only a small proportion of the national total. Because few respondents are required for a good sample and a very weak relationship exists between the size of the sample and the size of the population from which it is drawn, many of the citizens who are aware of these apparent anomalies are skeptical of the validity of the entire polling enterprise.

Statistical and probability theory explain why such small sample sizes suffice to generate valid results, but these theories are not very enlightening to people who lack an extensive mathematical background. More helpful perhaps is an analogy. To perform a blood test, a medical technician need only draw a drop or two of blood from the patient. This very small sample of the total amount of blood in the patient's body is sufficient to produce accurate results, because any one drop has properties identical to those of the remaining blood. Another analogy of sample size is a chef trying to decide whether to add more spices to a large kettle of soup. The chef might sample the soup's flavor by tasting one spoonful, certainly a very small sample. Now, all spoonfuls of soup may not be comparable unless the chef first carefully stirs the mixture. But if the soup is stirred properly, a spoonful would be sufficient to determine whether more spices should be added.

Because the major expense in public opinion polling is the cost of interviewing the selected sample, it is critical that the researcher select a sample that suits both the purposes and the budget of the project. There is no particular virtue in large samples. If poorly selected, they provide no guarantees of accurate results. The classic example is the infamous *Literary Digest* poll of 1936, which confidently predicted a sweeping victory for Republican presidential candidate Alf Landon based on a sample of more than two million people. In the end, though, incumbent Democratic president Franklin D. Roosevelt carried forty-six of the forty-eight states in the November election. The *Literary Digest* poll failed because of the unrepresentativeness of the respondents who were selected from telephone directories and automobile registrations, a procedure that skewed the sample to the upper end of the socioeconomic continuum. This method of sample selection had worked well for the *Literary Digest* in previous elections, but it failed in the depression year of 1936. Squire (1988) points out that the sample was only one of the problems affecting the *Literary Digest* poll in 1936. The additional problems with low response rates and a nonresponse bias were such that those who did respond to the poll were more likely to be for Landon than for Roosevelt.

About Sampling Error

One determinant of sample size is the amount of sampling error that can be tolerated in a poll. *Sampling error* is simply the difference between the estimates obtained from the sample and the true population value—for example, the percentage of people in the sample who approve of the president's performance versus approval of the president in the overall population. Investigators often select national samples of sufficient size to generate a sampling error of about 4 percent; this means that if the sample indicates, for example, that 52 percent of respondents approve of the president's performance, the actual value is likely to be in the range of 48–56 percent (52 plus or minus 4 percent). How likely it is that the actual value will fall within that range is measured by the *confidence level*. In this example a 95 percent confidence level would mean that in 95 out of 100 samples that might be selected, the sample would generate an estimate of approval within the range of 48–56 percent. One way to reduce the sampling error is to increase the sample size, but larger samples entail higher costs. A 4 percent sampling error is normally considered acceptable.

Several caveats about sampling error should be kept in mind. First, in some instances a 4 percent error will be too large in view of the predictions the investigator wants to make. For example, if the sample shows for an upcoming election that 51 percent of voters, with a 4 percent sampling error, are planning to vote Republican, the election outcome cannot be firmly predicted because the Republican vote could be as low as 47 percent or as high as 55 percent. But if the poll indicates that 70 percent plan to vote Republican, then a sampling error of 4 percent or even higher will scarcely affect the conclusions.

Second, although the sampling error of the overall sample may be only 4 percent, the sampling error associated with estimates based on subsets of the sample can be substantially higher, particularly for the smaller groups within the sample. In subgroup analysis the original sample is subdivided into a number of mutually exclusive subsets. For example, a researcher interested in comparing the political attitudes of Protestants, Catholics, and

Jews based on a national sample of about 1,500 respondents would sub-
divide the sample into these three religious groups. The sampling error
associated with estimates for the Jewish subgroup would be much higher
than those associated with the other groups, because Jewish respondents
would number only 40–60, reflecting the percentage of Jews in the overall population (likewise, the sample would contain 350–400 Catholics and
about 1,000 Protestants). To compare across religious *and* gender groups
simultaneously, the researcher would divide the same sample into six categories: male Protestants, male Catholics, male Jews, female Protestants,
female Catholics, and female Jews. The sampling error associated with
these classifications would be even larger. In general, as the original sample
is subdivided into increasingly smaller subsets, the sampling error becomes
larger and larger.

A 1985 controversy about the level of support enjoyed by President
Reagan among African Americans illustrates, among other things, the need
to be sensitive to the large sampling error associated with small subsets of
respondents. A CBS News/*New York Times* poll conducted in December
1985 became a major news story when it "showed" that 6 percent of black
respondents approved of President Reagan's performance and only 24 percent disapproved, a level of support dramatically higher than the president
had ever had (Clymer 1986a). About a month later, an ABC News/*Washington Post* poll found that only 23 percent of blacks approved of the job
the president was doing and that 63 percent disapproved. Which poll was
more accurate?

In retrospect, it seems clear that the positive results in the December
1985 CBS News/*New York Times* poll were misleading and incorrect.
The poll interviewed a national sample of 1,358 Americans of whom 150
were black. Thus, the sampling error for the estimates about blacks was
high (9 percent). By contrast, the ABC News/*Washington Post* survey
was based on a specially designed national sample of 1,022 African Americans. With a sampling error of 3.5 percent, it was much more reliable than
the CBS News/*New York Times* poll. Other polls conducted at about the
same time confirmed the ABC News/*Washington Post* results; a Gallup
survey showed Reagan with a 23 percent approval rating among blacks,
and a *Los Angeles Times* poll showed 37 percent support.

The next CBS News/*New York Times* poll took place in January
1986. This one was in line with other polls, showing the president with
37 percent support among blacks, thereby contradicting the December
1985 CBS News/*New York Times* survey. Adam Clymer, director of polling operations at the *New York Times,* attributed the discrepancy between
the two polls to a bad sample and sampling error: "It now appears that our
December poll had a very unrepresentative black sample, especially of

black men, and the findings plainly exceeded normal sampling error. This month's sample appears, on matters from education to household size, much more representative of the black population as a whole" (Apple 1986, A-14).

Although the controversy about black support for the president was resolved, Sussman (1986a) noted that a puzzle still remained: the January 1986 CBS News/*New York Times* poll showed the president to have a 37 percent approval rating, or one considerably higher than the 23 percent reported in the same month by the ABC News/*Washington Post* poll. He cited three possible reasons for the difference. The first was sampling error: the ABC News/*Washington Post* poll had an error of 3.5 percent, whereas the CBS News/*New York Times* poll had an error of 7 percent because there were 189 black respondents in the total sample of 1,581. Another source of divergence was the race of the interviewers. The CBS News/*New York Times* poll employed white and black interviewers, but the ABC News/*Washington Post* poll used black interviewers only, some of whom may have "sounded black" over the telephone. Thus black respondents to the ABC News/*Washington Post* poll may have been more negative toward the president because that seemed to be the "appropriate" black response. (The effects of interviewers' race are discussed in greater detail in the next chapter.) Finally, Sussman noted that the ABC News/*Washington Post* poll began with an explicit statement that it was a survey of blacks, perhaps leading respondents to take more of a black perspective and therefore to be more critical of the president.

Informing the Consumer about Sampling

Different survey organizations provide their audiences with different amounts of information about their sample surveys. Most tell the date of the interviews, the method of data collection, the size of the actual sample, and the sampling error of the overall sample. For example, on June 16, 1997, *Newsweek* provided the following information to its readers about a poll it had commissioned to assess Americans' opinions on the April 1995 Oklahoma City bombing and the fate of defendant Timothy McVeigh: "For this *Newsweek* poll, Princeton Survey Research Associates interviewed 751 adults 18 and older June 5–6. The margin of error is +/– 4 percentage points, +/– 9 percentage points for nonwhites."

News releases from the media vary in the amount of information they provide. For example, the Newark, New Jersey, *Star-Ledger*/Eagleton Institute at Rutgers University poll provides more information than other organizations, including a definition of sampling error. Its background memo released March 10, 1991, warned that "sampling error does not take into

account the possible sources of error inherent in any study of public opinion." The memo did not specify, however, the sources of these other non-
sampling errors. ABC News provides much more information about its
methodology than other media organizations and is more explicit about
other sources of error. For example, in its February–March 1986 release,
in addition to the standard information ABC News explained how the telephone sample was selected; informed readers that the survey responses
were "weighted by age, sex, education and race using the latest U.S. Census figures"; warned that in addition to sampling error "inaccuracy may occur from the wording of certain questions or the order in which they are
asked"; and presented "full results of poll questions in the order they
were asked." As for polling information provided in newspaper articles, the
New York Times and the *Washington Post* maintain an enviable standard
of reporting (see the conclusion of Chapter 6).

Obviously, the more information provided about the methodology
of a poll, the better consumers can judge the soundness of the poll results.
For example, consider two polls conducted in Chicago in the same week
in 1986. The polls obtained sharply dissimilar results for the mayoral election trial heats between incumbent mayor Harold Washington and former
mayor Jane Byrne. An ABC News/Station WLS survey showed Washington ahead of Byrne by a twenty-three-point margin (58 percent to her
35 percent), but a Northwestern University poll had Byrne ahead of Washington, 43 to 34 percent.

Paul Lavrakas analyzed the differences between the two polls and
pointed out three factors that might have affected the results. The first was
callbacks—that is, efforts made to interview respondents who initially could
not be reached for some reason. Because the Northwestern University survey was conducted over three evenings, in contrast to two for the ABC
News poll, and thus had more time for callbacks, the Northwestern survey
may have done a better job of tracking down hard-to-reach respondents. A
second difference was that the Northwestern survey weighted its results to
reflect the demographics of Chicago's adult population. The ABC News
poll did not weight its data and, according to Lavrakas, overrepresented
blacks in its sample, because it sought to have the distribution of blacks and
whites in the sample reflect the 1980 census estimates of Chicago's *overall* racial composition as opposed to its *adult* racial composition. Finally,
the trial heat question used by ABC News followed a question that asked
respondents to choose among three candidates—Byrne, Washington, and
Richard Daley, son of another former mayor. Because of hostility between supporters of Byrne and Daley, this question may have affected the
responses to the Byrne-Washington query so that Daley supporters opted
disproportionately for Washington. Although Lavrakas refused to conclude

that the Northwestern University poll results were likely to be sounder, his analysis does indicate how information about poll methodology can help consumers of public opinion polls sort out conflicting claims and results (Lavrakas 1986).

Total versus Actual Sample Size

When a sample of citizens is interviewed, not every question receives a response from every respondent. Some respondents may refuse to answer, other respondents may be screened out because of nonattitudes, and still others may have no opinion on the matter. Indeed, in some instances there may be a substantial difference between the total sample size and the actual number of people responding to or included in the reporting of the results of a particular question.

Consider the following hypothetical situation in which 1,500 Americans are asked about their vote preferences one month before an election. Perhaps only 80 percent of the sample are registered to vote, and only 60 percent of those registered will actually vote on Election Day. If the investigator wants to report the vote preferences of likely voters only and is able to identify that group (a difficult task), then the effective sample has shrunk from 1,500 to 720 ($0.80 \times 0.60 \times 1,500$) with an attendant increase in sampling error. Of these 720, 3 percent might refuse to reveal their preference, and another 22 percent might be unsure, thereby reducing the 720 to 540 likely voters with definite vote preferences, or just 36 percent of the original sample of 1,500. The 540 voters, then, are the actual sample out of the total sample. Of the 540 likely voters, 300 may intend to vote Democratic and 240 Republican, a 56 to 44 percent split. In reporting this split, the pollster also should describe the subset of the sample from which it is calculated.

A real-life example of the importance of reporting actual sample size is provided by a July 1985 ABC News/*Washington Post* poll on President Reagan's Strategic Defense Initiative, also known as "Star Wars" (Lardner 1985). The three questions and responses were:

Q. Have you read or heard about plans by the Reagan administration to develop weapons in outer space that could destroy nuclear missiles fired at the United States by the Soviet Union or other countries? Reagan calls the research on these weapons SDI, for Strategic Defense Initiative, and some people refer to it as "Star Wars."

Yes, have read or heard	84%
No, have not read or heard	16%
Don't know or no opinion	1%

Q. Supporters say such weapons could guarantee protection of the United States from nuclear attack and are worth whatever they cost. Opponents say such weapons will not work, will increase the arms race, and the research will cost many billions of dollars. How about you: would you say you approve or disapprove of plans to develop such space-based weapons?

Approve	41%
Disapprove	53%
Don't know or no opinion	5%

Q. (For those who approved) Currently the United States and the Soviet Union have an anti-ballistic missile treaty that prohibits both nations from developing certain weapons. Suppose the U.S. had to violate or abandon that treaty in order to develop the space-based weapons. Would you still favor development of those space-based weapons or not?

Yes, would still favor	63%
No, would not still favor	32%
Don't know or no opinion	5%

Fortunately, Lardner was very careful in his reporting of the responses to the last question, for without the appropriate qualifications, citizens might interpret the result as showing strong support for development of the weapons even if the United States had to scrap the treaty. Note that the 63 percent favoring SDI represents only 26 percent (0.41×0.63) of the original sample of 1,506 and only 22 percent ($0.41 \times 0.63 \times 0.84$) of those respondents who had read or heard about the plans initially. It would, then, be misleading and unscrupulous to release only the results of the last item without the necessary qualifiers. Unfortunately, advocates of causes have at times been highly selective in their use of poll information with the conscious aim of swaying the public to their position.

Response Rates

A growing concern among pollsters is the problem of nonresponse—that is, when citizens selected for the sample either refuse to participate in the interview or cannot be contacted. Refusals are attributed to several reasons, including the growing hostility to legitimate public opinion polling because of the excesses and intrusiveness of the telemarketing that bombards Americans. As for reaching Americans, it is now even more difficult because of the proliferation of technological barriers. According to Piekarski et al. (1999), 50 percent of households have answering machines, 25 percent have "Caller ID," and 6 percent have voice mail.

Also contributing to the increased difficulty in contacting respondents is the growing tendency of pollsters to conduct overnight polls on salient political topics such as presidential candidates' debate performance and the "bounce" produced by a national nominating convention. For overnight polls, there is insufficient time to do the multiple callbacks that may be needed to contact a member of the sample who was not at home or was otherwise unavailable when the first telephone call was made. As Kagay (1999) points out, most reputable pollsters make multiple calls to households over the multiple days that the poll is in the field in order to contact the designated respondent. These repeat calls are made at different times of the day to enhance the probability of a response. In many instances, interviewers leave phone messages explaining why they are calling and try to arrange a more convenient time to interview the respondent. Many polling organizations also utilize specially trained interviewers to re-contact respondents who had originally refused to participate in the survey to try to convert their refusals into completed interviews. But none of these special measures can be applied to an overnight poll in which the actual interviewing period might be four hours or less.

The American Association for Public Opinion Research has called on polling organizations to provide more systematic and comparable information about response rates for telephone, in-person, and mail surveys. For example, for telephone interviews AAPOR advocates that the disposition or outcome of telephone calls be made available to the users of polls so they can better evaluate the product. These outcomes would be: (1) a successful interview with an eligible case; (2) an eligible case that was not interviewed (for example, a refusal); (3) a noneligible case (for example, a fax line or a nonworking number); and (4) a case of unknown eligibility (for example, a constant busy signal). AAPOR recommends that survey organizations calculate and present response rates, cooperation rates, refusal rates, and contact rates. Traditionally, pollsters have provided little information about response rates. One exception to this is the *Columbus Dispatch*'s reporting of its mailed election surveys, which have an incredible track record for accuracy in election predictions (see Chapter 7) despite low response rates. In a September 2000 mail survey on the presidential race in Ohio, the *Dispatch* listed as one of many sources of error "nonresponse bias," which it defined as the possibility that those who responded to the mail survey might not reflect the views of those who did not respond. The *Dispatch* then told its readers that the response rate was 22 percent.

One finding that shows up repeatedly in the research on the characteristics of respondents and nonrespondents is that the residents of large metropolitan areas are less likely to participate in polls than those in rural areas. Other research has examined what happens to the properties of a sample when respondents who initially refused to be interviewed are converted to a successful interview through repeated callbacks and other methods. Wiese (1998) finds that the inclusion of "converted refusals" does not make the sample more representative of the population from which it was drawn and that "converted refusals" provide less complete information than respondents who initially were successfully interviewed.

The Pew Research Center for the People and the Press conducted an intriguing experiment to determine whether differential response rates affected the results of two identical surveys. The first survey was conducted over a five-day period, and the second was conducted over an eight-week period that allowed for greater efforts to contact mobile and reluctant respondents. The first survey had an overall response rate of 42 percent; the second a 71 percent response rate. Despite the large difference in response rates, the two surveys produced very similar results across a wide variety of questions. For example, there was no difference in the partisanship of the two samples or in their presidential preferences. Only on some race-related items were there differences between the two samples.

What conclusions can be drawn about the problem of response rates? Certainly it is important to monitor what is happening to response rates; AAPOR's recommendations, if followed, will be very helpful here. Declining response rates are less of a problem for those reputable survey organizations that work harder to secure completed interviews through multiple callbacks and other tactics. But for the overnight polls, low response rates can indeed be a serious problem and need to be recognized as such. If the percentage of refusals increases, additional research will be required on the fundamental question of whether survey respondents are indeed representative of nonrespondents. Obviously, high response rates are better than low rates, but lower rates do not automatically indicate that a poll is inaccurate. As America's communications technology continues to advance and as individual concerns about the intrusiveness of telemarketing and protection of privacy continue to grow, the problem of response rates will become an even greater challenge for public opinion polling.

Weighting the Sample

Samples are selected to be representative of the population from which they are drawn. Sometimes, however, adjustments must be made to a sample before the results of a poll can be analyzed and reported. These adjustments may be made for substantive reasons or because of biases in the characteristics of the selected sample. An example of adjustments made for substantive reasons is pollsters' attempts to determine who the likely voters will be and to base their election predictions not on the entire sample but on a subset of likely voters.

Weights are used to correct for biases—that is, to ensure that the sample's demographic characteristics more accurately reflect the population's overall properties. Because sampling and interviewing involve statistics and probability theory as well as logistical problems of contacting respondents, a sample may contain too few blacks, or too few men, or too few people in the youngest age category. Assuming that the true population proportions for sex, race, and age are known, the researcher, using weights, brings the sample numbers into line with the overall population values. For example, if females constitute 60 percent of the sample but 50 percent of the overall population, the researcher might weight each female respondent by five-sixths, thereby reducing the percentage of females in the sample to 50 percent (five-sixths times 60 percent).

A 1986 *Columbus Dispatch* preelection poll on the gubernatorial preferences of Ohioans illustrates the consequences of weighting. In August 1986 the *Dispatch* sent a mail questionnaire to a sample of Ohioans selected from the statewide list of registered voters. The poll showed that incumbent Democratic governor Richard Celeste was leading former GOP governor James Rhodes, 48 percent to 43 percent, with independent candidate and former Democratic mayor of Cleveland Dennis Kucinich receiving 9 percent; an undecided alternative was not provided to respondents (Curtin 1986a). Fortunately, the *Dispatch* report of its poll included the sample size for each category (unlike the practice of the national media). One table presented to the reader showed the following relationship between political party affiliation and gubernatorial vote preference (Curtin 1986b):

Gubernatorial Preference	Democrat	Republican	Independent
Celeste	82%	14%	33%
Rhodes	9	81	50
Kucinich	9	5	17
Total %	100	100	100
(N)	(253)	(245)	(138)

Given the thrust of the news story that Celeste was ahead 48 to 43 percent, the numbers in the table were surprising. Rhodes was running almost as well among Republicans as Celeste was among Democrats, and Rhodes had a substantial lead among independents. Based on the N's provided, one could calculate the actual number of Celeste, Rhodes, and Kucinich votes in the sample as follows:

Celeste votes = .82(253) + .14(245) + .33(138) = 287
Rhodes votes = .09(253) + .81(245) + .50(138) = 291
Kucinich votes = .09(253) + .05(245) + .17(138) = 58

The percentages calculated from these totals show Rhodes slightly *ahead,* 46 to 45 percent, rather than trailing. At first I thought there was a mistake in the poll or in the party affiliation and gubernatorial vote preference. In rereading the news story, however, I learned that the sample had been weighted. The reporter wrote, "Results were adjusted, or weighted, slightly to compensate for demographic differences between poll respondents and the Ohio electorate as a whole" (Curtin 1986b). Although the reporter informed readers that the data were weighted, nowhere did he say that the adjustment affected who was ahead in the poll. The adjustment was statistically valid because the poll respondents did not include sufficient numbers of women and blacks, two groups that were more supportive of the Democratic gubernatorial candidate. However, nowhere in the news story was any specific information provided on how the weighting was done. This example illustrates that weighting can be consequential, and it is typical in terms of the scant information provided to citizens about weighting procedures.

One ongoing problem in polling is the tendency of selected samples to overrepresent females and underrepresent males. This problem can be easily corrected by weighting the sample so that the proportion of male and female respondents in the sample reflects the overall population distribution. This solution, however, assumes that sampled males are representative of unsampled males. Males may be undersampled for several reasons. First, there are simply more female-only households than there are male-only households. Moreover, because fewer men live in male-only households and a higher proportion of men live in mixed households, the probability of a male being selected in the sample is lower than for a female. The second factor relates to how the actual respondent to be interviewed is determined. Typically, interviewers (in telephone polling) ask the person who answers the phone if they can speak with the oldest female or the second oldest male or whomever in the household. Sometimes the person who answers the phone is unwilling to transfer the interviewer to the household member requested. Because women are more likely to answer the phone in the first place and are less willing than men to bring their spouse to the phone, the number of male respondents is diminished. Finally, daytime calls are more likely to obtain female respondents because of the higher proportion of males who work outside the home.

Conclusion

For many Americans, sampling is the most problematic feature of public opinion polling. Many citizens doubt whether the "small" samples reported in the media can adequately represent the population of whatever entity is being studied. And if the response rates that characterize these "small samples" are low, citizens are likely to be even more skeptical. Citizens may question the wording of a poll, but it is difficult for them to offer informed criticism of sampling procedures unless the polling organization provides sufficient information about such matters as the size of the sample, sampling error and confidence levels, the dates of the interviews, response rates, and the method of interviewing. Even though sampling is considered to be a statistical and scientific procedure, sampling problems may undermine the results and interpretations of public opinion polls. Normally, however, citizens must trust the polling organization to select a good sample.

5 Interviewing and Data Collection Procedures

The interviewer plays a critical role in measuring public opinion. In general, polling organizations provide the public with little or no information about the interviewing process. Consequently, the consumers of polls cannot make independent judgments about the quality of the interviews and must assume that they were conducted competently. This is undoubtedly a safe assumption about the major polls.

Nevertheless, as someone who has agreed to be a respondent in public opinion, market research, and academic research surveys, I have been surprised by the obvious disparities in the training and competence of the interviewers. Often, when I am a respondent, I will ask the interviewer what a certain question means or complain about the range of alternatives available to me. Some interviewers are well trained to handle such reactions, but others are not. One interviewer agreed with my frustration about a particular item and informed me that there had been many complaints about the survey. Another interviewer, when I strenuously objected to the alternatives, pleaded with me to pick one of the given choices, because he did not know how to handle volunteered responses. In yet another situation the interviewer told me that she would place my aberrant response in the category in which she thought it would best fit.

In some surveys there is no live interviewer per se. The most familiar example is the self-administered, mailed questionnaire, typically in a paper/pencil format. Gaining popularity are the computerized self-administered questionnaire (CSAQ) and computer-assisted self-interviewing (CASI), which provide greater flexibility to pollsters. Finally, there is the growing phenomenon of Web-based Internet polls that are typically self-administered and raise a variety of issues about sampling, representativeness, and the like.

The purpose of this chapter is to alert the consumers of polls about the potential effects of the interviewing process on poll results. The first section describes the methods used to collect data and discusses the advantages and disadvantages of three approaches: mailed questionnaires, telephone interviews, and personal interviews. That section is followed by a closer look at the interview situation itself and factors such as the sex, socioeconomic status, race, and ethnicity of the interviewer that can affect responses. The chapter ends with a discussion of the advantages and limitations of Web-based Internet surveys.

Methods of Collecting Polling Information

Self-Administered Questionnaires

Mailed questionnaires are used frequently to assess opinions, especially by organizations with access to good mailing lists. As discussed in Chapter 1, interest groups often use mailed surveys in conjunction with their fund-raising efforts. Mailed questionnaires have several advantages, but the main one is their low cost. Because mailed surveys are self-administered by the respondent, no interviewers must be trained and supported, which dramatically reduces costs. Moreover, interviewer bias does not affect results. The privacy in which a mailed survey can be completed may reassure respondents about the anonymity and confidentiality of their responses and may encourage them to respond more frankly, particularly on sensitive topics. For example, a study by Aquilino (1994) shows that self-administered questionnaires used in the context of a personal interview generate a higher level of admitted illicit drug and alcohol use than do a telephone or personal interview without a self-administered questionnaire. Indeed, an extensive body of literature generally shows that self-administered questionnaires are more likely to produce higher estimates of illicit, illegal, or controversial behaviors than other modes of data collection in which an interviewer directly interacts with respondents (Tourangeau and Smith 1996). And in the area of race-related attitudes, Krysan et al. (1994) demonstrated that a mail questionnaire generated more negative views among white respondents to questions about racial integration and affirmative action than did personal interviews. The explanation given for this finding was straightforward: white respondents were more open and honest about their views in the privacy of the self-administered mail questionnaire setting. In a personal interview the pressure to be socially and politically correct came into play, resulting in responses more supportive of civil rights.

These advantages of mailed questionnaires are typically outweighed by their limitations. Foremost among these is the fact that response rates tend to be lower for mailed surveys than for telephone and personal interviews. However, this disadvantage may be lessening, in part because of the higher refusal rates in personal and telephone interviews (see Chapter 4) and because of improved techniques for generating satisfactory response rates to mailed questionnaires (Goyder 1985).

Researchers continue to investigate ways to improve response rates for mail surveys. A study by Fox, Crask, and Kim (1988) found that university sponsorship (as opposed to private business sponsorship) of a mail survey increased the response rate. Other important factors in improving response rates included notifying respondents about the survey beforehand by letter, sending the survey by first-class postage, using postcard follow-up, and providing return postage. Another significant factor w as the color of the paper on which the questionnaire was printed. According to James and Bolstein (1990), a monetary incentive to return the survey, along with follow-up mailings urging respondents to complete the questionnaire, increase response rates. Similar results are found in Yammarino, Skinner, and Childers (1991) and Church (1993), who reviewed a large number of studies of the factors that affect response rates.

A problem related to low response rates is ascertaining the extent to which respondents represent the actual population, a particularly acute problem when the response rate is low. If the respondents are representative of the broader population even when the response rates are low, there is less need to incur the costs required to increase the response rate. A study by Bernick and Pratto (1994) addressed the issues of response rates and the representativeness of respondents with a four-step process to survey registered voters' attitudes toward local government. They first sent the sample a letter, the questionnaire, and a postage-return envelope. One week later they sent a postcard. Two weeks later they sent a mailing similar to the first one. Finally, three weeks later, using certified postage, they sent a special mailing to those people in the sample who had not yet replied. This last mailing did stimulate responses, particularly among less-educated respondents. Moreover, early and late responders did differ somewhat in their attitudes, leading the authors to conclude that in this case it was worthwhile to expend the extra resources to enhance response rates. In other words, simply weighting or adjusting the respondents obtained from the first three mailings according to the known population distribution of educational levels would not have fully resolved the problem of the response bias in the sample.

Another limitation of mailed surveys is that much information cannot be collected in self-administered surveys. For example, one cannot be sure who actually completes a questionnaire—a serious limitation when surveying elite populations, such as members of Congress or state legislators who, because they are bombarded with mailed questionnaires, may have a staff person fill out the survey form. Also not available is information about respondents' reactions to a survey and about the environment in which a survey is completed. Because no interviewer is present to assist respondents who have difficulty with a questionnaire, instructions must be explicit and questions must be as unambiguous as possible. There is no opportunity for clarification.

Mailed questionnaires must not be too burdensome for respondents or the response rate will plummet. Whenever I receive a questionnaire in the mail, I first check the number of open-ended questions that would require me to write mini-essays. If there are many, I'm likely to toss the questionnaire into the circular file unless it addresses a topic of particular interest to me. Mailed questionnaires encourage response when they are largely limited to highly structured, fixed alternative questions. However, even the structured items are often annoying to citizens, particularly to political elites who complain that the political world is too complicated and their own opinions too complex to be captured in a fixed alternative item.

The burdens imposed by a mailed questionnaire are not uniform across the population. Poorly educated respondents will have more difficulty with a mailed survey, and illiterate persons may simply have to ignore it. In addition, there is no way of knowing the order in which any particular respondent answered the questions. Certainly, some people will read the entire survey before responding; others will start at the beginning and proceed sequentially. Thus the questionnaire may elicit different responses from individuals depending on the order in which they approach the questions. Finally, mailed questionnaires are inappropriate if an investigator needs a quick response to a topic such as a presidential debate or foreign policy crisis. Experienced researchers allow several weeks for questionnaires to be returned.

One response to some of the limitations of self-administered mailed questionnaires is computer-assisted self-interviewing in which respondents answer survey questions on a computer. CASI enables more flexibility in questionnaire design by allowing, for example, branching, in which respondents are presented with different survey questions depending on their responses to previous items. CASI reduces the number of errors that occur in the usual paper/pencil format and allows quick identification of any internal inconsistencies in item responses. Yet CASI maintains many of the privacy benefits traditionally associated with self-administered mailed questionnaires. Indeed, CASI appears to perform better than mailed questionnaires in generating accurate responses on sensitive topics. For example, Wright et al. (1998) found in a survey on smoking, alcohol, and drug use that adolescents overall reported higher levels of alcohol and drug use when queried by CASI than by self-administered paper questionnaires, although more mistrustful adolescents were less likely to report substance use in the computer-based survey than in the paper/pencil format. Another study (Harmon 1998) of risky sexual behavior among male teenagers found that respondents who listened to questionnaire items on earphones and saw them on a computer screen reported higher incidences of risky behavior than teens surveyed by the traditional paper/pencil method. For example, teens surveyed by computer were fourteen times more likely to report having sex with an intravenous drug user (2.8 versus 0.2 percent) and five times more likely to admit that they were often or always drunk or high when they had heterosexual sex (10.8 versus 2.2 percent). These findings suggest that computerized administration of polls may make respondents feel more comfortable about privacy issues and therefore more likely to offer honest responses about socially unacceptable and possibly illegal behavior. Much more work needs to be done in this area.

Telephone Interviews

Unlike mailed questionnaires, telephone surveys can be completed quickly (often in only two to four days and sometimes in a single evening), thereby providing an almost instantaneous reaction to a political event. Another advantage is that by using random-digit dialing techniques (see Chapter 4), researchers can easily pick a representative sample. Although more expensive than mailed questionnaires, telephone interviews are less costly than personal interviews, and they generate a good response rate (yet typically not as high as that for personal interviews). In some situations telephone interviewing may succeed where other methods can fail, perhaps because of the sensitivity of a topic or because respondents will not allow a stranger in their home to conduct a personal interview.

Telephone interviews also have shortcomings. Although most households today possess telephones, telephone interviews are still somewhat biased against respondents of low socioeconomic status who cannot afford phones. Also, respondents become fatigued more quickly in a telephone interview than in a personal interview, which limits the scope of a telephone survey (although recent experience indicates that telephone surveys can be lengthier than was originally thought). Another shortcoming is that training interviewers in order to avoid unwanted effects from the interviewing process adds to the cost of a project. Finally, use of the telephone eliminates the possibility of using visual aids during the interview unless materials are sent to respondents in a preliminary mailing.

Thanks to recent advances, telephone interviews are now faster, more efficient, and more accurate. The foremost of these is computer-assisted telephone interviewing (CATI). With CATI, interviewers sit at video display terminals and feed responses directly into a computer, thereby eliminating a separate keypunching step. A computer program controls the overall flow and logic of the interview. Among other things, the program ensures that questions are asked in the correct sequence and that responses are consistent with the question(s) being asked (Frey 1983, 144–145). Running totals are easily generated with CATI, so that survey results are available almost instantaneously. As CATI systems become more sophisticated, investigators who use them can save money, particularly as the sample size grows larger.

Personal Interviews

Personal interviews generally provide the richest and most complete information in public opinion polling and tend to have higher response rates. Respondents are willing to participate in lengthy personal interviews (in contrast to telephone interviews), particularly if the interviewer is skillful in developing a rapport with them. The presence of the interviewer is also helpful in other ways. He or she can assess respondents' problems with and reactions to the survey and can directly record not only the verbal responses of the interviewee but also nonverbal behavior such as fidgeting, nervousness, and other signs of unease or lack of interest in the interview situation. Moreover, the interviewer has more opportunities to ask follow-up questions and to probe in a personal interview than in a telephone survey.

The obvious drawbacks of personal interviews are their high cost and the danger of introducing substantial interviewer effects and biases. The cost of training interviewers, supporting them in the field, often with housing, meals, and transportation allowances, and paying their salary is steep. Because the interview is a social situation, poorly trained interviewers may alter the interpersonal dynamics of the interview and thereby influence respondents' answers in undesirable and often unpredictable ways. Such interviewer effects and biases are the topic of the next section.

Interviewer Effects in Public Opinion Polling

Interviewer effects can emerge in both telephone and personal interviews, although they are likely to be more pronounced in personal interviews because of the face-to-face interaction between the interviewer and the respondent. For most respondents, the personal interview is a new experience with all the attendant uncertainties and ambiguities of unfamiliar

activity. Unsure of how to behave, respondents may look to the interview situation for appropriate cues. The two most important sources of cues are the survey instrument itself (the questionnaire) and the person who administers the questionnaire, the interviewer. The cues provided by the survey instrument are direct (even if the questions are flawed); the cues provided by the interviewer may be far more subtle. If interviewers are inconsistent in the cues they give to different respondents, the reliability of the survey results may be undermined. At minimum, interviewers must not change the question wording, question order, or voice intonations from respondent to respondent. And because most polls use more than one interviewer, the interviewing process must be standardized as much as possible, which requires careful training of interviewers.

This emphasis on consistency and uniformity in the interviewing process reflects a concern with the *reliability* of the measuring instrument. One type of reliability measure is based on equivalence, the extent to which different investigators applying the same measuring instrument to the same individuals obtain consistent results. Ideally, the identity of the interviewer should not affect the responses that the questionnaire generates in the interview.

The reliability of an instrument can be distinguished from its *validity,* the extent to which the instrument measures what it is supposed to measure. For example, consider one of the political efficacy items discussed in Chapter 3: "Voting is the only way that people like me can have any say about how the government runs things." A "disagree" response to this item is considered an efficacious reply; it presumably means that the respondent believes that he or she can be influential in ways other than voting. But what if a respondent rejects this statement out of a belief that there is no way that people can have influence? In this case, a "disagree" response signals a lack of efficacy, and the item itself is not a valid indicator of the underlying concept of political efficacy. Because of the problem with validity, this item has been eliminated from the American National Election Studies.

An interviewer's general demeanor, competence, and performance have much to do with the success of the interview. Interviewers must be able to establish a rapport with respondents, making them feel at ease and receptive to the survey. If a rapport is not established, respondents may refuse to cooperate or fail to provide complete and accurate information to interviewers. Ideally, interviewers are well informed about the purposes of the research and the intention of specific questions so that they know whether a respondent has fully answered a question and how to ask follow-up questions for clarification. They should not, however, inject themselves into the interviewing process by making editorial comments about respondents' replies.

Although they should follow instructions carefully and ask all appropriate questions, interviewers also should be able to handle the unexpected, such as a respondent who volunteers additional information. Equally important, interviewers must record and transcribe responses as accurately as possible, even when the answers do not fall neatly into one of the predetermined response categories.

The difficulty of an interviewer's job depends on the nature of the questionnaire as well as on the characteristics of the respondents. For example, highly structured survey items require less guidance and judgment from an interviewer; relatively unstructured instruments require more. For interviews of political elites that use open-ended questions, an interviewer must not only be a good listener and prober who takes few or no notes during an interview, he or she must be able to write up the results of the interview after the question-and-answer session has ended. Sometimes such interviews are taped, which eliminates the need to take extensive notes, but taped interviews must be transcribed to be usable.

In addition to demeanor and skills, the personal characteristics of an interviewer can affect responses to a poll. For example, many interviewers are middle-aged women because this group is least threatening to male and female respondents, particularly in a personal interview in a home. Also, female interviewers often are able to establish a rapport more successfully than men.

Morin (1990) cites research that shows that men and women answer poll questions differently depending on the gender of the interviewer. In a poll on abortion conducted by the Eagleton Institute, women were much more likely to give pro-choice responses to female interviewers than to males; the response pattern for men was weaker. For example, when given the statement "The decision to have an abortion is a private matter that should be left to the woman to decide without government intervention,"

84 percent of the female respondents interviewed by women agreed, compared with only 64 percent of women interviewed by men. Seventy-seven percent of the male respondents interviewed by women agreed with the statement, compared with 70 percent of those interviewed by men.

A growing body of research indicates that women are more likely to give traditional, nonfeminist responses to male interviewers and more feminist responses to female interviewers. Likewise, men are somewhat more likely to give feminist responses to female interviewers than to males. Kane and Macaulay (1993) found that both men and women were more likely to express more egalitarian gender-related attitudes and more criticism of gender-related inequalities to female interviewers than to male interviewers. Huddy and Bracciodieta (1992) obtained similar results in their research except that they also found gender-of-interviewer effects on topics such as party identification and authoritarian attitudes, which are not directly related to gender. For example, both men and women gave more feminist, Democratic, and anti-authoritarian responses when interviewed by a female than a male. Therefore, on gender-related survey topics such as abortion and perhaps even on gender-neutral topics, researchers must be sensitive to the potential for interviewer-gender effects.

Like personal characteristics, the social distance between interviewers and respondents can influence an interview. If an interviewer appears to be of higher social status than a respondent, the respondent may tend to defer or acquiesce to the interviewer by providing answers intended to win approval. Even an interviewer's manner of speech can affect a respondent's replies, because a person's speech may reflect his or her geographical origin, social class, age group, or level of education.

An interviewer's race and ethnicity are additional factors that can affect responses to a poll (Schuman and Converse 1971; Hatchett and Schuman 1975–1976; Campbell 1981; Weeks and Moore 1981; Cotter, Cohen, and Coulter 1982). When black respondents are queried about the American political system, they are more likely to give supportive, positive answers to white interviewers than to black interviewers. Likewise, white respondents are less likely to reveal attitudes of racial hostility when interviewed by blacks than when interviewed by whites. A January 1987 New York Times/WCBS-TV News poll of New Yorkers' reactions to a racially motivated attack on some young black men in the Howard Beach section of New York City found that the race of the interviewer had a substantial effect on responses, even in telephone interviews, because, as pointed out earlier, interviewers may "sound" black or white. An earlier study by the same organizations had shown that telephone respondents can correctly identify the race of the interviewer about three-fourths of the time. In the

Howard Beach poll, which asked whether the lawyer for one of the black victims had acted responsibly, nearly half the black respondents interviewed by whites thought he had not, and about one-fourth thought he had. But among blacks interviewed by fellow blacks, the results were reversed (Meislin 1987). In late 1993 and early 1994 a major national telephone survey of African Americans was conducted using only black interviewers. (Morin 1995b). Even though respondents were not told the race of the interviewer, 76 percent of the sample correctly thought the interviewer was black; 14 percent incorrectly thought the interviewer was white; and the remaining 10 percent either did not know or thought the interviewer was of some other race. A comparison of the answers of respondents who correctly believed they were being interviewed by blacks with those who incorrectly thought they were interviewed by whites revealed substantial differences in the responses. For example, only 17 percent of the respondents who thought they were queried by African Americans agreed with the statement "American society is fair to everyone," compared with 31 percent agreement for those who believed their interviewer was white. Likewise, 84 percent of blacks who thought they were questioned by interviewers of their own race agreed with the statement "The American legal system is unfair to blacks," compared with 72 percent agreement for those queried by interviewers incorrectly perceived to be white. Finally, Davis (1997) found that black respondents in a survey were likely to be more accommodating and deferential to white interviewers, even to the point of taking contradictory stances in evaluations of political figures and political parties.

Similar patterns of race-of-interviewer effects occurred in a 1989 ABC News/*Washington Post* poll (Morin 1989b). On a number of race-related questions, white responses shifted about 5–10 percent depending on the race of the interviewer. For some questions the effect was greater. For example, 62 percent of whites interviewed by whites said that most of the problems now faced by blacks were "brought on by blacks themselves"; only 46 percent of white respondents interviewed by blacks gave that same response. A study by Anderson, Silver, and Abramson (1988) found that "blacks interviewed by whites were much more likely to express warmth and closeness toward whites than were blacks interviewed by blacks" (p. 289). Finally, a study by Finkel, Guterbock, and Borg (1991) of race-of-interviewer effects in a preelection poll in the 1989 Virginia gubernatorial contest between black Democrat Douglas Wilder and white Republican Marshall Coleman showed that white respondents interviewed by black interviewers were more likely to state a preference for Wilder (52.2 percent) than those queried by white interviewers (43.8 percent). This pattern was particularly pronounced among white Democrats and among whites who were less sure of their vote intention.

A study by Reese and colleagues (1986) on the effects of interviewer ethnicity—white versus Hispanic—found that ethnicity also affected the responses to certain questions, especially items that related to the culture of the interviewer. When Anglos were asked questions by Hispanics about aspects of Mexican American life, they responded more sympathetically than when they were asked the same questions by fellow Anglos. Why? The general explanation is that respondents try not to give answers that might offend an interviewer, particularly on matters that relate to the interviewer's race and ethnicity.

Internet Polling

Pollsters would benefit greatly from using the Internet to conduct public opinion polls of representative samples of citizens. First, they could interview large numbers of citizens in a quick and economical fashion. Moreover, they could provide respondents with audio and video materials as part of the interviewing process. Internet surveys could be self-administered, but an interviewer, either live or recorded, also could participate. Finally, via Internet polling researchers could tabulate and analyze data very rapidly.

With all these potential advantages, what factors are preventing the widespread use of Internet polling? Certainly the most obvious factor is that about half of all Americans do not have direct access to the Internet. Today's Internet users are more likely to be younger, better educated, more affluent, and white and male. But this description is likely to change rapidly in the not-too-distant future. Indeed, some observers compare the Internet today to the early days of the telephone. And just as telephone access became almost universal in American households, so too will Internet availability.

But even if Internet access and use were widespread, the most significant flaw in many Internet polls is that respondents are not selected through some scientific sampling procedure. Instead, respondents are self-selected in that they choose whether or not to participate in the survey. Obviously, such respondents may not be representative of the overall population, perhaps because they are more interested in the topic of that particular survey or perhaps because they have been stimulated by various groups to take part in the survey. Then there is the problem of respondents who participate in a survey more than once.

Internet surveys with self-selected or voluntary samples are essentially nonprobability samples, which means that sampling error cannot be calculated nor can probability statements be made about the relationship between the sample results and the true population parameters. There is simply no sampling list from which a probability sample can be collected. This problem, however, is not an inevitable shortcoming of Internet polls. Morin (2000a, 2000b) notes that companies are developing new techniques that use elements of both random-digit dialing and Internet polling. As one example, Morin cites a company that selects random samples of American households using random-digit dialing techniques. These selected households are then given free Internet access as well as free WebTV hardware, thereby eliminating the bias in Internet access and enabling pollsters to interview representative samples via the Internet. Some observers, however, might argue that providing households with Internet access contaminates the selection process. It is likely that Internet access will become almost universal on its own in the near future. Moreover, in some settings today, such as many university campuses, access to computers, e-mail, and the Internet is universal, *and* comprehensive lists of university populations do exist. Given these conditions, Internet polling of representative samples of university communities is very feasible.

In the ongoing debate about the viability of Internet polling, some scholars, such as Taylor and Terhanian (1999), tout online polling as the wave of the future and are less concerned about its nonprobability features. Instead, they talk about the utility of quota sampling and the effectiveness of weighting as ways of overcoming the shortcomings of voluntary, self-selected samples. Other scholars, such as Mitofsky (1999), are skeptical about jumping on the Internet bandwagon, at least until the problem of sampling lists and frames are resolved, especially if the researcher wants to generalize the sample results to a broader population.

Whatever the arguments, Internet polling will continue to grow. For many practitioners, the information collected in Internet polling is useful even if it cannot be generalized to larger populations. But technical developments and expanded access to the Internet will likely facilitate progress in making Internet surveys more scientific. In the meantime, the results of Internet surveys should be viewed with caution, particularly if they are conducted by entities with an agenda to promote. The National Council on Public Polls (NCPP), skeptical about the reliability of many Internet surveys, has provided journalists with ten questions they should address before reporting the results of Internet polls. According to the NCPP, if an Internet survey is not designed to be representative and if there is no evidence that it is representative, its results should not be reported. The NCPP also essentially dismisses self-selected, call-in polls. Yet, despite the NCPP's admonitions to journalists and the media to be careful about publicizing and reporting Internet polls, Web-based surveys are becoming more prominent, and many are even sponsored by the media themselves. The next chapter will discuss the role of the media in the polling enterprise.

Conclusion

The method of interviewing and the actual conduct of the interview measurably affect the responses to a public opinion poll. In most instances consumers of polls are in a weak position to evaluate these effects, mainly because pollsters provide little information about interviewing procedures. Nevertheless, consumers might raise a number of questions about the interviewing process, particularly if they have been selected to be respondents in a poll. For example, consumers who refuse to complete a mailed questionnaire might ask themselves why. Is it because the subject matter is of no interest, because the questions are too simplistic, or because the questionnaire is too time-consuming? Consumers who choose to participate in a survey might examine their reactions to question wording and question order, to the overall experience itself, or to other specific elements of the questionnaire.

One question that poll consumers will never be able to answer is whether the same results would have been obtained had a different interviewing method been used. Some research suggests that the choice of interviewing method can affect the responses because of the different interpersonal dynamics that characterize different interviewing modes. For example, in two studies on substance use, personal interviews showed higher levels of alcohol and drug use by respondents than did telephone interviews (Johnson 1989; Aquilino and Losciuto 1990).

Respondents to personal or telephone polls also should make some mental notes about the skill of the interviewers. How effective was the interviewer in establishing a good climate for the interview? How well did the interviewer handle the respondent's questions and problems? Did the interviewer do or say anything that seemed to lead the person to respond in certain ways? Did the interviewer have any characteristics or traits that either facilitated or hindered the interview? The answers to these and other questions should alert poll respondents to biases that can influence the interviewing process and the answers it generates.

6 The Media and the Polls

The media's role in public opinion polling is essentially twofold: to inform the public of poll results and to sponsor polls. The print and electronic media, especially newspapers and television, are the major sources of what Americans learn about polls, because most citizens do not have direct access to reports prepared by polling organizations. And because the media are the sources Americans rely on, citizens need to recognize that many organizations that sponsor surveys try to manipulate the media to cover poll results in ways that promote the organizations' objectives. Likewise, candidates often seek advantageous media coverage of private campaign polls by selectively leaking results.

Some of the most publicized and widely disseminated public opinion polls are sponsored by the national television networks and their local affiliates, the major news magazines, and newspapers throughout the country. Thus the media generate public opinion data, which in turn become the subject matter for news stories presented by these same media. For some observers, this situation raises questions about a conflict of interest—that is, the definition of what is newsworthy may be unduly influenced by media-sponsored polls on particular topics. In addition, the fact that the media make substantial investments in developing their capability for public opinion polling may result in a tendency to use that capability even when it is not appropriate to the topic at hand.

Because of the media's pivotal role in developing citizens' awareness of polling, this chapter evaluates the media's reporting of public opinion polls, both those sponsored by the media and those sponsored by other organizations. The discussion focuses on two distinct aspects of poll coverage: the treatment of the polls' technical features (for example, sampling error and question wording) and the presentation of substantive results and interpretations based on the polling data. The chapter concludes by considering some caveats in the reporting of polls.

──→   Standards for Reporting Results

Because media reporting of polls may not always be reliable, various organizations have adopted standards to govern the disclosure of poll results to citizens. For example, the National Council on Public Polls, a group of polling organizations, has adopted the following Principles of Disclosure:

> All reports of survey findings of member organizations, prepared specifically for public release, will include reference to the following:
>
> —sponsorship of the survey;
> —dates of interviewing;
> —method of obtaining the interview;
> —population that was sampled;
> —size of the sample;
> —size and description of the subsample, if the survey report relies primarily on less than the total sample;
> —complete wording of questions upon which the release is based;
> —the percentages upon which conclusions are based.

The recommendations go on to state:

> When survey results are released to any medium by a survey organization, the above items will be included in the release. . . .
>
> Survey organizations reporting results will endeavor to have print and broadcast media include the above items in their news stories and make a report containing these items available to the public upon request.

The American Association for Public Opinion Research has its own code of conduct, one part of which specifies the standards for disclosure of how a poll was conducted. AAPOR advocates that at the minimum the following items be disclosed:

1. Who sponsored the survey, and who conducted it.
2. The exact wording of questions asked, including the text of any preceding instruction or explanation to the interviewer or respondents that might reasonably be expected to affect the response.
3. A definition of the population under study, and a description of the sampling frame used to identify this population.
4. A description of the sample selection procedure, giving a clear indication of the method by which the respondents were selected by the researcher, or whether the respondents were entirely self-selected.

5. Sizes of samples, and, if applicable, completion rates and information on eligibility criteria and screening procedures.
6. A discussion of the precision of the findings, including, if appropriate, estimates of sampling error, and a description of any weighting or estimating procedures used.
7. Which results are based on parts of the sample, rather than on the total sample.
8. Method, location, and dates of data collection.

Effectiveness of the Standards

But how much protection do these standards provide for consumers of public opinion research, assuming that polling organizations adhere to them? The answer is that they provide less protection than is apparent at first glance, although they have contributed to improved media coverage of the polls. One reason the standards are not as effective as they appear is that they apply primarily to survey organizations and pollsters who release results rather than to the media that are covering the results. However, in some cases, when the survey organization and the disseminator of the results are part of the same news organization, coverage of in-house polls is usually more in line with the NCPP and AAPOR standards.

Here is an example of how the standards may be applied when the survey organization and the disseminator of the results are the same. The results of a CBS News/*New York Times* poll may emanate from four distinct sources: (1) the story that appears in the *New York Times*; (2) the report presented on the "CBS Evening News"; (3) the news release issued by the *New York Times*; and (4) the news release prepared by CBS News. The first two sources are readily available to citizens; the latter two are not. Normally, the news releases prepared by CBS News and by the *New York Times* and the news story in the *Times* comply closely with the NCPP and AAPOR standards; the story presented on the "CBS Evening News" is less complete because airtime is limited.

If the organization reporting the poll is different from the group that sponsored it, the poll release and the actual news story may show major discrepancies in meeting the NCPP and AAPOR recommendations. For example, most newspapers do not conduct their own polls. Instead, they rely on syndicated polls from organizations such as Gallup and Harris, or on news releases in the public domain that are issued by polling organizations. In these situations the NCPP recommends that the sponsoring organization attempt to ensure that the medium that reports its results conforms to the NCPP standards. But there really is no way to enforce this requirement with news organizations once the poll release has become a public docu-

cathy®   **by Cathy Guisewite**

ment. Moreover, the interests of the sponsoring organization may not be well served by full disclosure of the technical features of the poll, particularly when the sponsoring organization has manipulated the poll to generate a desired set of results. Overall, then, compliance with the standards is voluntary. Because organizations may choose not to observe them or may not be able to observe them, the effectiveness of the standards is diminished.

Another reason the NCPP and AAPOR standards are less effective than they might be is that they do not specify reporting of all the technical aspects of a poll that can markedly affect the results. For example, the NCPP standards recommend reporting the "complete wording of questions on which the release is based." Complete wording is not necessarily identical to the complete questionnaire—that is, without an entire survey instrument it is difficult to ascertain whether question order and placement have influenced the results reported in a release. Likewise, the second AAPOR standard is a very subjective recommendation. Different polling organizations might very well disagree about the meaning of "instruction or explanation . . . that might reasonably be expected to affect the response." For the major news organizations this standard is less of a concern, because their releases typically include entire questionnaires showing the order in which items were asked. Moreover, the television networks and major newspapers are willing to distribute complete poll releases to interested citizens.

A more serious problem arises, however, when a news organization prepares a news analysis based on a subset of items from a questionnaire and does not inform readers or viewers about question wording and question order. Thus the news analysis may or may not accurately represent the content of the entire survey. Obviously, the items chosen for analysis and the perspective given to those selected items can dramatically affect the resulting coverage.

The NCPP and AAPOR standards ignore other technical specifications. For example, NCPP standards do not require reporting of adjustments made to a sample, such as weighting (used to achieve demographic representativeness—see Chapter 4) or filtering (used to identify likely voters within a sample). A poll release will often state that weighting and filtering have been done, but in most cases it will not tell how. As a result, the poll consumer, ill equipped to assess the soundness of the poll, is at the mercy of the decisions made by the news organizations. For example, pollsters use different methods to identify likely voters, which can generate divergent predictions of election outcomes (see Chapter 7).

Finally, the NCPP and AAPOR recommendations do not include response rates and the procedures, such as callbacks, that are used to increase the response rate. Poor response rates may require adjusting the interviewed sample to make it representative of the broader population. If respondents who are called back multiple times in order to complete an interview differ in systematic ways from respondents who are interviewed on the first attempt, then the decision on whether to use multiple callbacks can affect the substantive findings of the poll. Unfortunately, in most situations poll consumers receive little if any information about response rates and related matters.

Observing the Standards

How closely do the media actually conform to the NCPP and AAPOR standards in their reporting of polls? An early study by Miller and Hurd (1982) examined how well three newspapers—the *Chicago Tribune,* the *Los Angeles Times,* and the *Atlanta Constitution*—followed the AAPOR guidelines. In a sample of 116 polls reported between 1972 and 1979, compliance was highest for sample size (reported 85 percent of the time) and sponsorship (reported 82 percent of the time), and lowest for sampling error (reported only 16 percent of the time). Miller and Hurd found no marked trend indicating improved poll reporting over time, but they did find that compliance with the AAPOR standards on sampling error was better for election polls than for nonelection surveys. In general, compliance was better when newspapers reported on their own in-house polls than on polls provided by external sources. When newspapers did not publish information called for by the AAPOR standards, in some instances the external polls had not provided the information, but in other instances the newspapers had simply edited out that information (Miller and Hurd 1982, 246).

Another study (Salwen 1985b) examined the reporting of public opinion polls by the *Detroit News* and the *Detroit Free Press* in presidential election years from 1968 to 1984. Salwen did find improvement over time in the reporting of some of the information required by AAPOR, although the exact question wording and the timing of the poll were reported less frequently (about 28 percent and 61 percent of the time, respectively) and reporting on those aspects showed no improvement during the sixteen-year period. Reporting of sampling error did improve over time, but in 1984 only 50 percent of the news stories about polls mentioned sampling error. Like Miller and Hurd, Salwen found that newspapers did a much better job of presenting the methodology of their in-house polls than of polls from external sources.

Overall, Miller and Hurd and Salwen did see positive signs that newspaper reporting of polls had improved over the years. They attributed the improvement to increased collaboration between journalists and social scientists, the availability of readable books and texts on polling, and the increased frequency of in-house polls (newspapers do a better job of reporting their own polls because of local interest in them and because reporters have greater access to information about their technical aspects).

The positive findings of these studies must be tempered by the fact that they both dealt with major daily newspapers of reasonably high quality. One might expect such papers to have expertise and competence in reporting polls. Moreover, many of the polls the researchers analyzed were election surveys, which are more likely to report information such as sample size and sampling error than are nonelection surveys. Another study by Salwen (1985a), however, found that for question wording and method of interviewing, reports of nonelection polls were more descriptive than those of election polls, a finding speculatively attributed to the fact that question wording and interviewing method are more self-evident in election polls and therefore need not be reported. In smaller daily and weekly newspapers without the resources to conduct in-house polls and employ their own survey research experts, poll coverage is probably much poorer.

If newspaper reporting falls short of the NCPP and AAPOR standards, what must television's coverage be like? Newspapers have obvious advantages in reporting polls. One is that they provide the reader with hard copy that can be reread and referred to, in contrast to the television message which (unless taped) "disappears" as soon as it is presented. Another is that newspapers can more easily present a lot of information, such as full question wording. Television, with its severe time and space constraints, is less likely to do so.

Paletz and colleagues (1980) conducted one of the few empirical studies of the treatment of polls by network television. They examined every poll reported on the CBS and NBC evening news shows and in the *New York*

Times in 1973, 1975, and 1977, years deliberately chosen to avoid presidential elections. Their conclusion was that the television networks generally did a poorer job of reporting details about polls than did the *Times,* although the latter's performance was not stellar. (Keep in mind that during the 1970s the networks and the *New York Times* had not yet begun extensive in-house polling; in-house polls are better reported than external surveys.) Among the findings was that the sponsor of a poll was almost never mentioned on the networks and mentioned only about 25 percent of the time in the *Times.* Sample size was presented in two-thirds of the *Times* stories, but in only 26 percent of the television reports. The time of interviewing was given in 43 percent of the *Times* accounts and in 30 percent of the television reports. And in only 30 percent of the *Times* stories and 5 percent of the television reports was the complete wording of particular questions provided. Beyond these details, the report provides virtually no other technical information about the polls (Paletz et al. 1980, 504–505).

An analysis of Australian television coverage of election polls (Smith and Verrall 1985) generally concurs with Paletz and his colleagues that television coverage is superficial and lacking in methodological details. Smith and Verrall argue that the heterogeneity of the television audience requires that coverage be kept brief and simple. One way to foster brevity and simplicity is to omit methodological information.

As the available evidence suggests, then, the media could do a much better job of adhering to the NCPP and AAPOR standards in reporting poll results, especially for surveys not conducted in-house. Such adherence would enable citizens to become more technically proficient in assessing and evaluating poll results. Methodological sophistication in poll reporting is increasing as journalists, political practitioners, and even the media audience acquire survey research skills. Moreover, as more media organizations conduct their own in-house polls and ignore polls from other sources, the overall quality of poll reporting will probably improve. Nevertheless, "the way methodological information about polling is reported in the media tends more to reassure than alert the audience about the possible defects of poll data" (Paletz et al. 1980, 506).

In 1994 two examples of excellent reporting of the mechanics of a poll appeared in the *Columbus Dispatch.* That year, the newspaper conducted its own in-house mail surveys and commissioned the Gallup Organization to conduct statewide telephone polls on the 1994 elections in Ohio. About its own poll, the *Dispatch* said:

> The Dispatch poll was based on returns from 1,456 registered Ohioans who intend to vote Nov. 8. *The Dispatch* bought a computerized list of all registered Ohio voters. A *Dispatch* computer randomly chose those

to receive ballots, modeled as closely as possible after the state's official ballot layout. Voters receiving the ballots were asked to describe themselves by party affiliation, age, sex, race, education, income, religion, union membership and how they voted for president in 1992 and governor in 1990. Ballots of different colors were sent to various regions of the state so *The Dispatch* could ensure that each area was represented in proportion to its actual voting strength. The areas, patterned on groupings of the state's media markets, are: northeast (20 counties); central (20 counties); southwest (8 counties); northwest (12 counties); west (14 counties); and southeast (14 counties). The standard margin of sampling error in a scientific poll of the size conducted by *The Dispatch* is plus or minus 2.5 percentage points in 95 out of 100 cases. This means that if a scientific poll is conducted 100 times, in 95 cases the result will not vary by more than 2.5 percentage points from the result that would be obtained if all registered voters in Ohio were polled and responded. Error margins are greater for poll subsamples. Like all polls, *The Dispatch* Poll is subject to possible error other than sampling error. Other sources of error can be unintentional bias in the wording of questions, data entry error or nonresponse bias. Nonresponse bias means that those who responded to the poll may not necessarily reflect the views of those who did not participate. The response rate was 19 percent. The results were adjusted slightly to compensate for demographic differences between poll respondents and the Ohio electorate as a whole. Although precautions are taken to ensure that the sample reflects the demographic characteristics of the Ohio electorate, precise estimates for total possible error cannot be calculated. The poll was designed, conducted and financed by *The Dispatch*. (*Columbus Dispatch* 1994a, 5)

About the Gallup poll, the *Dispatch* reported the following information provided by the Gallup Organization:

The results of the Gallup survey are based on telephone interviews with a randomly selected statewide sample of 803 registered voters, conducted Tuesday through Thursday. Data were weighted to ensure appropriate representation by age, sex, education, race and geographical location. Household telephone numbers were generated by a computer to ensure that all areas of the state were represented in proportion to the actual population in that area. This method ensures that both listed and unlisted telephone numbers are included in the sample. Respondents were asked whether they were registered to vote in their precinct or election district. For all respondents—registered or not—information was obtained on their gender, age, education and race, so that the overall sample of registered and unregistered adults could be weighted to conform to the census statistics. Registered voters also were asked their likelihood of voting and how interested they were in the election. These two questions were used to compute a "likely voter" category, which includes 483 respondents. For results based on the statewide sample of 803 registered voters, one can say with 95 percent confidence that the error attributed to sampling and other random effects could be plus or minus 4 percentage points. For results based on the "likely voter" category, the margin of error is plus or minus 5 percentage points. In addition to sampling error, question wording and practical difficulties in conducting surveys can introduce error or bias into the findings of public opinion polls. (*Columbus Dispatch* 1994b, 2)

Note that in addition to the standard information about sampling error and confidence levels, both of these descriptions discussed weighting or adjusting the data and mentioned the different sampling error for subgroups. They also mentioned other sources of error, although they did not develop these points. It is to the credit of the *Dispatch* that it commissioned an outside poll for results that could be compared with the results of its in-house surveys.

Substantive Interpretation of Polls

Without access to the complete results of polls, citizens cannot easily evaluate how well the media report on the technical aspects of polling. It is even more problematic for them to evaluate how well the media describe and interpret the substance of public opinion polls. Because interpretation of polling data can be highly judgmental and value laden, it may be difficult to demonstrate that one particular interpretation is superior to another except in cases where obvious misreadings of the data have occurred or where blatant biases have been built into the analysis. Even a simple description can pose a problem if time and space constraints force the media to cover only a subset of the items on a topic.

This section presents several examples illustrating how the media use and interpret polls and how much leeway the media have in deciding what parts of a poll to emphasize. The first example deals with Americans' reactions to the U.S. bombing of Libya as measured in a CBS News/*New York Times* poll conducted in April 1986. At the time of the poll the government of Libya was sponsoring terrorism and was hostile to the American military presence in the Mediterranean Sea. After several incidents, the United States launched a retaliatory air attack against Libya. The reports of the poll in a CBS News release, in the *New York Times,* and on the "CBS Evening News" were consistent, the lead being that Americans overwhelmingly approved of the bombing by a margin of 77 percent to 14 percent, even though a plurality of 43 percent thought it would lead to more terrorism, and 30 percent thought it would reduce terrorism. The *Times,* of course, presented far more details about the poll's results than did the "CBS

Evening News," but the overall consistency of both reports suggested a common interpretation.

In addition to asking citizens whether they thought the Libyan bombing would reduce or increase terrorism, respondents were asked a related item about the efficacy of American military action in general: "If the United States made it a policy to take military action against a government it believes has trained or financed terrorists, do you think that would reduce terrorism in the long run, or would it only make things worse?" Fully 57 percent said it would reduce terrorism; 27 percent thought it would make the risk worse. In their treatment of this item, the *Times* story and the CBS press release differed. The *Times* reported this question at the very end of an article that ran forty-four column inches, while in a twelve-paragraph CBS press release the item was detailed in the fourth paragraph. Neither the *Times* nor CBS News made much of the discrepancy between citizens' doubts that the Libyan bombing would reduce terrorism and their belief that a policy of taking military action against terrorist governments would reduce terrorism. But imagine the divergent portrayals of public opinion that could be painted if one or the other item had been reported, but not both. One headline might read, "Americans question effectiveness of Libyan bombing," while another might proclaim, "Americans support military response to terrorism."

A good example of the choices that face the analyst is Adam Clymer's *New York Times* story on attitudes toward abortion, based on a survey of Americans conducted in late 1985. In Clymer's view, the wording of questions about abortion has a tremendous impact on citizens' responses, a "clear indication of uncertainty and conflict" in the public's attitudes on the topic (Clymer 1986b). Three items in the survey illustrate the complexity of popular attitudes:

> What do you think about abortion? Should it be legal as it is now, legal only in such cases as saving the life of the mother, rape or incest, or should it not be permitted at all?

Legal as is now	40%
Legal only to save mother, rape or incest	40%
Not permitted	16%
Don't know, not ascertained	4%

> Which of these statements comes closest to your opinion? Abortion is the same thing as murdering a child, or abortion is not murder because a fetus isn't really a person.

Murder	55%
Not murder	35%
Don't know, not ascertained	10%

Do you agree or disagree with the following statement? Abortion sometimes is the best course in a bad situation.

Agree	66%
Disagree	26%
Don't know, not ascertained	8%

Markedly different stories could be written based on this survey, depending on which items are emphasized and how particular items are
interpreted. By focusing only on the first item, a reporter could write a pro-
choice story that points out that 40 percent of Americans favor the current
abortion law, another 40 percent favor legalized abortion in limited circumstances, and only 16 percent oppose abortion outright. Another reporter
could write an antiabortion story based on the first item, by stressing that
56 percent of the sample (40 percent plus 16 percent) favor limiting somewhat the current availability of abortion. Likewise, the second item could be
used to document an antiabortion story that emphasizes that a majority of
Americans think abortion is murder. But a story based only on the third
item would suggest that a strong majority of Americans think abortion is
sometimes the best course of action. Clymer's article reflects the complex
and even contradictory nature of popular attitudes on abortion; imagine
the advocacy piece he could have written if he had adopted a blatantly pro-
choice or antiabortion perspective.

News articles in the *New York Times, Washington Post,* and other
major newspapers that include polling data usually integrate the polling
information into the body of the article, often presenting detailed breakdowns of the data and a reasonable amount of information about the poll
and its characteristics. Newspapers not only use polls to supplement a
news story, but also print articles in which polls are the subject.

By contrast, news magazines such as *Time* and *Newsweek* often commission polls to use as sidebars to news stories. Sometimes the poll results
are placed in a separate box, with little reference made to them in the accompanying story. For example, a four-page story about the beating of a
black man by Los Angeles police officers appeared in the March 25, 1991,
issue of *Time,* which also had commissioned a poll on the subject. The story
carried no mention of the poll; it was presented simply as an inset in the article (see box next page). Note the scant analysis of the poll. Even though
a black-white comparison would have been of interest, no breakdown by
subgroups is shown (perhaps the sample size would have not allowed for a
reliable comparison). Also, no statement is made about any filtering or
screening of those people who had not heard or read about the incident.

The following examples suggest that media reports of polls conducted
by other organizations are particularly susceptible to misinterpretation and

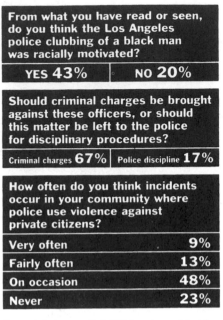

From what you have read or seen, do you think the Los Angeles police clubbing of a black man was racially motivated?

| YES 43% | NO 20% |

Should criminal charges be brought against these officers, or should this matter be left to the police for disciplinary procedures?

| Criminal charges 67% | Police discipline 17% |

How often do you think incidents occur in your community where police use violence against private citizens?

Very often	9%
Fairly often	13%
On occasion	48%
Never	23%

From a telephone poll of 500 American adults taken for TIME/CNN on March 13 by Yankelovich Clancy Shulman. Sampling error is plus or minus 4.5%. "Not sures" omitted.

---

faulty reporting. Jan Werner (2000) criticizes a *New York Times* report (Glanz 2000) of a survey sponsored by People for the American Way on citizens' attitudes toward teaching evolution and creationism. The *Times* headline read, "Poll Finds That Support Is Strong for Teaching 2 Origin Theories," and the first paragraph of the news story claimed that "an overwhelming majority of Americans think that creationism should be taught along with Darwin's theory of evolution in the public schools." But Werner notes that a more careful reading of the poll's results shows that the *Times* headline and lead are inaccurate. Eighty-three percent of respondents favored teaching evolution in schools, but there was not overwhelming support for teaching creationism as scientific theory. In fact, 79 percent of Americans thought there was a place for creationism in the curriculum of public schools, but only 30 percent thought it should be taught as scientific theory; 49 percent believed it should be taught as a religious belief.

Krosnick (1989) investigated the *New York Times* coverage of a poll commissioned by Aetna Life and Casualty on the public's attitudes toward the civil justice system and tort reform; the poll was conducted by Louis Harris and Associates. Aetna had a vested interest in tort reform. When the poll was completed, Aetna issued a press release that began, "An overwhelming majority of Americans support a number of specific reforms to improve the nation's civil justice system." Throughout the press release and the Harris report of the survey results were assertions that Americans supported and favored many changes. The survey questions themselves, however, did not ask respondents whether they supported or favored these changes; instead, the questions asked whether respondents found these changes to be acceptable. Clearly, to find something acceptable is not the same thing as supporting or favoring it. Nevertheless, the news story on the poll that appeared in the *New York Times* failed to recognize this distinction and made strong claims that the poll results demonstrated "broad public support for *changes* in the civil justice system" and "reflected the public's *demand* for reform" (Krosnick 1989, 108). As Krosnick concluded, the *Times* coverage of the poll results most likely overstated public support for the changes that Aetna desired.

A close look at another *New York Times* article reveals how a reporter can become so creative in describing poll results that he or she fails to convey to the reader what the results really mean. In 1990 the Graduate School of the City University of New York commissioned a major national survey about religion in the United States. One item in the survey asked Americans what their religion was, and 7.5 percent responded that they had no religion. At the state level, Oregon led the nation with 17 percent of its population reporting "no religion." The *New York Times* story about this poll began with the simple declarative sentence "The state with the highest proportion of [atheists] is Oregon" (Goldman 1991). This lead may draw the reader into the story, but it also distorts the meaning of the poll results: having no religion does not necessarily mean denying the existence of a higher being.

A more serious example of media misreporting and misinterpreting of polls occurred in the late 1970s as the U.S. Senate considered ratification of the treaties that would lead to Panamanian control of the Panama Canal. Smith and Hogan (1987) found that as the debate progressed in the Senate, many media organizations were reporting that public opinion was shifting toward support of the treaties—a finding that, if true, would obviously make it easier for senators sympathetic to the treaties to vote for ratification. But when Smith and Hogan examined the myriad poll results from this period, they found a pattern of stable opinion (which was hostile to the treaties), not one of change. They attributed the misleading interpretations to the variety of questions asked by different polling outfits, flaws in these questions, misinterpretation of key findings, and other factors. Here, though, the key point is their evaluation of how different media actually reported the polls. They wrote:

> In general, CBS and the *New York Times* provided accurate and perceptive accounts of public opinion on the treaties. But the *Time, Newsweek,* and NBC stories . . . display serious flaws. During the crucial period of Senate deliberation (January through April 1978) all claimed a massive shift in approval based on comparison of responses to different questions asked, in most cases, by different pollsters. Furthermore, the coverage is littered by errors of fact and inference and shows little understanding of the complex issues involved. . . .
>
> Equally disturbing are certain common omissions. After January 1978, most findings of continued public opposition were simply ignored. . . . Also omitted were the methodological details that would have allowed an educated reader or viewer to discover the misinterpretations embedded in the media coverage. Only two articles, both in the *New York Times,* provided the complete text of a question; only one, also in the *Times,* included all of the information required by the American Association for Public Opinion Research (AAPOR) Standards of Disclosure for poll reports. In *Time* and *Newsweek* almost no information was given. (Smith and Hogan 1987, 27)

Morin (1998) has pointed out that much of the media coverage (including some of his own) of the U.S. role in Bosnia in the late 1990s ignored poll results indicating strong support for some form of multilateral involvement and instead emphasized public opposition to U.S. involvement. Likewise, the coverage of domestic policy issues is often flawed. Morin (1997d) cites the work of Jacobs and Shapiro, who investigated how the media use polls to report on entitlement programs. Their conclusions are very critical, claiming that news stories often fail to provide context and background from which to interpret survey data. They also point out that polling on topics such as entitlements is focusing increasingly on the politics (for example, the performance of various political actors) of the issue rather than the substance. Certainly it is possible that the way the media portray public opinion on controversial issues such as the canal treaties or Bosnia or entitlements may affect the public policy decisions that are ultimately made.

Sometimes the media use pseudo-polls of self-selected respondents to embellish a news story in a misleading way. For example, in 1980 ABC News inappropriately used a telephone call-in poll to gauge reactions to the presidential debate (see Chapter 7). More recently and on a less-consequential issue, ABC again used a pseudo-poll as part of its coverage when genuine polling data were available (Morin 1996a). ABC's news magazine show "20/20" devoted a segment to physical attraction—that is, whether women were satisfied with their physical appearance and what aspects of the physical appearance of women were most important to men. ABC's own scientific survey on these topics had found that the vast majority of women were satisfied with their physical attributes. The show decided, however, to build its story about physical attractiveness around a pseudo-poll conducted by *Self* magazine, and it went on to report that 50 percent of the women who completed the magazine survey and mailed it in said "they were inadequate because of their breast size." But the genuine poll that ABC itself conducted found quite different results: only 23 percent of respondents had ever wished their breasts were a different size, and, unlike the thrust of the "20/20" segment, with its emphasis on breast enlargement, more than half of the dissatisfied women in the genuine poll had wished that their breasts were smaller, not larger. In this case, then, entertainment values overrode any responsibility to use appropriate polling data.

The statistical analysis most commonly presented in poll stories is simple percentage distributions for individual questions in the survey—something that most adults understand. Sometimes media reports include a breakdown by demographic subgroups, such as men and women or blacks and whites, but they seldom offer a cross-tabulation that shows the relationship between two survey items. Moreover, measures of association, correlation analysis, and multivariate statistical analyses almost never appear in news stories, probably out of the media's fear of intimidating and alienating the audience. It is fair to say, however, that the media's statistical interpretation of poll results is reasonably accurate as far as it goes, in part because poll coverage is not very ambitious given the media's perception of what their audiences want and are able to comprehend.

Media, Polls, and the News Reporting Emphasis

The media are frequently criticized for elevating polls to such a position of prominence that the polls themselves become regular topics for news stories. Indeed, some observers complain that the media in their role as sponsors of polls have gone into the business of *creating* the news rather than simply *reporting* it. More and more media have developed their own polling capabilities, and, as mentioned earlier, in order to justify this sizable expenditure they may increasingly report poll-based stories that are not newsworthy in the traditional sense. Fitzgerald, Rule, and Bryant (1998) document the rise of poll-based reporting on television news and the growing tendency of the networks to use their own polls. Consider this hypothetical example. A news organization conducts a poll on American attitudes toward mass transportation. Even though this topic is not on the national agenda and not a focal point for public debate, the news organization publishes a story reporting the results of this survey. Such a story comes very close to being news that is created by the media rather than news that is coverage of real events. The media also come close to generating news in their constant reporting of presidential popularity polls; the latest blip in the trend line of presidential popularity becomes fodder for a news story.

Another concern is that as more news organizations develop their own polling capabilities, they will increasingly fail to cover polls conducted by their rivals. Most of the media pollsters query citizens on matters such as presidential election trial heats, but usually their news reports do not mention the competition's results, particularly when those results disagree with their own.

The media's treatment of election polls has received especially harsh criticism. The most common complaint is that the media treat elections as sporting events—the comparison is usually to horse races (see Chapter 7)—and use the polls to help handicap the outcome. Indeed, Fitzgerald, Rule, and Bryant (1998) found that between 1969 and 1996 only four topics accounted for 90 percent of the poll-based subjects covered by TV news, and number one on the list was candidates and elections. Campaign coverage by the media frequently emphasizes candidates' relative electoral standing, often as measured by the polls (Broh 1980; Asher 1992), rather than their stances on the issues. As Robinson and Sheehan (1983, 252) argue:

> The main problem with polling . . . is that it is objective and so "newsworthy" (at least for the moment) that it drives out all other forms of news. Polls have a higher priority in the newscast than most other forms of campaign reporting. And, of course, polls tend to be among the least substantive kinds of political journalism.

In the 1988, 1992, 1996, and 2000 presidential campaigns, much of the criticism of presidential election polls focused on their frequency, their intrusiveness, their inconsistency, and the quality of media coverage of these polls. For example, Elving (1989) notes that in August 1988 fourteen major polls on the Dukakis-Bush presidential contest had results that varied by nineteen percentage points, a situation that generated confusion and annoyance with the polls. In defending their enterprise, many pollsters deflected criticism by shifting the blame to the media. Elving cites some pollsters' criticisms of how the media handled the polls in 1988:

> "Did I see [1988] polls that annoyed me? No, but I did see reporting on them that did," says Linda DiVall of American Viewpoint Inc. "I wish the press had less desire to be conclusive and say the race is over when it's 10 points and it's May."

Ed Goeas, president of Tarrance & Associates, says newspaper polls can be manipulated by the campaigns. "When newspaper polls are in the field the campaign can learn of it and do things to pump their guy up."

But, Goeas contends, the real problems come when the data are in hand: "Newspapers are hurting the credibility of the industry because they are not prepared to analyze the data correctly." . . .

"They're getting better, but I am always amazed at how many reporters are covering polls . . . without training or background," says Bud Lewis, the veteran pollster for the *Los Angeles Times*. "It's like sex—everybody thinks they're good at it automatically."

The 1992 elections offer another example. In the pre-convention period, different polls had either George Bush or Ross Perot ahead (though not by large margins). The media coverage of these polls was often very dramatic and definitive, with little recognition in many cases of how unstable early presidential preferences can be (Morin 1992d). Likewise, the post-convention polls showed dramatic swings in support for Bill Clinton and Bush. Harwood (1992) argues that the media did a poor job of accounting for these swings, often simply attributing them to the convention "bumps" that each candidate received, when in fact much of the fluctuation might have stemmed from the limitations inherent in the polls themselves.

A similar situation occurred in the pre-convention period in the 1996 presidential campaign. Most polls in May 1996 showed Clinton with a sizable double-digit lead over Bob Dole. Most of the next round of poll results in mid-June showed Clinton still ahead by a double-digit margin but a smaller one than in May. Of the June polls, the one that received the greatest media attention was the survey that showed the smallest gap between Clinton and Dole; the *Time*/CNN survey revealed that Clinton's lead had dropped from 56 to 34 percent to 49 to 43 percent. Why did the media focus on the *Time*/CNN poll when other polls showed Clinton with a larger lead? The answer is probably twofold. First, the media love a close horse race that generates excitement, and that is what the *Time*/CNN poll provided. Second, the *Time*/CNN poll showed the greatest fluctuation over time, which intrinsically made it more interesting to the media.

In the 2000 election, the Bush/Gore trial heat poll results bounced around substantially through the Republican and Democratic conventions, past Labor Day, and into the presidential debates in October. This volatility perplexed some observers and led others to be critical of the media for their breathless reporting of slight changes in poll standing.

Other problems inherent in media-sponsored public opinion polling reflect the structural characteristics of the polling and news-reporting enterprises. Ladd (1980, 576) questions whether polling and journalism can

ever fit together well, given that *newsworthiness* for the media is characterized by speed and timeliness, whereas good polling, despite the current
technology for quick assessments of public attitudes, requires "extensive,
time-consuming explanation and exposition." This potential conflict is ex-
acerbated by the space and time constraints faced by news organizations.
Consequently, the media are often unable to present a poll-based story
that includes complete details about the poll itself as well as adequate substantive background and context. Ladd also argues that good reporting is
generally sharply focused with relatively unambiguous conclusions; good
survey research, however, usually reveals uncertainty, ambiguity, and low
levels of public information and interest on matters of public policy. Often
the portrait of public attitudes revealed by polls is a complex, contradictory
one that may not make a "good" news story.

The media's treatment of polls also is shaped by the capabilities of
journalists to analyze and report on the polls. Because of changes in the
curriculum of university journalism programs, reporters are becoming
increasingly skillful in reporting on polls. Even so, characteristics of the
journalism profession will continue to affect how polls are presented and
discussed. Crespi (1980, 473) argues that journalistic requirements affect
polling in both positive and negative ways:

Positive	**Negative**
Journalistic requirements place a high value on factual documen-tation of poll results, in the form of actual percentages rather than fuzzy generalizations.	There is a preoccupation with re-porting numbers, the "objective" poll results, with a corresponding lack of interest in their underlying meaning or patterning.
Subjective editorializing is deval-ued insofar as poll reports are con-cerned, reducing the likelihood that the personal views of poll-sters will introduce bias.	Superficiality and lack of analysis too often characterize coverage of even the most complicated issues.
Attention is focused on opinion regarding specific events and is-sues, thereby making poll results relevant to the real-life experi-ences and problems of the public, and to the political process.	Topics that can be expected to create front-page headlines dom-inate, leading to a spasmodic coverage of the agenda of public concerns.
Sensitivity to changes in public opinion, resulting from the effects of events, is enhanced.	There is limited continuing cover-age of long-term trends, and back-ground news is often neglected.

Conclusion

The relationship between polling and the media can be difficult and complex. But if poll sponsors recognize both the uses and limitations of polls, the relationship also can be very beneficial and informative to citizens. The media, however, need to take whatever steps are necessary to ensure that they provide their audiences with sufficient information to make informed judgments. Reporting sample size and sampling error is the beginning of good poll coverage by the media, not the end. Standard practice should include presenting question wording and question order, factors that can have a much greater effect on the responses than can sampling error.

Beyond this, the journalism profession must be more sensitive to and reflective about the possible linkages between polls and news coverage. The media can easily play an agenda-setting role by bringing certain issues to the public's attention through news reporting, sponsoring and conducting polls on these issues, and reporting the results of their polls which will reinforce the visibility of an issue to the electorate. Indeed, citizens can become highly concerned about an issue even though its prominence is largely due to media coverage and media-sponsored polls. For example, Morin (1994a) says that public concern about drugs in the late 1980s and fears about crime may have been largely media driven, both by media coverage of the issues themselves and by media coverage of polls on these issues. He points out that in January 1989, only 19 percent of poll respondents cited drugs as the most important problem facing the nation. By October of the same year, the percentage had increased to 53. But less than a year later, only 16 percent of Americans named drugs as the country's major problem. He attributes much of the rise and fall in the public's concerns about drugs to the media's heavy attention to the drug problem followed by media inattention to drugs.

Journalists also need to be more perceptive about the frailties and limitations of polls and about how the reporting of polls can influence people in unintended ways. Gawiser and Witt (second edition), in a pamphlet sponsored by the National Council on Public Polls, compiled a list of twenty questions that journalists should ask about poll results. Their elaborations of and answers to the following questions should be required reading for journalists.

1. Who did the poll?
2. Who paid for the poll and why was it done?
3. How many people were interviewed for the survey?
4. How were those people chosen?
5. What area: nation, state, or region—or what group: teachers, lawyers, Democratic voters, etc.—were these people chosen from?

6. Are the results based on the answers of all the people interviewed?
7. Who should have been interviewed and was not?
8. When was the poll done?
9. How were the interviews conducted?
10. What about polls on the Internet or World Wide Web?
11. What is the sampling error for the poll results?
12. Who's on first?
13. What other kinds of mistakes can skew poll results?
14. What questions were asked?
15. In what order were the questions asked?
16. What about "push polls"?
17. What other polls have been done on this topic? Do they say the same thing? If they are different, why are they different?
18. So I've asked all the questions. The answers sound good. The poll is correct, right?
19. With all these potential problems, should we ever report poll results?
20. Is this poll worth reporting?

The *New York Times* and the *Washington Post* usually do a good job of informing their readers about the technical features of their surveys. For example, a *Times* article on the presidential candidates in 2000 included the following polling information:

> The latest *New York Times*/CBS News Poll is based on telephone interviews conducted Wednesday through Sunday with 1,462 adults throughout the United States. Of these, 1,131 said they were registered to vote.
>
> The sample of telephone exchanges called was randomly selected by a computer from a complete list of more than 42,000 active residential exchanges across the country.
>
> Within each exchange, random digits were added to form a complete telephone number, thus permitting access to both listed and unlisted numbers. Within each household, one adult was designated by a random procedure to be the respondent for the survey.
>
> The results have been weighted to take account of household size and number of telephone lines into the residence, and to adjust for variations in the sample relative to geographic region, sex, race, age, and education.
>
> Some findings regarding voting are additionally weighted in terms of an overall "probable electorate," which uses responses to questions dealing with voting history, attention to the campaign, and likelihood of voting in 2000 as a measure of the probability of respondents' turning out in November. The method assumes approximately 50 percent turnout in November. In theory, in 19 cases out of 20 the results based on such samples will differ by no more than three percentage points in either direction from what would have been obtained by seeking out all American adults.

For smaller sub-groups, the margin of sampling error is larger.

In addition to sampling error, the practical difficulties of conducting any survey of public opinion may introduce other sources of error into the poll. Variations in the wording and order of questions, for example, may lead to somewhat different results. (Berke and Elder 2000)

Note that in addition to the standard items, the *Times* briefly explained random-digit dialing, explicitly stated that the data had been weighted, directly acknowledged and explained that some findings were based on a subset of respondents called "the probable electorate," discussed sampling error for the entire sample and for subgroups, and mentioned other sources of errors in polls. Overall, this is a thorough yet concise statement of the factors that can influence poll results. Moreover, a comparison of this disclaimer to that used by the *Times* ten years earlier reveals that much more information is now being provided. But even as the media are becoming increasingly responsible and thorough in reporting the technical details of polls, one must wonder whether readers actually read and can understand this information. The person who wishes to be a discerning consumer of polls must take some responsibility for utilizing the technical polling information provided by the media. And when the media (or other polling outfits) do not provide basic information about their polls, the consumer should be wary. Finally, even when the media provide technical information about their polls, they always must ensure that the substance of their stories accurately reflects the polling data. Only conscientious, well-trained reporters and editors can guarantee this.

☑ 7 Polls and Elections

Of the various kinds of polls, election surveys are probably the most familiar to Americans. Like surveys on presidential performance, election surveys receive substantial and continuing coverage in the media. They also generate the most controversy, particularly when preelection polls incorrectly predict the Election Day outcome. Although the most prominent election polls focus on the presidential contest, polling has expanded to include congressional contests as well as many state and local races. Indeed, American-style campaigns replete with polling, media ads, and "spin doctors" have spread throughout the world, including countries such as Russia that are in transition from authoritarian to democratic regimes. In such nations the accuracy of election polls is spotty, a point developed later in this chapter.

Sponsors of Election Polls

Election polls are sponsored by a variety of organizations and individuals, such as candidates for office, political parties, and the media. The candidates and parties use polls as research tools, collecting information in order to devise and implement winning campaign strategies. Typically, candidate-sponsored polls survey citizens on their sociodemographic characteristics, their perceptions of the candidates, and their views on issues. The candidates can then determine how well they are running overall, how their campaigns are going within electorally important subgroups, and how campaign events and media advertising affect their standing among the voters.

As for the mass media, election polls are a central focus of their election coverage. Indeed, the media have been criticized (Asher 1992, 273–278) for treating elections as if they were horse races, emphasizing not what the candidates say on the issues, but their relative standing in the polls: Who's ahead? Who's behind? Who's gaining? Who's falling back in the pack? Yet media polls also often go beyond recording levels of support for the candidates by addressing topics such as patterns of support for the candidates among groups of voters defined by their demographic characteristics and issue stances.

The distinction between candidate- and media-sponsored polls is often blurred. This is particularly so when candidates try to manipulate the media so that the results of both kinds of polls show the candidates in the best possible light, or at least minimize the damage caused by an adverse poll result. It is not uncommon for candidates to selectively leak their own polls to gain a helpful story in the media. Candidates may also criticize the accuracy of media-sponsored polls to minimize their negative effects.

This chapter describes the types and uses of polls common to election campaigns. It examines candidates' and parties' attempts to use polls for purposes other than research and to manipulate media coverage of polls. It also covers the role of polling during the presidential primary season and general election and how and why polls can go wrong in making election predictions. The chapter concludes with a speculative analysis of how polls can affect the way citizens vote.

Types of Election Polls

The differences among the many kinds of election polls are found less in their methodologies than in the purposes they serve. For example, some of the candidate- and party-sponsored polls, such as tracking surveys, serve as the private tools of a campaign; media-generated surveys, such as exit polls, often become topics of public controversy. It is important for consumers of public opinion polls to be aware of the different kinds of surveys and what they can say about elections.

Benchmark Survey

A benchmark survey is usually commissioned by a candidate after he or she decides to seek office. It collects standard information about the candidate's public image and positions on issues and about the demographics of the electorate in order to provide a baseline for evaluating the progress of a campaign. Three important pieces of information often gathered in a benchmark survey are the candidate's name-recognition level, the candidate's electoral strength vis-à-vis that of the opponents, and citizens' assessments of an incumbent officeholder's performance.

One problem with a benchmark survey is its timing. The earlier it is done, the less likely it is that the respondents will know anything about the challenger and the more likely it is that the political and economic situation will change dramatically as the election nears. Nevertheless, useful information can be collected about voters' perceptions of the strengths and weaknesses of the incumbent, their perceptions of the ideal candidate, and their views on major policy issues. The results of a benchmark survey normally are not publicized or leaked unless they show the candidate doing surprisingly well.

Trial Heat Survey

Technically, a trial heat survey is not a survey but a question or series of questions within a survey. Trial heat questions pair competing candidates and ask citizens for whom they would vote in that contest.

Typically, a trial heat question reads: "If the election were held today, would you vote for X or Y?" Sometimes questions are asked about hypothetical matches, particularly in the earlier stages of the presidential selection process. For example, early in 2000 many polls paired various potential Republican nominees such as Gov. George W. Bush and Sen. John McCain against the candidates for the Democratic nomination, Vice President Al Gore and former U.S. senator Bill Bradley. The results of these trial heat questions facilitate the "horse race" emphasis in media coverage of election campaigns. Indeed, such questions are fun and often become the grist for interesting political speculation and gossip.

Several caveats apply to the results of trial heat questions. The most important one is that much can change between the time a question is asked and the actual voting on Election Day. This is best illustrated by the dramatic fluctuations in support for the presidential candidates in 2000. For example, a Reuters/MSNBC/Zogby poll in early August of that year gave Bush a seventeen-point lead over Gore; by early October the poll was indicating that Gore had a four-point lead. The same dramatic changes can occur over a much shorter time period. For example, a *New York Times/WCBS-TV* poll done less than two weeks before the 1993 New Jersey gubernatorial contest showed incumbent Democratic governor Jim Florio with a 49 to 34 percent lead among registered voters over his Republican opponent Christine Todd Whitman (and an even larger lead among likely voters). But on Election Day Whitman was the victor. Likewise, in California's 1994 gubernatorial race Democratic challenger Kathleen Brown was more than twenty points ahead of the Republican incumbent, Pete Wilson, in trial heat polls conducted months before the election. But on Election Day Wilson defeated Brown by a fifteen-percentage-point margin.

Trial heat questions asked far in advance of an election measure name recognition more than anything else, particularly in less-prominent elec-

CARLSON, © 2000 *Milwaukee Sentinel.*
Reprinted with permission of Universal Press Syndicate.

tion contests. Thus the consumers of such surveys must be careful not to view trial heat placements as immutable, nor should they be surprised when the standing of the candidates changes dramatically over the course of the campaign. Moreover, because the results of a trial heat question depend on how the question is constructed, consumers must be careful in assessing the results. For example, when the political party affiliation of the candidate is given, the outcome is bound to be affected. With well-known candidates, it makes little difference whether party affiliation is mentioned, but in races between less well known candidates, it can make a substantial difference if the question is phrased "Mary Doe versus Joe Blitz" or "Mary Doe, the Democrat, versus Joe Blitz, the Republican."

Tracking Polls

Tracking polls provide the most up-to-date information on which to base changes in campaign strategy and media advertising. A tremendous resource for candidates, these polls are often conducted on a daily basis near Election Day in order to monitor closely any late shifts in support. Because tracking polls are expensive, they rely on *rolling samples.* For example, samples of 100 different people may be collected on four consecutive days. Although an *N* of 100 is small and has a large sampling error, an *N* of 400 is much more reliable. But much can happen between the first and fourth day of interviewing, perhaps making the oldest interviews less interesting to the campaign. Thus on the fifth day another 100 people are interviewed and added to the sample, and the first 100 responses are discarded. And on the sixth day another 100 people are interviewed, and the 100 interviews done on the second day are eliminated. This procedure guarantees an overall sample of 400 that includes 100 new interviews each day, thereby allowing a close and timely monitoring of voters' reactions to the campaign. One danger of tracking polls is that any single day's interviews could be highly aberrant; the candidate and campaign must be careful not to overreact to what might be only a statistical blip.

Tracking polls were very prominent in the 2000 presidential campaign. As Election Day approached, the results of various media-sponsored tracking polls converged to yield predictions very close to the actual election outcome. But throughout the campaign one particular tracking poll—that conducted by the Gallup Organization for CNN and *USA Today*—showed dramatic fluctuations over very short time periods. For example, one set of results showed Gore ahead by eleven points, yet two days later Bush was up by seven. This substantial volatility surprised observers who questioned the accuracy of the Gallup results. It turned out that one reason for the results was the dramatic variation in the proportion of Democrats and Republicans in their samples over short periods of time (Morin and Deane 2000). Thus when the sample had relatively more Democrats, Gore did better and vice versa. Gallup argued that the short-term fluctuations in the distribution of partisanship were genuine. Other polling organizations made different decisions and weighted their results so that the proportion of Democrats and Republicans did not vary as much with each night's sampling, and thus their results did not show as much volatility. This example certainly demonstrates the effect of weighting on poll results (see Chapter 4).

Cross-sectional versus Panel Surveys

When the major polling organizations conduct multiple polls over time on an election contest, they generally use a *cross-sectional design* in which different samples of citizens are selected for each round of interviewing. For example, in the 2000 presidential contest a CBS News/*New York*

Times poll conducted in mid-October showed Bush ahead of Gore 46 to 44 percent, with 4 percent for Ralph Nader and 1 percent for Pat Buchanan—both minor-party candidates. Another CBS News/*New York Times* survey conducted in early November showed Bush ahead 47 to 42 percent, with 5 percent for Nader and 1 percent for Buchanan. Each of these surveys provides a picture of where the electorate stood at a single point in time, and each is based on a different sample. A comparison of the two surveys reveals that the Bush lead went from 2 percent to 5 percent (subject to sampling error) and that the *net* gain for Bush was 3 percent. But what pattern of movement produced this net gain? Perhaps 1 percent of Gore supporters moved to Bush and another 1 percent of Gore supporters shifted to Nader. But perhaps 10 percent of Gore supporters moved to Bush and 1 percent of Gore supporters went to Nader, while 9 percent of Bush supporters changed to Gore. Both of these hypothetical scenarios yield a net gain of 3 percent, but the total percentage of citizens who changed their preferences varies dramatically—2 percent in the first instance and 20 percent (10 + 1 + 9) in the second case.

Unfortunately, cross-sectional surveys reveal only the net change; they cannot tell poll consumers about the gross change or about the pattern of individual changes that produced the net result. Thus cross-sectional surveys are fine for revealing net changes in the relative standing of the candidates, but a *panel design* is needed if the total volatility of voters' attitudes and preferences is the chief concern.

In a panel survey, the same individuals are interviewed two or more times—a more costly and difficult process because the same respondents must be located repeatedly, which is no easy task in view of the mobility and mortality of respondents. For example, panel surveys of college students conducted over a period of months or years can be burdensome because of the high mobility of that group. Another problem is that respondents may not be willing to participate in multiple interviews; moreover, respondents who do agree to be reinterviewed may differ in distinct ways from those who do not. A final problem with panel surveys is that the experience of being interviewed at one point in time may affect the respondent's answers at the next interview. Despite these difficulties, panel surveys provide better information about the dynamics of the campaign and of voter decision making than do cross-sectional surveys.

Focus Groups

Focus groups can be an important campaign tool even though the voter may never hear of them. Technically, focus groups are not polls but in-depth interviews with a small number of people (usually ten to twenty) who often are selected to represent broad demographic groups. A focus group might watch a candidate debate and offer reactions, thereby helping the candidate to prepare better for the next debate. Or a group might be asked to react to a political commercial so that campaign managers can gain some insight into the commercial's effectiveness before spending money to air it. Focus group discussions also are useful in raising and developing questions that later may be incorporated into a public opinion poll.

The effectiveness of focus groups was probably illustrated most famously in the 1988 election, when the Bush campaign team called on a group to identify the "hot button" issues later used with devastating effect against his Democratic opponent, Massachusetts governor Michael Dukakis, in the general election. The campaign team invited two dozen New Jersey residents to a local hotel to talk about the candidates. Many of the participants were blue-collar and Catholic Democrats who had supported Reagan, but intended to vote for Dukakis even though they knew little about him. Because these Reagan Democrats were seen as critical to a Bush victory, the focus group leader pushed until issues were identified that moved participants away from support for Dukakis. These issues turned out to be Dukakis's opposition to the death penalty, his opposition to a bill requiring Massachusetts schoolchildren to recite the Pledge of Allegiance, and his support of a weekend furlough program for prisoners (among them the infamous Willie Horton). The reactions of the focus group participants told the Bush team that it had found the issues needed to undermine the Dukakis campaign. It would have been much more difficult to generate this information through a public opinion survey. As Bush campaign manager Lee Atwater commented, "Focus groups give you a sense of what makes people tick and a sense of what's going on with people's minds and lives that you simply don't get from reading survey data" (Grove 1988b).

Morin (1992e) has pointed out that focus groups have become very popular among the media; newspapers and television networks frequently commission them. Although Morin applauds focus groups as another tool for journalists, he warns that the media often fail to recognize the limitations of this methodology. Certainly one caveat is that focus groups are not mini-public opinion surveys. Focus groups may suffer from problems of external validity—that is, the results of the focus group may not be generalizable to any broader population, because the participants in a focus group may not be representative in who they are and how they were selected. Nevertheless, the process of intensive discussion within a focus group may provide insights into what factors are motivating citizens, insights not readily revealed by a standard public opinion survey. In the early 1990s a report prepared for the Kettering Foundation relied heavily on focus group methodology (Harwood

Group 1993). Entitled "Meaningful Chaos: How People Form Relationships with Public Concerns," the report argued that if political leaders really want to engage citizens in key public policy concerns, they and the media may need to devise new ways of reaching this goal. Among the report's recommendations is a call for more "mediating institutions" where citizens can interact directly and discuss the issues of the day. The Kettering report was sensitive to the limitations of the focus group methodology. In the appendix on methodology, the report stated (p. 49):

> There are, of course, limitations to group discussions. The research is qualitative. Thus, the observations detailed in this report should not be mistaken for findings from a random sample survey. They are, technically speaking, hypotheses, or insights, that would need to be validated by reliable quantitative methods before being considered definitive. Still, the insights are suggestive of how citizens view public concerns and their relationships to them.

In observing focus group sessions dealing primarily with local government topics such as the quality of city services or the performance of the local school system, I have been struck by how often the sessions take a critical and negative turn. One focus group participant relates a particular horror story, leading other participants to join in with their own awful anecdotes. Soon the focus group becomes a gripe session. Would public opinion polls on the same topics elicit as much intensely negative content? I doubt it. A 1996 book on gender relations by Roberta Sigel that employed both focus groups and surveys supports my speculation. In general, Sigel's focus group data—more than her survey information—showed women to be angry about gender discrimination and the mistreatment they had endured as women. Sigel attributed the differences in the focus group responses and the survey responses in part to methodological differences in the two modes of data collection. In other words, focus groups do not yield the same kinds of information as surveys and polls. Focus groups are fine research tools for certain purposes, but citizens should be wary of accepting general descriptions and explanations of people's attitudes and behavior based solely on a focus group.

Deliberative Opinion Polls

A deliberative opinion poll combines elements of both the focus group and the standard public opinion poll—that is, it brings together a representative group of citizens, provides them with information and the opportunity for discussion on issues, and then polls them on these issues. The rationale and need for deliberative polls are presented by Fishkin (1992,

1996), who argues that public opinion surveys measure what the public thinks, but not what they would think if they had the opportunity to meet and become immersed in the issues through discussion about and study of the issues. Logistically, a deliberative poll is an expensive and challenging undertaking, because it requires bringing together a representative sample and providing fair and balanced materials about the issues at hand.

The first major deliberative poll in the United States took place in Austin, Texas, in January 1996 in the context of the presidential election (Merkle 1996; Winkler 1996). A representative sample of Americans was first surveyed about their opinions in three main issue areas: foreign policy, the economy, and family concerns. Then a subset of the sample attended the National Issues Convention in Austin, where after extensive presentations and discussions on the same issue domains, members of the subset were polled again to determine whether and how their views had changed. Attitude changes did occur. For example, support for U.S. military engagement abroad rose, and support for a flat income tax declined. The respondents' views about the biggest problems facing American families moved toward economic concerns and somewhat away from the breakdown of traditional family values.

The key question rising from this deliberative poll is how much can its users generalize its conclusions to the broader population? Fishkin (1996) would argue that because there was a representative sample, a similar attitude change might be expected in the population at large. But one of the major criticisms of Fishkin's claim is that citizens in the real world and the election campaign itself do not operate like the National Issues Convention (Mitofsky 1996). Most people do not take the time to learn nor are they exposed to information about the issues or candidates in such a concentrated, in-depth fashion. Even though small group discussions may occur in the real world, much of what citizens experience and learn comes directly from campaign ads, news coverage, and the like. Moreover, critics faulted the representativeness of the 1996 sample as well as the intrusive effects of television, which heightened the awareness of the respondents that they were participating in a very special event. This awareness might have unduly influenced citizens' reactions to the deliberative polling experience.

Even if the real world prospects for deliberative polling are less than its adherents believe, the rationale for the enterprise is clear. Traditional public opinion polls capture what is immediately on the voters' minds and, as noted in Chapter 2, they often are plagued by nonattitudes. Moreover, candidates tend to treat citizens' opinions as something to manipulate through political advertising and campaign rhetoric. A deliberative poll, by contrast, can reveal what citizens think once they are informed about an issue. Whether such results would ever constrain candidates or influence politics and elections remains doubtful. Interest in deliberative polls waned in the 2000 election.

Exit Polls

Exit polls, as noted in Chapter 1, are interviews with voters as they leave polling places. These very visible and controversial polls typically ask voters for whom they voted. They also collect some information on the issue positions and demographic characteristics of the respondents. The most prominent exit polls are conducted by the major news organizations to predict and explain presidential election outcomes as well as the results of congressional and major state-level races.

Exit polls have several advantages and uses. First, they are polls of actual voters, so they avoid the enduring problem faced by preelection surveys: determining who will actually vote. Second, exit poll samples are collected in many states, allowing state-by-state analysis of the presidential election—an endeavor not feasible with national surveys of 1,500 respondents, which are not amenable to breakdowns by state. (For details on how exit poll samples are selected, see Levy 1983.) Third, exit polls can be tabulated quickly, allowing almost instantaneous predictions and descriptions of election outcomes. Indeed, this advantage became a central selling point for exit polls as the networks competed with each other to be the first to call an election. Finally, exit polls generate rich information that enables both journalists and social scientists to understand better the factors that help to shape the voters' choices.

Exit polls are generally accurate, although recent developments in the mechanics of how Americans vote might affect the predictive ability of exit polls. For example, numerous states are making it easy to vote by absentee ballot, and some states are experimenting with voting prior to Election Day. Clearly, these votes will not be captured by Election Day exit polling. Moreover, there is evidence that exit polls overrepresent the well educated and affluent, because they are more willing to fill out the exit poll forms (Morin 1994e).

On rare occasions, exit poll results are inaccurate. For example, an exit poll in the 1989 Virginia gubernatorial race showed the black Democratic candidate, Douglas Wilder, winning by 10 percent of the vote when he actually won by less than 1 percent. The explanation for this inaccuracy is that some white respondents in the exit poll indicated that they had voted for Wilder when they had not (Traugott and Price 1992). As another example, the 1992 exit poll in the GOP presidential primary in New Hampshire showed George Bush with only a six-point margin over Republican challenger Pat Buchanan when his lead in the actual vote count was sixteen points. The discrepancy was attributed in part to the greater intensity of Buchanan supporters and their greater willingness to participate in the exit polling (Mitofsky 1992; Morin 1992b). This misleading exit poll actually affected news coverage of the New Hampshire primary by reporting Buchanan's showing as stronger than it actually was. A similar situation occurred in 1996, this time in the Republican presidential primary in Arizona. Using exit polls, three television networks projected that Republican Bob Dole would finish third in the Arizona primary behind Steve Forbes and Pat Buchanan. Based on Dole's projected third-place finish, media commentators described his Arizona performance as weak and raised questions about the direction of his campaign. But it turned out that the exit poll projections were wrong; in the actual vote totals Dole finished a close second to Forbes, with Buchanan coming in third. As was the case in New Hampshire in 1992, the exit poll's overestimation of the Buchanan vote was attributed to the greater intensity of his voters who were eager to participate in the exit polling (Carter 1996).

Exit polls created a storm of controversy on election night in 1980 and again in 2000. Although the national preelection polls had indicated a close race between Jimmy Carter and Ronald Reagan in 1980, the results from the eastern time zone revealed that a Reagan landslide (especially in the electoral college) was developing. What troubled many observers was that within minutes after the polls closed in a state, the networks would declare—on the basis of exit polls and not official election returns—that Reagan had carried that state. By 8:30 p.m. Eastern Standard Time (EST), it was clear from exit poll results that Reagan had won enough states to ensure his election, no matter what happened in those states west of the Mississippi, where the polls were still open (strong Reagan states in any event). Thus the networks declared Reagan the victor while parts of the country were still voting. Moreover, Carter conceded the election before all of the polls had closed. Understandably, many concerns were raised about the effects of media declarations of victory when some voters had not yet cast their ballots. There were reports that voters in line at polling booths left when they heard that the presidential race was already decided and other citizens decided not to go to the polls at all. In 1984 Democrat Walter Mondale wisely waited until the polls were closed on the West Coast before conceding, as did Michael Dukakis in 1988.

Did the early call of the 1980 presidential election actually deter citizens from voting? The empirical evidence is mixed. Works by Jackson and McGee (1981) and Jackson (1983), based on a January 1981 reinterview of respondents who had been part of a national election sample months earlier, claimed that a combination of factors, including the early projections based on exit polls and Carter's early concession, reduced overall turnout by 6–12 percent. Epstein and Strom (1984), using different analysis procedures, challenged these findings, claiming that only four of forty-five respondents in the survey who decided on Election Day not to vote attributed their decision to their knowledge that Carter had lost. These four respondents represented only 1 percent of the total number of registered nonvoters in the sample ($N = 395$). Had they voted, the overall turnout would have increased by only 0.2 percent. Using official election returns from congressional districts, Delli Carpini (1984) found that the early call of the 1980 election did depress turnout in both the presidential and congressional contests to the detriment of Democratic candidates. He argued that in some five to fourteen congressional contests the Republican margin of victory was less than the advantage the GOP gained from the early reporting of the presidential outcome. Critical of all of the empirical studies of the effects of early reporting in 1980, Sudman (1986) concluded that congressional district turnout was depressed by 1–5 percent. The early projections had no significant impact on the outcome of the presidential race in 1980, but in state and local contests turnout effects, no matter how small, could have been much more consequential. In these elections fewer votes are cast, and the margin between victory and defeat is sometimes very small.

In the 2000 election, the major television networks twice made predictions about the outcome of the presidential contest in the key state of Florida that never should have been made. Early on election night, the networks projected Vice President Gore as the winner—a prediction issued even though the polls in western Florida were still open. Much later in the evening, the networks projected that Governor Bush had won Florida—another forecast that had to be withdrawn, but a forecast that nonetheless gave Bush a major strategic advantage in the post-election Florida recount battle.

The media's tendency to project election results for a state before that state's polls are closed raises concerns about the media's behavior. Although there is some dispute (Busch and Lieske 1985) about how late in the day exit polls must be taken in order to obtain a representative sample and make accurate projections, it is clear that if the polls close in a state at 7:30 p.m., exit polls could in most cases accurately predict the winner by late afternoon. Yet widespread reporting of such projections by the media could measurably depress turnout within the state. The television networks claim they are very careful not to make projections about a state until after its polls have closed, but a 1983 study by the League of Women Voters (LWV) and the Committee for the Study of the American Electorate pointed to numerous instances in which 1982 election projections were

broadcast while the polls were still open. In the 2000 election, there were deliberate leaks of exit poll results while the polls were still open in some of the early key primary states. Only the threat of lawsuits prevented certain media outlets from prematurely leaking exit poll results for the general election. And even some of the major television news anchors have become careless about revealing exit poll results for a state before that state has completed voting. Indeed, all too often network news people are heard speculating on election night that the early exit poll results suggest that it will be a good evening for a particular candidate.

The opposition to exit polls has been fierce in many circles. Newspaper columnist Mike Royko once urged readers to lie to exit poll interviewers, thereby undermining the usefulness of the entire enterprise. Some pollsters have been critical of exit polls and early projections. Although Roper (1985) and others believe that exit polls have few if any effects on elections, they argue that their use should still be curtailed because most citizens believe that exit polls can influence election outcomes. Exit polls, they claim, cause citizens to lose confidence in the electoral process and become increasingly suspicious of the mass media.

Congress and state governments have sharply criticized exit polls as well. The U.S. House Task Force on Elections conducted hearings in 1985 on the news industry's use of exit polls and called for voluntary restraint on the part of the media (Swift 1985). The state of Washington went further. Recognizing that it would be difficult to prohibit the reporting of election projections and results, the state legislature passed a law making it a misdemeanor to conduct any exit interviews within 300 feet of the polls (Abrams 1985). The obvious intention of this law was to make the collection of exit data far more difficult. It was ultimately invalidated in federal court. In 2001 congressional committees are once again holding hearings and state legislatures are once again considering legislation that would restrict the conduct and/or reporting of exit polls.

The controversy surrounding exit polls will likely continue to heat up every two years. The networks argue strenuously that government-imposed limitations on the reporting of exit polls would be a form of censorship and a violation of their First Amendment rights. Also, the news organizations note that if the polls were open simultaneously for twenty-four hours in all fifty states, the problem of early projections would be resolved. State officials reject this option as too expensive and point out that the networks could still make premature projections for those states for which they had sufficient information. Broder (1984) has proposed the Canadian solution: the networks could begin their election coverage by time zone from east to west, beginning each regional broadcast just as polls in that region are closing. Thus the networks might begin election coverage in the East at 8:00 p.m. EST, in the Midwest at 9:00 p.m. EST, in the Mountain States at 10:00 p.m. EST, and on the Pacific Coast at 11:00 p.m. EST.

Consumers of exit polls should carefully evaluate the news reports throughout Election Day. Any news about patterns of vote choices among various groups is most likely based on the exit polls completed to that point. Consumers should ask themselves whether such reports might affect their likelihood of voting and their actual choice of candidate. They also should note the time of the announcement of any election projections; if the projection is made before the polls have closed, then it is based on exit polls and not on official election returns, because the latter are not available until after the polls close. Then, is the projection for a state contest or a national race? If the latter, consumers should note whether the polls are still open in some states. Finally, consumers should try to keep a mental list of the number of early projections that subsequently are contradicted by the actual vote totals.

It is unlikely that exit polls will ever be regulated except by the self-policing of the networks themselves. In the early days of exit polling, the television networks, aiming to beat the competition and to improve ratings, invested heavily in the technology of polling and election coverage. (The polls play a somewhat different role for newspapers, which are not in a competition to predict election outcomes on election night. Instead, newspapers use exit polls primarily to describe voting patterns and to explain why the election turned out as it did.) Beginning, however, with the 1990 midterm elections, the competition among networks was somewhat mitigated when ABC, NBC, CBS, and CNN decided to conduct one joint exit poll under the auspices of the Voter News Service (VNS) rather than separate ones as in the past. The major reason for this change was financial; exit polling is very expensive. But as Schneider (1989) has pointed out, when different exit polls have been conducted for the same election, the results have differed; multiple polls enabled investigators to compare the results and decide which polls were more likely on target.

The creation of the Voter News Service did have the benefit of temporarily eliminating the competition among networks to be the first to issue election projections; in 1990 and 1992 it was VNS and not the individual networks that made the election projections. In 1994 ABC decided to make its own projections based on VNS data and scooped its competition in a number of races. Since then, more networks have chosen to hire their own analysts to predict election outcomes based on VNS data and thus the competitive pressure to be the first to call an election is once more a factor in election night coverage.

Push Polls

Push polling gained notoriety in the 1996 elections even though the practice had been ongoing for years, particularly in U.S. House races and in some state and local contests. As push polling has become more common, the American Association for Public Opinion Research and the National Council on Public Polls have condemned the practice. AAPOR has described push polling as

> a telemarketing technique in which telephone calls are used to canvas potential voters, feeding them false or misleading "information" about a candidate under the pretense of taking a poll to see how this "information" affects voter preferences. So-called "Push polls" are not polls at all. They are a form of political telemarketing whose intent is not to measure public opinion but to manipulate it—to "push" voters away from one candidate and toward the opposing candidate. Such polls defame selected candidates by spreading false or misleading information about them. The intent is to disseminate campaign propaganda under the guise of conducting a legitimate public opinion poll. (AAPOR 1997)

The NCPP further explains the difference between legitimate political polls and push polls:

> [Legitimate political polls] use samples representative of all voters. "Push Polls" use telephone banks to canvass large numbers of voters. Legitimate polls may seek out weaknesses of candidates and attempt to ascertain the impact on voters of knowledge of these weaknesses, as well as issues and other facets of a political campaign. "Push Polls" attack selected candidates. The intent of legitimate polls in each case is research; a sample is interviewed, not a canvass, and the survey is not designed to deceive. . . . The results of "Push Polls" should never be reported by the media, but the use of such polls by a candidate may, of course, be a legitimate news story. (NCPP 1995)

In 1996 a push poll was used in a Republican congressional primary in Texas (Clymer 1996). Representative Greg Laughlin was the preferred choice of the Republican Congressional Committee, which financed a push poll designed to hurt the other two contenders, Ron Paul and Jim Deats. About 30,000 calls were made. If respondents said they preferred Ron Paul, they were asked if they would still support him if they knew that Paul supported legalization of drugs, pornography, and prostitution. Likewise, if respondents said they favored Deats, they were asked how strong their support was given his campaign debt of $200,000 and four previous unsuccessful attempts for office. The information provided to respondents was misleading, however, and designed to push them away from Paul and Deats and toward Laughlin. In the 2000 presidential primaries, a major controversy emerged in the South Carolina Republican primary when the McCain campaign accused the Bush team of engaging in massive push polling. The Bush campaign denied the charge, pointing out that the thousands of phone calls being made were simply advocacy calling, not done under the guise of a poll. The intent, the Bush camp said, was to disseminate negative information about Sen. John McCain to South Carolina voters.

It is perfectly legitimate in survey research to present respondents with information to see how it affects their opinions. For example, in surveys about support for a balanced budget, respondents who favor a balanced budget might be asked whether they would still support a balanced budget if it meant reductions in spending on Social Security or Medicare or some other program area. Likewise, in surveys about support for American military engagement abroad, respondents who support such involvement might be asked whether they would still support such an activity if it cost American lives or a substantial amount of money. What makes the push polling enterprise so objectionable is that the information provided the respondents is most often inaccurate. Moreover, the push polling is conducted as if it were a legitimate public opinion survey trying to ascertain citizens' attitudes when in fact it is trying to influence voters' attitudes and behavior.

Given that push polling and legitimate survey research may seem very similar on the surface, how can citizens protect themselves from push polls? The American Association of Political Consultants, another organization that has denounced push polling, has provided some helpful hints for spotting such polls. First, reputable polling begins by providing the name of the sponsor of the research or the organization conducting the research; push polls typically do not provide this information. Second, legitimate telephone surveys usually last at least five minutes and often much longer; the typical push poll is less than a minute in duration. A third sign of a push poll, more apparent to the media than the average citizen, is the number of calls made in a particular election contest. The fact that thousands and thousands of calls have been made to citizens about a particular race is a clear sign that push polling is under way, because most genuine polls require fewer than a thousand respondents. Indeed, when the media hear of such an activity they should publicize and condemn it. And citizens who believe they have been called as part of a push poll might tip off their local media in the hope that the media would investigate and expose the situation. Because push polling is more likely to be used in less-visible, lower-level elections where media scrutiny is often less extensive, it is important that citizens be particularly vigilant in such circumstances.

Uses of Polls by Candidates

Candidates use polls to test the political waters in a variety of ways. Prospective candidates might commission a private poll and also examine public polls to assess their chances. Their assessments of results can steer their expectations and actions. For example, bad poll news might lead to a decision not to seek office. In 1986 New Yorker Geraldine Ferraro decided not to run for the U.S. Senate against incumbent Republican senator Alphonse D'Amato in part because poll results showed her trailing substantially. A party organization with the financial resources to conduct polls and to provide other election services may use this capability to provide services to recruit candidates. At the national level the Republican Party has been much better able than the Democrats to offer such assistance to its candidates and would-be candidates because of its more successful fund-raising operations based on computerized direct mail.

Sometimes candidates will use positive poll results to generate campaign contributions or to deter contributions to their opponents. In 1985 Idaho's Democratic governor, John Evans, sent the results of a poll he had conducted to many political action committees (PACs) and potential contributors. The poll showed Evans in a virtual tie with the state's Republican U.S. senator, Steve Symms, in a trial heat for Symms's Senate seat. Evans's action was clearly a signal to contributors that he had a good chance of unseating Symms in the 1996 election and therefore was worthy of their donations (Rothenberg 1985, 11). Evans ultimately lost, however, by a narrow margin.

Often when published polls show a candidate running poorly, the candidate will try to minimize the potential damage to fund-raising and volunteers' morale by attacking the credibility and relevance of the poll. "The only poll that counts is the poll taken on Election Day," the candidate might argue, and then cite examples of how the polls have been wrong in the past. In a systematic analysis of reactions of the 1992 Bush campaign to negative poll results, Bauman and Herbst (1994) found three dominant responses. First was the (often valid) assertion that it was too early to give much credence to poll results. Second was an attack on the pollsters themselves and the journalists who reported the polls. Finally, the campaign tried to counter the results of published polls with the results of its own private polls. In other instances, the attack on a poll may be more methodological, challenging the sample or question wording or question context.

Whatever the merits of these criticisms, it is clear that a candidate "harmed" by polls has a strong incentive to cast doubt on their credibility so that a campaign is taken seriously. If a campaign is not taken seriously, it will have difficulty raising money and attracting other resources, such as free media coverage.

Sometimes candidates deliberately manipulate aspects of their campaign or the polling process to generate results that will advance their candidacies. For example, in the four-way contest for the Republican nomination for governor of Ohio in 1982, one of the candidates, Seth Taft, scheduled his early television advertising to go on the air before the Ohio Republican Party conducted a statewide poll assessing the standing of the candidates. The poll showed Taft running first, thereby enhancing his credibility. Undoubtedly, his famous last name and the skillful timing of his commercials gave Taft an early advantage in the polls, but he eventually lost the primary. To demonstrate greater electoral strength than they actually have, candidates often schedule television commercials and mailings in conjunction with party- and media-sponsored polls.

Candidates and campaign managers are also very skillful in selectively leaking information from in-house, private polls to improve their chances of winning. Sometimes these in-house polls are deliberately designed to generate the desired results. For example, before asking a trial heat question about the contenders, pollsters might ask a series of issue questions or candidate qualification items that will predispose the respondent to support one candidate over another. But in leaking the results of the trial heat item to the media, no information will be provided about the questions that preceded it. A candidate can also try to control poll results through sample selection. For example, if a candidate is thought to be more popular among women than men, interviewing might be conducted mainly during the day to obtain a predominantly female sample. When the results of the poll are leaked, however, pollsters will not mention the gender composition of the sample, thereby inflating the standing of the candidate.

Voters and reporters should be wary of such selective leaking. One tip-off is the refusal of a campaign to reveal additional information about a poll, such as question wording and question order. Although this kind of manipulation is not widespread, many campaigns use whatever tactics they believe will work, because the objective of most campaigns is to win. Consumers can only hope that they can exercise good judgment in evaluating election poll results and that reporters and other journalists will not be easily victimized by manipulative campaigns.

Polls in the Presidential Selection Process

Polls are used at all stages of the presidential selection process. During the primary season, media polls in key states are common, as are national polls measuring the presidential preferences of Democrats and Republicans throughout the nation. During the general election, the major news organizations and the campaigns themselves regularly conduct polls. When a major campaign event occurs, such as a televised debate between the presidential contenders, a slew of polls follows immediately to assess the effect of the event on the campaign.

One result of the ubiquity of polls in presidential campaigns is the increasingly prominent role of pollsters. Over the past two decades, individual pollsters such as Pat Caddell, Richard Wirthlin, and Stanley Greenberg achieved celebrity status during the Carter, Reagan, and Clinton campaigns. Today such pollsters are part of the core strategy group that decides themes and tactics, media advertising, public speaking schedules, and other key aspects of the campaign.

Polls do much more than simply reflect the current standing of the candidates in the presidential contest. The polls themselves and the reporting of them shape the very course of the campaign. They also have been instrumental in campaign fund-raising, although their impact has lessened in this area. Since 1976, presidential campaigns in the general election have been publicly funded, leaving major party nominees free from worry that poor poll performance will cut off the flow of money to their campaigns. In 1968, however, many Democrats complained that the early polls showing Hubert Humphrey losing the election badly hindered fund-raising so that even when it became clear near the end of the campaign that Humphrey had a chance to win, the money available for the final push was inadequate. In contrast to the general election, during the primary season eligible candidates today receive only partial public funding, and the public matching funds they do receive depend on the ability of the candidates to attract private financial support. Thus bad poll results, as well as poor primary and caucus showings, may deter potential donors from supporting a failing campaign.

The Caucus and Primary Season

The combined effect of polls and media coverage of polls is particularly critical during the caucus and primary season for at least two reasons.

First, many candidates may seek a party's presidential nomination. In 1988, for example, six Republicans and seven Democrats sought party nominations. Unable to cover all candidates equally, the media give more attention to the most serious and viable candidates, with viability defined by a candidate's standing in the polls.

Second, the caucuses and primaries are a sequence of elections in which media coverage of the outcome in just one state can dramatically affect later polls and primaries. For example, in 1984 John Glenn's campaign conducted a poll in New Hampshire about one week before that state's primary. The actual interviewing was conducted around the time of the Iowa precinct caucuses in which Glenn did much worse than expected. The media coverage of the Iowa results stressed how badly the Glenn campaign was hurt there. Consequently, Glenn's New Hampshire survey showed that interviews completed before the reporting of his poor finish in Iowa had him running much more strongly in New Hampshire than did interviews completed after the reporting of the Iowa results. The combined effect of media coverage and the polls is particularly significant in Iowa and New Hampshire, the states in which the formal process of selecting delegates for the parties' national nominating conventions begins. Thus the "winners" in Iowa and New Hampshire almost invariably enjoy a sizable gain in support in the national polls because of the positive and extensive media coverage they receive.

The presidential primary season is something of a sequential, psychological game in which the perception that a candidate is running strongly, as reflected in good poll results, makes it easier for the campaign to attract money, volunteers, and media coverage; bad poll results have the opposite effect. But strong performance in the polls is itself a function of the amount and content of media coverage that a candidate receives. This is why Iowa and New Hampshire are so critical. Because they are small states in which both a personal and a media campaign can be conducted, they enable a relatively unknown and/or underdog candidate, such as Jimmy Carter in 1976 or Gary Hart in 1984 or Bill Clinton in 1992 or John McCain in 2000, to do better than expected and thus receive substantial media coverage. This coverage can move a candidate higher in the public opinion polls, which in turn enhances the candidate's media coverage and credibility.

During the primary season, then, candidates appeal for support on the grounds that they are more electable than their opponents as demonstrated by the polls. Probably the best examples of this phenomenon occurred in 1976 and, earlier, in 1968. In 1976 Gerald Ford and Ronald Reagan were locked in a tight battle for the Republican presidential nomination; the winner would most likely face former Georgia governor Jimmy

Carter in the general election. The Ford campaign conceded the South to Carter no matter who won the GOP nomination, but argued, citing public opinion polls, that Ford was the much stronger candidate to run against Carter nationwide (Phillips 1976). In 1968 Nelson Rockefeller's campaign to win the GOP nomination also depended heavily on the public opinion polls, because he knew he would have great difficulty winning presidential primaries and caucuses. Rockefeller challenged Richard Nixon, the front-runner, to cosponsor fifty state polls to see which candidate was the strongest. Rockefeller also commissioned and released polls of key electoral vote states that showed him running better than Nixon against Democratic candidate Hubert Humphrey (Crossley and Crossley 1969, 7). Rockefeller hoped to sway Republican delegates to his cause by the argument that he was the strongest candidate the party could offer.

Presidential Debates and the General Election

The interaction between poll results and media coverage is well illustrated by the treatment of the presidential and vice-presidential debates before the general election. Often polls taken immediately after a debate produce very different results than do polls taken a few days later. The difference is attributable to the dominant media message in the interim. For example, a CBS News/New York Times poll conducted immediately after the first Reagan-Mondale debate in 1984 showed that 43 percent of respondents thought Mondale had won the debate, 34 percent thought Reagan had won, and 16 percent saw it as a tie—a nine-point Mondale advantage overall. Two days later, a CBS News/New York Times poll gave Mondale a forty-nine-percentage-point advantage (66 percent thought Mondale was the winner, 17 percent favored Reagan, and 10 percent saw it as even). The only explanation for this massive shift in sentiment was the intervening news coverage of the debate, which focused heavily on the president's poor performance and for the first time explicitly raised the question of his age.

Another example of influential media coverage is provided by polls conducted after the second Ford-Carter debate in 1976. In that debate President Ford mistakenly asserted that Eastern Europe was not under the domination of the Soviet Union, when, in fact, at the time Soviet troops were stationed in Poland and the Polish government, among others in the region, was following the dictates of Moscow. Telephone polls immediately after the debate showed Carter winning, but only by a narrow margin. When Ford received negative media coverage after the debate for his mistake, his campaign officials did not display much skill at putting the matter to rest. As a result, Carter's narrow margin changed in the follow-up polls, which showed that Americans overwhelmingly viewed him as the winner of the debate.

"Winning" a debate may be less a matter of a candidate's actual performance than a function of the media's coverage and interpretation of that performance. This is why the call-in poll sponsored by the ABC News organization after the Carter-Reagan debate in 1980 was particularly offensive. ABC News invited its viewers to call one of two numbers to indicate whether they thought Reagan or Carter had won; the call cost fifty cents. Despite the self-selection and economic biases inherent in this procedure and the technical difficulty many citizens experienced in trying to complete their calls, ABC News announced that Reagan had won the debate by a two-to-one margin over Carter. Ideally, Americans would have dismissed this instant poll as foolish and unsound. Unfortunately, because it was the first large-scale reaction to the debate to be publicized, the poll and ABC's reporting of it shaped subsequent perceptions of who won the debate. After the first Bush-Gore presidential debate in 2000, scientific polls generally showed Gore to be the victor, albeit by a small margin. Many Internet and radio call-in polls, characterized by self-selected and unrepresentative samples, showed Bush to be the big winner. Fortunately, when the media discussed the debate polls, they focused on the scientific ones. The media were criticized, however, for their reliance on instant and overnight polls.

As polling has become an integral part of media coverage of major campaign events such as convention speeches and presidential debates, the media have increasingly utilized overnight and instant polls as part of their coverage. The NCPP, however, has urged caution in the use of such polls:

> One issue where news values and good polling methods clash is the media's appetite for "instant" polls which provide an immediate reaction to dramatic events. . . .
>
> A key question for poll watchers, and the media who report polls, should always be *"How many days was the survey in the field?"* In general, the quality of the sample improves the longer the survey is in the field. . . .
>
> All surveys fail to interview many people . . . because they are on vacation, on a business trip, visiting, shopping, eating out or just too busy to take the call. That is why the most reliable telephone surveys make three, four or more calls, on different days, to try to complete an interview. Obviously, this is not possible for polls that are conducted overnight or over a few hours, and their response rates are much lower.
>
> Given the very real possibility that those who are not interviewed, because they are not available, have even slightly different opinions than those who are interviewed, overnight polls, with their very low response rates, are much more likely to have substantial biases than polls with multiple call-backs over several days. (NCPP 2000)

Polls also played a big role in the presidential debate of 1980. The League of Women Voters, the sponsor of the debate, decided to invite candidates whose popular support in public opinion surveys was more than 15 percent. The real issue was whether independent candidate John Anderson would meet the 15 percent test. The Carter strategists wanted Anderson excluded, because they believed that Anderson drew more votes from Carter than from Reagan, an effect that might be heightened if Anderson had the opportunity to share the same platform with Reagan and Carter. When Anderson did meet the test, Carter boycotted the debate, leaving the platform to Anderson and Reagan. The League's use of polls in this fashion sparked much controversy among pollsters (see Dionne 1980; Knap 1980). What would the League have done had Anderson gotten only 13 percent? Would it have factored in sampling error? How would it have treated the undecided respondents? It was fortunate that Anderson clearly met the standard.

In the 1996 presidential election, public opinion polls again played a role in determining which candidates would be allowed to participate in the presidential debates. Unlike in 1980, all independent and minor-party candidates were excluded from the debates, including Ross Perot. In response, Perot and other candidates went to court to overturn the decision, but to no avail. The decision had been made by the Commission on Presidential Debates, a ten-person body composed of five Republicans and five Democrats who determined the debate format and the debate participants. The Democratic and Republican nominees (Clinton and Dole) were automatically included, but the candidates of other parties, to participate in the debates, had to demonstrate that they had a realistic chance of being elected president—that is, they had to show evidence of a national organization, national newsworthiness, and national enthusiasm for their candidacies (Hernandez 1995). One indicator of national enthusiasm was a candidate's standing in the public opinion polls. The commission, after judging that Ross Perot's low standing in the polls, and other evidence, made it unlikely that he could win, excluded him from the debates.

Presidential debates should not be cluttered with scores of mostly frivolous candidates, but was the decision to exclude Perot appropriate? After all, Perot was on the ballot in all fifty states, he had received 19 percent of the popular vote in 1992, and he had more than $20 million in public funding to finance his 1996 campaign. Although the polls used by the commission to exclude Perot showed him with the voting support of only about 5 percent of the American people, other polls showed that more than 70 percent of Americans wanted Perot included in the presidential debates. Moreover, Perot's 5 percent in the polls when the commission made its decision in 1996 was close to his support level at a comparable point in the 1992 election campaign, yet ultimately he got almost a fifth of the vote in 1992.

As Perot learned, the use of poll standing to exclude a candidate from the presidential debates creates a self-fulfilling prophecy. If a candidate is showing poorly in the polls, the exclusion of that candidate from the most visible events of the presidential campaign can only further hurt the candidate as the campaign moves into its final critical weeks. This was particularly hurtful for Perot, who had millions of dollars to put into his campaign in the final weeks. But all of these dollars could not replace the loss of visibility and credibility he suffered because of his absence from the presidential debates.

A similar situation occurred in 2000 when the presidential debate commission again decided to use poll standing as one criterion for inclusion in the presidential debates. The commission chose a 15 percent standard as evidenced in a set of polls conducted shortly after Labor Day. The two most prominent minor-party candidates—Ralph Nader and Pat Buchanan—could not meet that standard and thus were excluded from the debates. This situation was particularly frustrating to Buchanan who, as the nominee of the Reform Party, had received $12 million in public funding based on the Reform Party's performance in the 1996 election.

When and Why Election Predictions Are Wrong

The vast majority of polls are on target. Nevertheless, sometimes pollsters can make notorious mistakes, such as in the *Literary Digest* poll of 1936 (discussed in Chapter 4) and the 1948 presidential election polls that indicated that Republican Thomas Dewey would beat Democrat Harry Truman. The bad call in 1948 is widely attributed to the quota method of sampling employed by the polls and, more important, to the fact that polling stopped too far in advance of the election and therefore did not reflect the movement of many Democratic defectors back to Truman. In fact, the last polls showed Dewey with only a five-point lead over Truman, and the trend in the polls had been one of a declining Dewey advantage.

National polls have been off target in other important races. In 1980, for example, they failed to predict the magnitude of Reagan's victory. Most polls showed a very tight race even though Reagan beat Carter by ten percentage points. Again the poor predictions were attributed to the fact that many polls did not continue right through to the end of the campaign and thus did not capture the last-minute surge to Reagan by the undecideds and independents. The state-level polls in 1980 were far more accurate in predicting a sizable Reagan victory.

In 1982 the polls projected landslide victories for incumbent Republican governors in Illinois and Pennsylvania, but the incumbent governors barely eked out a win. The polls also incorrectly predicted that Tom Bradley would win the California gubernatorial contest and Bill Clements the race for governor of Texas. And in 1988 the polls incorrectly predicted Bob Dole as the victor in the New Hampshire GOP primary, which George Bush won by nine points. Last-minute vote changes, emerging economic problems, and the inability to foresee turnout accurately among various subgroups were all cited as explanations for the polls' faulty projections.

In 1992 the general election presidential polls were quite accurate overall, although critics expressed concerns about the deluge of sometimes-conflicting polls and the media reporting of them. One specific set of criticisms focused on the Gallup tracking polls conducted toward the conclusion of the campaign. The polls, which received substantial media attention (Traugott 1992), generated concerns about the actual selection of respondents, the method by which undecided voters were allocated to candidates, and, most important, a shift in poll analysis from registered voters to likely voters. These concerns created some confusion among the media and the public as to how much the gap between Clinton and Bush had actually narrowed.

In 1996 the preelection polls correctly predicted that Clinton would be reelected, but some of the polls substantially overestimated his margin of victory. For the U.S. House vote in 1996, even the polls conducted just before the election yielded widely varying estimates, with some predicting a sizable Democratic victory, others a smaller Democratic win, and others a narrow GOP victory. Political scientist Everett Carll Ladd (1996) described 1996 as a very bad year for pollsters—"an American Waterloo." Ladd criticized the polls for overstating Clinton's margins and blamed the polls and the media for contributing to the low voter turnout by dampening voter interest in the outcome because of their predictions of a major Clinton win. Pollsters defended the polls; Newport (1997) and Morin (1997a) found the 1996 polls generally on target. Perhaps the real problem with election polls is not their accuracy but how they are reported. Too many polls dominate news coverage of the election and contribute to the horse race mentality. Small changes in poll standing often are given too much attention, creating breathless news stories when there really is no news. In the meantime, the subtleties of poll interpretation frequently are lost, particularly as they relate to the methodological aspects of the polls. And the media tend to focus on their own polls and ignore those of the competition.

The performance of the polls in 2000 was generally quite good, with most of the national polls converging toward the end of the campaign to show a very close contest between Bush and Gore. Probably the worst experience (other than the Florida fiasco discussed earlier) for the pollsters in

2000 was the New Hampshire Republican primary. There, John McCain scored a landslide victory over George W. Bush when most polls were showing a much closer contest. Part of the problem for pollsters in New Hampshire was that independents could vote in either party's primary, and many of them voted for McCain in the GOP primary. Moreover, as Smith and Hubbard (2000) note, the turnout among the "undeclared" or independents was much higher than normal in 2000.

The accuracy of predictions depends on several factors. The rest of this section examines four of the factors that affect election predictions: the timing of preelection polls, the treatment of undecided voters, the estimation of voter turnout, and the changing political and economic climate.

Timing of Polls

The timing of a preelection poll influences its accuracy; the closer to the election the poll is conducted, the more accurate its results are likely to be (Felson and Sudman 1975). Late polls can capture the effects of last-minute events and campaign activities that may influence outcomes. By contrast, early polls primarily reflect name recognition and perceptions of incumbents' performance. When voters have little information about the candidates, their attitudes about those candidates are highly volatile once they acquire some new information about the contenders. For that reason, the presidential primary polls often have a poorer track record than the general election polls. In the primaries, especially the early ones with a large field of candidates, information levels are low and voters' commitments to candidates are weak.

In a comprehensive analysis of the factors affecting the accuracy of preelection polls, Crespi (1988) found that the most important factor was how close to Election Day the preelection poll was conducted. The next most important factor was margin of victory, and then either turnout or whether the election was a primary. These findings suggest that polls would be more accurate if they did a better job of identifying likely voters and monitoring trends in voters' preferences in the latter stages of a campaign. This suggestion is directly relevant to the failure of the polls to predict Bush's comfortable win in the 1988 New Hampshire Republican primary. Why were most of the polls so wrong? The Gallup Organization explained that it stopped polling too early (by 4 p.m. on Sunday before the Tuesday election) and therefore did not capture late-breaking developments (Grove 1988a). The one poll that correctly predicted Bush's victory was the CBS survey, which involved a tracking poll on the Sunday and Monday before the election (Morin 1988a), thereby reinforcing Crespi's advice to poll as close to the election as possible. Lau's (1994) analysis of the accuracy of the 1992 presidential polls found that polls conducted over multiple days were more accurate than overnight polls. He also found that tracking polls were more accurate than standard polls and that polls that interviewed on both weekdays and weekends were more accurate than weekday-only polls.

Treatment of Undecided Voters

When respondents claim to be undecided they can mean different things. Some genuinely cannot choose among the candidates, because they do not have enough balanced information to make a choice. But this probably does not happen very often. Others may know very little about one or more of the candidates and therefore may be unwilling or unable to make a choice. Finally, "undecided" may be a safe answer for those who do not want to reveal their election choices to the interviewer.

Evidence for this third possibility is provided by the secret ballot technique long used by the Gallup Organization. In this procedure respondents are given a ballot by the interviewer, asked to mark their choices, and then requested to drop the folded ballot into a box. Perry (1979) points out that this approach yields an undecided rate that is about one-third to one-fourth as large as that obtained when respondents are asked their vote preference by means of a standard survey item. (Note that the secret ballot technique can be used only with personal interviews.)

Pollsters may simply ignore undecided respondents and tabulate results only for those respondents who have already made up their minds—a highly flawed procedure if the undecideds differ in major ways from the decideds. Another way of handling the undecideds is to report their numbers, but then to assume that the undecideds will split in the same way that the decideds already have. Thus if 60 percent of decideds vote Democratic, 60 percent of the undecideds will be allocated to the Democratic Party. This is probably a reasonable rule when both candidates are equally well known, and when there is no reason to suspect that anything unusual is going on among the undecideds.

When one candidate is well known and the other is not, the treatment of the undecideds is more problematical. In a race between a well-known, long-term incumbent and a relatively unknown challenger, an undecided vote can reflect poorly on the incumbent. In 1978 Ohio state representative Charles Kurfess challenged incumbent governor James Rhodes for the GOP gubernatorial nomination. Rhodes had already served three four-year terms as governor and was seeking a fourth; he was the well-known warhorse of the Ohio Republican Party. The benchmark survey conducted for the Kurfess campaign showed that respondents favored Rhodes over Kurfess, 66 to 6 percent, with 28 percent undecided. The final election results were 67 to 33 percent in favor of Rhodes. Without panel data it is impossible to conclude definitively that most of the undecideds moved to support Kurfess. Nevertheless, it seems plausible that the undecided vote in this case was actually a negative comment on the incumbent; in response to another question, the undecideds overwhelmingly preferred a new candidate for governor.

The 1986 contest for the Ohio GOP gubernatorial nomination illustrates the danger in ignoring undecideds. The candidates were the incumbent governor, James Rhodes, now seeking his fifth term, and state senators Paul Gillmor and Paul Pfeifer, who were not yet household names in the state. Most observers gave the two "Pauls" little chance to win because they would probably split the anti-Rhodes vote. At an important stage of the campaign, a major media-sponsored poll that received extensive coverage showed Rhodes with 70 percent of the vote, Gillmor with 19 percent, and Pfeifer with 11 percent. Media coverage of the poll focused only on those respondents who had already made up their minds. Moreover, the actual wording of the question—"Will you support James Rhodes, Paul Pfeifer, or Paul Gillmor for Governor in the Republican primary?"—did not include an undecided category. And nowhere in the newspaper reports of the poll was there any mention of the proportion of respondents who volunteered that they were undecided (Miller 1986; Kostrzewa 1986a).

In the end, the pollsters' and the media's decision to ignore the undecideds yielded a very high and widely publicized estimate of Rhodes's strength that unwittingly aided his campaign by making his lead seem insurmountable and his nomination inevitable. Had the undecideds been considered, Rhodes's nomination would not have been a certainty, particularly if the poll's consumers believed that an undecided response in a choice between a sixteen-year former governor and two less well known challengers was a negative reaction to that long-term incumbent. Ultimately, Rhodes, Gillmor, and Pfeifer received 48, 39, and 13 percent of the vote, respectively. The closeness of the outcome surprised many reporters and commentators and led them to wonder what might have happened had the Gillmor campaign been taken more seriously. Yet, influenced by the poll results, they had found it difficult to view the Gillmor effort as viable and had focused instead on the inevitability of Rhodes's nomination. (Rhodes lost badly in the general election.)

The behavior of undecided voters also partially accounts for the failure of preelection polls to mirror closely the outcome of the two prominent contests in 1989—for mayor of New York City and for governor of Virginia. Although polls accurately predicted the winners as David Dinkins in New York and Douglas Wilder in Virginia, the poll estimates of their margins of victory were much too high. Wilder won in Virginia by less than

1 percent, yet the preelection polls were suggesting a double-digit margin. In New York, Dinkins won by about 2 percent, even though the polls showed him between fourteen and twenty-one points ahead (Balz 1989). These contests received a lot of media coverage, because both Dinkins and Wilder would be the first black Americans to be elected to their respective positions. If, as pollsters increasingly believe, whites who are undecided in a contest between a black and a white candidate vote heavily for the white candidate, then one reason for the polling errors in the Dinkins and Wilder contests was the behavior of the heavily white undecided voters. Other factors contributing to poll discrepancies in the Dinkins and Wilder victories were race-of-interviewer effects, turnout effects, and last-minute changes in voter preferences. The fact remains, however, that white citizens gave an undecided response to an interviewer querying on a black-versus-white contest, even though they had already decided to support the white candidate.

Estimating Turnout in Elections

Probably the most difficult task pollsters face is estimating which of their respondents will actually vote. If the survey preferences of voters and nonvoters were identical, then this task would not be a problem. But often there are marked differences between the two groups.

Pollsters use a variety of means to predict whether a person will vote. The Gallup Organization has used a subsample of likely voters from the overall sample of all possible voters (Perry 1979, 320–321). Among the items in the survey are the respondents' stated intention to vote, registration status, reported frequency of past voting, awareness of where to vote, interest in politics in general, interest in the particular election, and intensity of vote preference. Thus in Gallup's final survey for the presidential election in 1976, when all respondents were considered Carter led Ford 48 to 43 percent, Eugene McCarthy and others received 4 percent, and undecideds and those who refused to participate amounted to 5 percent. But when the survey considered only likely voters, Carter led 48 to 46 percent, the other candidates received 2 percent, and undecideds or those refusing to respond to the poll made up 4 percent.

Other pollsters use similar procedures for determining likely voters. For example, Peter Hart has used respondents' reports of registration status, past voting in other races and current intention to vote, interest in and perceived importance of the election, and awareness of the candidates and where to vote (Goldhaber 1984, 49). In 1998 a CBS News/*New York Times* poll identified likely voters as those who said they voted in either 1996 or 1994, who said they were paying attention to the current campaign, and who said they would definitely vote in November. Respondents who voted in both 1994 and 1996 were defined as "more likely voters" (Kagay 1998). One interesting result of the CBS News/*New York Times* classification was that the more likely a respondent was to vote, the more that person tended to be pro-Republican. For example, among registered voters in the 1998 poll the sample preferred Democratic to Republican congressional candidates by a margin of 45 to 37 percent. But among likely voters the Democrats led by only 47 to 42 percent, and among the most likely voters Republicans led 48 to 44 percent.

When tracking polls did not correctly predict the outcome of the 1988 New Hampshire primary, ABC News/*Washington Post* pollsters changed the way they determined who the likely voters would be (Morin 1988b). In their New Hampshire polling, the ABC News/*Washington Post* pollsters had simply asked self-described registered voters the following question: "Were they certain to vote, would they probably vote, were the chances 50–50, or would they probably not vote?" Anyone who said he or she was certain to vote was considered a likely voter. This method resulted in a sample whose projected turnout rate was twice as high as the real percentage, because people often say they will vote even when they will not; they want to portray themselves as good citizens. In view of the New Hampshire results, ABC News/*Washington Post* decided to establish multiple criteria for determining a likely voter. Among them, the respondent had to say he or she was certain to vote and had to have voted in 1986. Other factors also were considered, including strength of commitment to a candidate. This more stringent test of likely voters generated more accurate results, but also resulted in more interviews with registered voters being tossed aside when making election predictions.

A somewhat different approach has been taken by the *Columbus Dispatch,* which uses mailed questionnaires. As discussed in Chapter 4, mailed questionnaires have low response rates, and the representativeness of those people who do reply is uncertain. The *Dispatch* partially corrects for these problems by mailing questionnaires to samples selected from lists of registered voters. In 1994 and 1995, the *Dispatch* once again used its mailed questionnaires, but also commissioned telephone surveys by the Gallup Organization. Overall, the *Dispatch* results were much more accurate than the Gallup telephone polls, most likely because the mail poll did a better job of estimating the likely electorate. Anyone who completes a mailed questionnaire probably has a level of motivation indicative of a likely voter; the Gallup screen for likely voters simply consisted of registered voters who said they were likely to vote.

Visser et al. (1996) conducted an extensive comparative analysis of the performance of the *Dispatch* mail poll and the telephone polls conducted by the University of Akron and the University of Cincinnati in Ohio elections between 1980 and 1994. Overall, the election predictions of the final *Dispatch* poll were much more accurate than those generated by the telephone surveys. Numerous reasons were given for the *Dispatch* superiority: a larger sample size, a questionnaire that closely resembled the actual ballot, response categories that minimized undecided answers and eliminated the need to allocate undecided respondents, and sampling and response procedures that produced more representative samples. Thus, contrary to conventional wisdom, mail questionnaires with an average response rate of only 25 percent were actually more accurate than telephone surveys. Even more surprising, for the final preelection *Dispatch* polls the deadline for receipt of the mailed surveys by the newspaper was typically the Thursday before Election Day. Therefore no information was gathered over the last weekend before the election, a time when sizable shifts in voter preference might occur, and yet the *Dispatch* polls were still more accurate. The lesson of the *Dispatch* experience may lead some pollsters to rethink some of the conventional wisdom.

The Changing Political and Economic Climate

Surveys predict best when there is a normal voter turnout pattern. This observation applies to the polls in 1982. They performed poorly because they consistently underestimated the Democratic turnout, which was higher than expected that year because of the deepening economic recession and the effective efforts by labor unions and black organizations to mobilize participation among their rank and file members. Moreover, although voter turnout is usually low among the unemployed, the 1982 election may have been atypical because many of the newly unemployed had been regular voters and therefore participated at a higher-than-expected rate (Rothenberg 1983, 8).

The 1982 contest that probably did the most damage to the polls' reputation was the Illinois gubernatorial election. Most polls predicted that incumbent Republican governor James Thompson would score a fifteen- to twenty-point victory over Democrat Adlai Stevenson III (Kohut 1983; Day and Becker 1984). But when the votes were tabulated, Thompson narrowly won by less than 0.2 percent.

Kohut (1983) and Day and Becker (1984) tested numerous hypotheses about the inaccuracy of the Illinois polls. They ruled out some, such as last-minute shifts in preference that were missed by the polls; polls were conducted to the very end of the campaign, and they still showed Thompson winning by a large margin. A poor estimate of the likely voters also was ruled out as the cause of the polls' inaccuracies. Instead, the polls' poor performance seems to have been caused mainly by an upsurge in straight-ticket voting among Democrats, including some who preferred Thompson to Stevenson but still cast a straight Democratic vote. In Chicago, the Democratic organization had devoted many resources to a "Punch 10" (that is, vote straight Democratic) media campaign, an effort that was particularly effective in black areas where it was part of an overall anti-Reagan theme (Kohut 1983, 42; Day and Becker 1984, 613). Thus a good part of the Illinois poll debacle stemmed from political organization and mobilization, developments that are difficult to anticipate and assess by means of a poll.

A more recent example of inaccuracy occurred in the 1994 midterm elections, where the Republican victory was more sweeping than had been indicated by the polls conducted weeks before the elections. Perhaps part of the discrepancy was attributable to the difficulty in estimating the likely Democratic and Republican turnout, but events in the ten days before the elections also may have affected the results. The extensive and visible campaigning by President Clinton, for example, may have served to nationalize many of the local contests to the advantage of the GOP. The polls conducted right before Election Day were largely on target in predicting the Republican sweep as many races broke in favor of the GOP over the final weekend of the campaign.

How Preelection Polls Affect Voters

Speculation about how polls affect voters has been widespread and contradictory. Some observers argue that polls that show one candidate ahead of another increase the incentives for supporters of the trailing candidate to change their preference and climb on board the winning candidate's bandwagon. Others emphasize underdog effects: sympathetic voters, they claim, rally around the candidate the polls show to be losing. Little strong evidence supports either of these views. The bandwagon effect would require that leading candidates consistently increase their margin, and the underdog effect predicts that the losing candidate will inexorably gain on the leader. These simple kinds of effects have not shown up consistently in surveys.

An experimental study by de Bock (1976) found some evidence that the reporting of disheartening poll results weakened the support and turnout motivation among a candidate's adherents. However, this finding seems to be more a function of the experimental design itself, in which exposure to the negative polls was much more direct than would be the case in the real-world setting. Other experimental studies have shown that polls can encourage support for the underdog, although the effects are not strong (Marsh 1984).

A 1985 ABC News/*Washington Post* poll attempted to address the

PUBLIC OPINION POLLS DEFINITELY DO **NOT** INFLUENCE VOTERS!

I ADMIT OPINION POLLS **DO** INFLUENCE CAMPAIGN CONTRIBUTORS....

...AND CAMPAIGN SPENDING **DOES** INFLUENCE VOTERS...

ANYONE CAN CHANGE HIS OPINION.

POLLSTERS

By Renault for McClatchy Newspapers

© The Sacramento Bee.

question of the effects of polls on voter choice. The survey asked a sample of Americans whether they were aware of whom the polls had favored in the 1984 election and whether the polls had influenced their voting behavior (Sussman 1985f). Seventy-eight percent correctly knew that the polls had picked Reagan to win, 7 percent said Mondale, and 15 percent did not know or remember what the polls had said. Among the 78 percent who knew the polls had predicted a Reagan victory, 4 percent said it helped them decide for Reagan, 4 percent said it helped them decide for Mondale, and 93 percent said it had no effect. Sussman concluded that the preelection polls could not have had any significant impact on the vote split, because the pro-Mondale and pro-Reagan effects almost canceled each other out.

Anyone using Sussman's study, however, should weigh three factors. First, asking people to recall their views seven months after the election is risky—people simply forget. Second, Sussman's procedure requires people to remember explicitly that the polls had influenced them; polls can influence voters even though they may not be aware of it. Third, some people might not be willing to admit that the polls affected their vote lest they appear to be making decisions on inappropriate grounds. Despite these reservations, Sussman's conclusion seems plausible in general and certainly so for the 1984 election.

Bandwagon and underdog effects can and do occur, but their magnitude is small and probably inconsequential. Polls may have an indirect effect on voters through their impact on campaign contributors, campaign workers, and media coverage, as illustrated by the Renault cartoon. In addition to affecting voting behavior, polls can influence public opinion itself, a topic addressed in Chapter 9. For example, if people become aware of changes in public opinion on an issue, that information may lead them to support the position favored by the trend. Or if they learn that their views are not shared by their fellow citizens, they may become unwilling to express their views. The very act of polling people can sensitize them to politics and campaigns in general and can encourage them to seek out information or become more involved. Given the prominence of polls in elections and in political discourse in general, it is important for citizens to understand both the positive and the manipulative uses made of polls, regardless of original intent.

Conclusion

By and large, election polls in the United States are very accurate, particularly those conducted and sponsored by reputable media and polling organizations. In other nations where the history of polling and free elections is much shorter, the track record of polls is far less impressive. For example, in December 1993 in the first multiparty election ever held in Russia, the pollsters' performance was abysmal. As Shlapentokh (1994) notes, the pollsters failed to predict the victorious party and even the order in which the parties would finish. In other countries polling is problematic for several reasons, some of them technical and some cultural. For example, it may be very difficult to pick a good sample; telephone ownership may not be widespread, and other information about residential units, especially in rural areas, may be flawed. Citizens in countries with traditions of totalitarian governments and repression may be wary about being interviewed by strangers and therefore may not participate in polling or give answers that reflect their true views. As one Russian analyst commented about the difficulties of polling in the former Soviet Union, "You are talking about sampling 30,000 villages and more than 1,000 cities. You must go to places that have for decades despised authority and then ask people their most personal fears about the future. And they are supposed to tell people they have never met what is on their mind" (Specter 1996).

Fortunately, these technical and cultural problems are less prevalent in the United States and the track record of American election polls is quite impressive. What is of greater concern is how the polling enterprise affects the behavior of citizens in a democratic nation. We return to the issue of how the polls affect citizens and society in the last chapter.

8 Analyzing and Interpreting Polls

Thus far we have considered how public opinion surveys are conducted, how they are reported in the media, and how they influence elections and campaigns. This chapter focuses on the end products of public opinion surveys—the analysis and interpretation of poll data.

Interpreting a poll is more an art than a science, even though statistical analysis of poll data is central to the enterprise. An investigator examining poll results has tremendous leeway in deciding which items to analyze, which sample subsets or breakdowns to present, and how to interpret the statistical results. Take as an example a poll with three items that measure attitudes toward arms control negotiations. The investigator may construct an index from these three items, as discussed in Chapter 3. Or the investigator may emphasize the results from one question, perhaps because of space and time constraints and the desire to keep matters simple, or because those particular results best support the analyst's own policy preferences. Another possibility: the investigator may examine results from the entire sample and ignore subgroups whose responses deviate from the overall pattern. Again, time and space limitations or the investigator's own preferences may influence these choices. Finally, two investigators may interpret identical poll results in sharply different ways depending on the perspectives and values they bring to their data analysis; the glass may indeed be half full or half empty.

As the preceding example suggests, the analysis and interpretation of data entail a high degree of subjectivity and judgment. Subjectivity in this context does not mean deliberate bias or distortion, but simply professional judgments about the importance and relevance of information. Certainly, news organizations' interpretations of their polls are generally done in an unbiased fashion. But biases can slip in—sometimes unintentionally, sometimes deliberately—when, for example, an organization has sponsored a poll to promote a particular position. Because this final phase of polling is likely to have the most direct influence on public opinion, this chapter in-

SURE, I'M AGAINST TEACHING EVOLUTION IN SCHOOL.

I'M ALSO AGAINST MATH, ENGLISH AND HISTORY.

THAVES 12-26

FRANK & ERNEST reprinted by permission of Newspaper Enterprise Association, Inc.

cludes several case studies to illustrate the judgmental aspects of analyzing and interpreting poll results.

Choosing Items to Analyze

Many public opinion surveys deal with multifaceted, complex issues. For example, a researcher querying Americans about their attitudes toward tax reform might find initially that they overwhelmingly favor a fairer tax system. But if respondents are asked about specific aspects of tax reform, their answers may reflect high levels of confusion, indifference, or opposition. And depending on which items the researcher chooses to emphasize, the report might convey support, indifference, or opposition toward tax reform. American foreign policy in the Middle East is another highly complex subject that can elicit divergent reactions from Americans, depending on which aspects of the policy they are questioned about.

Some surveys go into great depth on a topic through multiple items constructed to measure its various facets. The problem for an investigator in this case becomes one of deciding which results to report. Moreover, even though an extensive analysis is conducted, the media might publicize only an abbreviated version of it. In such a case, the consumer of the poll results is at the mercy of the media to portray accurately the overall study. Groups or organizations that sponsor polls to demonstrate support for a particular position or policy option often disseminate results in a selective fashion that enables them to put the organization and its policies in a favorable light.

In contrast with in-depth surveys on a topic, *omnibus surveys* are superficial in their treatment of particular topics because of the need to cover many subjects in the same survey. Here the problem for an investigator becomes one of ensuring that the few questions employed to study a specific topic really do justice to the substance and complexity of that topic. It is left to the consumer of both kinds of polls to judge whether they receive the central information on a topic or whether other items might legitimately yield different substantive results.

The issue of prayer in public schools is a good example of how public opinion polling on a topic can be incomplete and potentially misleading. Typically, pollsters ask Americans whether they support a constitutional amendment that would permit voluntary prayer in public schools. In response, more than three-fourths of Americans say they would favor such an amendment. But this question misses the mark. Voluntary prayer by individuals is in no way prohibited; the real issue is *organized* voluntary prayer. Yet many pollsters do not include items that tap this aspect of the voluntary prayer issue. Will there be a common prayer? If so, who will compose it? Will someone lead the class in prayer? If so, who? Under what circumstances and when will the prayer be uttered? What about students who do not wish to participate or who prefer a different prayer?

The difficulty with both the in-depth poll and the omnibus survey is that the full set of items used to study a particular topic is usually not reported and thus the consumer cannot make informed judgments about whether the conclusions of the survey are valid. Recognizing this, individuals should take a skeptical view of claims by a corporate executive or an elected officeholder or even a friend that the polls demonstrate public support for or opposition to a particular position. The first question to ask is: What is the evidence cited to support the claim? From there one might examine the question wording, the response alternatives, the screening for nonattitudes, and the treatment of "don't know" responses. Then one might attempt the more difficult task of assessing whether the questions used to study the topic at hand were really optimal. Might other questions have been used? What aspects of the topic were not addressed? Finally, one might ponder whether different interpretations could be imposed on the data and whether alternative explanations could account for the reported patterns.

When people cite poll results, they may be tempted to seize on those that support their position and ignore those that do not. The problem is that one or two items cannot capture the full complexity of most issues. For example, a *Newsweek* poll conducted by the Gallup Organization in July 1986 asked several questions about sex laws and lifestyles. The poll included the following three items (Alpern 1986, 38):

> Do you approve or disapprove of the Supreme Court decision upholding a state law against certain sexual practices engaged in privately by consenting adult homosexuals? [This question was asked of the 73 percent who knew about the Supreme Court decision.]

Disapprove	47%
Approve	41%

In general, do you think that states should have the right to prohibit particular sexual practices conducted in private between consenting adult homosexuals?

No	57%
Yes	34%

Do you think homosexuality has become an accepted alternative lifestyle or not?

Yes	32%
No	61%
Don't know	7%

Note that the first two items tap citizens' attitudes toward the legal treatment of homosexuals, and the third addresses citizens' views of homosexuality as a lifestyle. Although differently focused, all three questions deal with aspects of gay life. It would not be surprising to see gay rights advocates cite the results of the first two questions as indicating support for their position. Opponents of gay rights would emphasize the results of the third question.

An Eyewitness News/*Daily News* poll of New York City residents conducted in February 1986 further illustrates how the selective use and analysis of survey questions can generate very different impressions of popular opinion on an issue. This poll asked a number of gay rights questions:

On another matter, would you say that New York City needs a gay rights law or not?

Yes, need gay rights law	39%
No, do not need gay rights law	54%
Don't know/no opinion	8%

On another matter, do you think it should be against the law for landlords or private employers to deny housing or a job to someone because that person is homosexual or do you think landlords and employers should be allowed to do that if they want to?

Yes, should be against law	49%
No, should not be against law	47%

Volunteered responses

Should be law only for landlord	1%
Should be law only for employers	8%
Don't know/no opinion	3%

Although a definite majority of the respondents oppose a gay rights law in response to the first question, a plurality also believe that it should be illegal for landlords and employers to deny housing and jobs to persons because they are homosexual. Here both questions address the legal status of homosexuals, and it is clear which question gay rights activists and gay rights opponents would cite in support of their respective policy positions. It is not clear, however, which question is the better measure of public opinion. The first question is unsatisfactory because one does not know how respondents interpreted the scope of a gay rights law. Did they think it referred only to housing and job discrimination, or did they think it would go substantially beyond that? The second question is inadequate if it is viewed as equivalent to a gay rights law. Lumping housing and jobs together constitutes another flaw, because citizens might have divergent views on these two aspects of gay rights.

Additional examples of the importance of item selection are provided by the polls taken to gauge Americans' attitudes about the Iraqi invasion of Kuwait in 1990. Early in the Persian Gulf crisis, various survey organizations asked Americans, using different questions, how they felt about taking military action against Iraq. Not surprisingly, the organizations obtained different results.

Do you favor or oppose direct U.S. military action against Iraq at this time? (Gallup, August 3–4, 1990)

Favor	23%
Oppose	68%
Don't know/refused	9%

Do you agree or disagree that the U.S. should take all actions necessary, including the use of military force, to make sure that Iraq withdraws its forces from Kuwait? (ABC News/*Washington Post,* August 8, 1990)

Agree	66%
Disagree	33%
Don't know	1%

Would you approve or disapprove of using U.S. troops to force the Iraqis to leave Kuwait? (Gallup, August 9–12, 1990, taken from *Public Perspective,* September/October 1990, 13)

Approve	64%
Disapprove	36%

(I'm going to mention some things that may or may not happen in the Middle East and for each one, please tell me whether the U.S. should or should not take military action in connection with it). . . . If Iraq refuses to withdraw from Kuwait? (NBC News/*Wall Street Journal,* August 18–19, 1990, taken from *Public Perspective,* September/October 1990, 13)

No military action	51%
Military action	49%

Note that the responses to these questions indicate varying levels of support for military action even though most of the questions were asked within two weeks of each other. The first question shows the most opposition to military action. This is easily explained: the question concerns military action *at this time,* an alternative that many Americans may have seen as premature until other means had been tried. The other three questions all indicate majority support for military action, although that support ranges from a bare majority to about two-thirds of all Americans. It is clear which question proponents and opponents of military action would cite to support their arguments.

Throughout the Persian Gulf crisis, public opinion was highly supportive of President George Bush's policies; only in the period between October and December 1990 did support for the president's handling of the situation drop below 60 percent. For example, a November 1990 CBS News/ *New York Times* poll showed the following patterns of response:

Do you approve or disapprove of the way George Bush is handling Iraq's invasion of Kuwait?

Approve	50%
Disapprove	41%
Don't know/NA	8%

Likewise, an ABC News/*Washington Post* poll in mid-November reported:

Do you approve or disapprove of the way George Bush is handling the situation caused by Iraq's invasion of Kuwait?

Approve	59%
Disapprove	36%
Don't know/NA	5%

Some opponents of the military buildup tried to use these and similar polls to demonstrate that support for the president's policies was decreasing— earlier polls had indicated support levels in the 60–70 percent range. Fortunately, the *Washington Post* poll cited above asked respondents who disapproved of Bush's policy whether the president was moving too slowly or too quickly. It turned out that 44 percent of the disapprovers said "too slowly" and 37 percent "too quickly." Thus a plurality of the disapprovers preferred more rapid action against Iraq—a result that provided little support for those critics of the president's policies who were arguing against a military solution.

Shortly before the outbreak of the war, the *Washington Post* conducted a survey of American attitudes about going to war with Iraq. To assess the effects of question wording, the *Post* split its sample in half and used two different versions of the same question followed by the identical follow-up question to each item.

Version 1

As you may know, the U.N. Security Council has authorized the use of force against Iraq if it doesn't withdraw from Kuwait by January 15. If Iraq does not withdraw from Kuwait, should the United States go to war against Iraq to force it out of Kuwait at some point after January 15 or not?

Go to war sometime after January 15	62%
No, do not go to war	32%

How long after January 15 should the United States wait for Iraq to withdraw from Kuwait before going to war to force it out?

Do not favor war at any point	32%
Immediately	18%
Less than one month	28%
1–3 months	8%
4 months or longer	2%

Version 2

The United Nations has passed a resolution authorizing the use of military force against Iraq if they do not withdraw their troops from Kuwait by January 15. If Iraq does not withdraw from Kuwait by then, do you think the United States should start military actions against Iraq, or should the United States wait longer to see if the trade embargo and economic sanctions work?

U.S. should start military actions	49%
U.S. should wait longer to see if sanctions work	47%

How long after January 15 should the United States wait for Iraq to withdraw from Kuwait before going to war to force it out?

U.S. should start military actions	49%

For those who would wait:

Less than a month	15%
1–3 months	17%
4 months or longer	9%

Morin (1991) points out how very different portraits of the American public can be painted by examining the two versions with and without the follow-up question. For example, version 1 shows 62 percent of Americans supporting war against Iraq, while version 2 shows only 49 percent.

These different results stem from inclusion of the embargo and sanctions option in the second version. Thus it appears that version 2 gives a less militaristic depiction of the American public. Responses to the follow-up question, however, provide a different picture of the public. For example, the first version shows that 54 percent of Americans (18 + 28 + 8) favor going to war within three months. But the second version shows that 81 percent of Americans (49 + 15 + 17) favor war within three months. The point, of course, is that the availability of different items on a survey can generate differing descriptions of the public's preferences.

The importance of item selection is illustrated in a final example on the Gulf War from an April 3, 1991, ABC News/*Washington Post* poll conducted just after the conflict. It included the following three questions:

Do you approve or disapprove of the way that George Bush is handling the situation involving Iraqi rebels who are trying to overthrow Saddam Hussein?

Approve	69%
Disapprove	24%
Don't know	7%

Please tell me if you agree or disagree with this statement: The United States should not have ended the war with Iraqi President Saddam Hussein still in power.

Agree	55%
Disagree	40%
Don't know	5%

Do you think the United States should try to help rebels overthrow Hussein or not?

Yes	45%
No	51%
Don't know	4%

Note that the responses to the first item indicate overwhelming approval for the president. But if one analyzes the second question in isolation, one might conclude that a majority of Americans did not support the president and indeed wanted to restart the war against Saddam Hussein. But the third item shows that a majority of Americans oppose helping the rebels. The lesson of this and the previous examples is clear. Constructing an interpretation around any single survey item can generate a very inaccurate description of public opinion. Unfortunately, advocates of particular positions have many opportunities to use survey results selectively and misleadingly to advance their cause.

The health care debate in 1993 and 1994 also provides examples of how the selection of items for analysis can influence one's view of American public opinion. *Washington Post* polls asked Americans whether they thought the Clinton health plan was better or worse than the present system (Morin 1994b). In one version of the question, the sample was given the response options "better" or "worse," and in the other version respondents could choose among "better," "worse," or "don't know enough about the plan to say." The following responses were obtained:

Version 1		*Version 2*	
Better	52%	Better	21%
Worse	34%	Worse	27%
Don't know (volunteered)	14%	Don't know enough	52%

Clearly, very different portrayals of American public opinion are presented by the two versions of the question. The first version suggests that a majority of Americans believed that the Clinton plan was better than the status quo, while the second version suggests that a plurality of citizens with opinions on the issue felt that the Clinton plan was worse. It is obvious which version of the question supporters and opponents of the Clinton health plan would be more likely to cite.

Another example from the health care reform area deals with Americans' feelings about the seriousness of the health care problem. Certainly, the more seriously the problem was viewed, the greater the impetus for changing the health care system. Different polling organizations asked a variety of questions designed to tap the importance of the health care issue (questions taken from the September/October 1994 issue of *Public Perspective*, 23, 26):

> Louis Harris and Associates (April 1994): Which of the following statements comes closest to expressing your overall view of the health care system in this country? . . . There are some good things in our health care system, but fundamental changes are needed to make it better. . . . Our health care system has so much wrong with it that we need to completely rebuild it. . . . On the whole, the health care system works pretty well and only minor changes are necessary to make it work.
>
> | | |
> |---|---|
> | Fundamental changes needed | 54% |
> | Completely rebuild it | 31% |
> | Only minor changes needed | 14% |
>
> NBC/*Wall Street Journal* (March 1994): Which of the following comes closest to your belief about the American health care system—the system is in crisis; the system has major problems, but is not in crisis;

the system has problems, but they are not major; or the system has no problems?

Crisis	22%
Major problems	50%
Minor problems	26%

Gallup (June 1994): Which of these statements do you agree with more: The country has health care problems, but no health care crisis, or, the country has a health care crisis?

Crisis	55%
Problems but no crisis	41%
Don't know	4%

Gallup (June 1994): Which of these statements do you agree with more: The country has a health care crisis, or the country has health care problems, but no health care crisis?

Crisis	35%
Problems but no crisis	61%
Don't know	4%

Certainly anyone trying to make the case that health care reform was an absolute priority would cite the first version of the Gallup question in which 55 percent of the respondents labeled health care a crisis. But anyone who wants to move more slowly and incrementally on the health care issue would likely cite the NBC News/*Wall Street Journal* poll in which only 22 percent of Americans said there was a crisis. Health care reform is the kind of controversial public policy issue that invites political leaders to seize on such poll results to advance their positions. But when they do, citizens should be sensitive to how politicians are selectively using the polls.

Schneider (1996) has provided an excellent example of how examination of a single trial heat question may give a misleading impression of the electoral strength of presidential candidates who include the incumbent president. A better sense of the candidates' true electoral strength is achieved by adding to the analysis information about the incumbent's job approval rating. For example, in a trial heat question in May 1980 incumbent president Jimmy Carter led challenger Ronald Reagan by 40 to 32 percent, yet at the time Carter's job rating was quite negative: 38 percent approval and 51 percent disapproval. Thus Carter's lead in the trial heat item was much more fragile than it appeared; indeed, Reagan went on to win the election. Four years later, in May 1984, President Reagan led challenger Walter Mondale by ten percentage points in the trial heat question. But Reagan's job rating was very positive: 54 percent approval compared with 38 percent disapproval. Thus Reagan's ten-point lead looked quite

Reprinted with special permission of King Features Syndicate.

solid in view of his strong job ratings, and he won overwhelmingly in No-vember. Finally, in April 1992 incumbent president George Bush led chal-lenger Bill Clinton by 50 to 34 percent in the trial heat question, a huge margin. But Bush's overall job rating was negative—42 percent approval versus 48 percent disapproval. Bush's lead over Clinton, then, was not as strong as it appeared, and Clinton ultimately won the election.

By collecting information on multiple aspects of a topic, pollsters are better able to understand citizens' attitudes (Morin and Berry 1996). One of the anomalies of 1996 was the substantial number of Americans who were worried about the health of the economy at a time when by most ob-jective indicators the economy was performing very well. Part of the an-swer to this puzzle was Americans' ignorance and misinformation about the country's economic health. For example, even though unemployment was substantially lower in 1996 than in 1991, 33 percent of Americans said it was higher in 1996 and 28 percent said the same. The average estimate of the unemployment rate was 20.6 percent when in reality it was just over 5 percent. Americans' perceptions of inflation and the deficit were similar; in both cases Americans thought that the reality was much worse than it actually was. It is no wonder that many Americans expressed economic in-security during good economic times; they were not aware of how strongly the economy was performing.

Sometimes it is tempting to speculate broadly about citizens' opinions and policy preferences based on their responses to particular survey items. In many cases, the speculations and projections would be incorrect, but only the use of additional polling questions would confirm the mistake. For example, in 1999 a survey conducted for CNN–USA Today by the Gallup Organization asked Americans, "Do you support the 'don't ask, don't tell' policy on homosexuality in the military?" Fifty percent of respondents said they supported the policy and 46 percent opposed it, suggesting a sharply divided citizenry with only the barest majority in favor of letting gays serve in the military. Fortunately, the survey asked a follow-up question to those 46 percent of Americans who opposed "don't ask, don't tell": "Do you oppose it because you think homosexuals should be able to serve openly in the military, or because you believe homosexuals should not be able to serve in the military under any circumstances?" In response to this question, the 46 percent broke down into 35 percent who said that gays should be able to serve openly, 8 percent who said they should never be able to serve, and 3 percent who cited no reason for their stance. Thus inclusion of the second item reveals a portrait of American public opinion that is much more supportive of gays serving in the military.

Two polls on abortion demonstrate that while support for the use of abortion may have weakened in recent years, one cannot conclude that citizens are therefore more likely to favor legally restricting abortion rights. A 2000 *Los Angeles Times* poll (Rubin 2000) found that more than half of Americans thought abortion should be either totally illegal or legal only in cases of rape, incest, or when the mother's life was in danger. Yet more than two-thirds of Americans said the decision to have an abortion should be left to the woman and her doctor. Even among the 57 percent of respondents who believed abortion to be murder, more than half agreed that the decision to have an abortion should be left to the woman. A 1998 *Columbus Dispatch* poll of Ohioans obtained similar results (Rowland 1998). Only 27 percent of Ohioans believed that abortion should be generally available; 15 percent said that abortion should be available but under stricter limits; 43 percent said that abortion should be against the law except in cases involving rape, incest, and the life of the mother; and 15 percent believed that abortion should not be permitted at all. Moreover, 51 percent of Ohioans believed that abortion was an act of murder. These results might suggest that Ohioans would be supportive of government action to limit or prohibit abortions, but that was not the case. Ohioans were asked to agree or disagree with the following statement: "Even in cases where I might think abortion is the wrong thing to do, I don't think the government has any business preventing a woman from having an abortion." Fully 66 percent of respondents agreed with this statement and only 27 percent disagreed. Again, the general lesson here is to not automatically assume knowledge of citizens' policy prescriptions based on their opinions on an issue; rather, ask specific questions about issue opinions and policy preferences. Some citizens may not like abortion, but they may be unwilling to impose their views on others. Likewise, some citizens may reject gun ownership for themselves, but that does not mean they would prevent their fellow citizens from owning guns. And some citizens may oppose mercy killings and doctor-assisted suicides, but that does not mean they support stiff criminal penalties to punish these actions.

The final example in this section focuses on how the media select what citizens learn about a poll even when the complete poll and analyses are available to the citizenry. *Sex in America: A Definitive Survey* by Robert T. Michael et al., was published in 1994, along with a more specialized and comprehensive volume, *The Social Organization of Sexuality: Sexual Practices in the United States,* by Edward O. Laumann et al. Both books are based on an extensive questionnaire administered by the National Opinion Research Center to 3,432 scientifically selected respondents. The enterprise was a genuine public opinion survey on sexual behavior, unlike the sex pseudo-polls discussed in Chapter 1.

Because of the importance of the subject matter and because sex sells, media coverage of the survey was widespread. How various media reported the story indicates how much leeway the media have and how influential they are in determining what citizens learn about a given topic. For example, the *New York Times* ran a front-page story on October 7, 1994, entitled "Sex in America: Faithfulness in Marriage Thrives After All." Less-prominent stories appeared in subsequent issues, including one on October 18, 1994, inaccurately entitled "Gay Survey Raises a New Question."

Two of the three major news magazines featured the sex survey on the covers of their October 17, 1994, issues. The *Time* cover simply read "Sex in America: Surprising News from the Most Important Survey since the Kinsey Report." The *U.S. News and World Report* cover was more risqué, showing a partially clad man and woman in bed; it read "Sex in America: A Massive New Survey, the Most Authoritative Ever, Reveals What We Do Behind the Bedroom Door." In contrast, *Newsweek* simply ran a two-page story with the lead "Not Frenzied, But Fulfilled. Sex: Relax. If you do it—with your mate—around twice a week, according to a major new study, you basically wrote the book of love."

Other magazines and newspapers also reported on the survey in ways geared to their readership. The November issue of *Glamour* featured the survey on its cover with the teaser "Who's doing it? And how? MAJOR U.S. SEX SURVEY." The story that followed was written by the authors of the book. While the cover of the November 15, 1994, issue of *The Advocate* read "What That Sex Survey Really Means," the story focused largely on what the survey had to say about the number of gays and lesbians in the population. The lead stated, "10%: Reality or Myth? There's little authoritative information about gays and lesbians in the landmark study *Sex in America*—but what there is will cause big trouble." Finally, the *Chronicle of Higher Education,* a weekly newspaper geared to college and university personnel, in its October 17, 1994, issue headlined its story "The Sex Lives of Americans. Survey that had been target of conservative attacks produces few startling results."

Both books about the survey contain a vast amount of information and a large number of results and findings. But most of the media reported on topics such as marital fidelity, how often Americans have sex, how many sex partners people have, how often people experience orgasm, what percentages of the population are gay and lesbian, how long sex takes, and the time elapsed between a couple's first meeting and their first sexual involvement. Many of the reports also presented results for married versus singles, men versus women, and other analytical groupings. Although most of the media coverage cited above was accurate in reporting the actual survey results, it also was selective in focusing on the more titillating parts of the survey, an unsurprising outcome given the need to satisfy their readerships.

Examining Trends with Polling Data

Researchers often use polling data to describe and analyze trends. To isolate trend data, a researcher must ensure that items relating to the topic under investigation are included in multiple surveys conducted at different points in time. Ideally, the items should be identically worded. But even when they are, serious problems of comparability can make trend analysis difficult. Identically worded items may not mean the same thing or provide the same stimulus to respondents over time because social and political changes in society have altered the meaning of the questions. For example, consider this question:

Some say that the civil rights people have been trying to push too fast. Others feel they haven't pushed fast enough. How about you? Do you think that civil rights leaders are trying to push too fast, are going too slowly, or are they moving at about the right speed?

The responses to this item can be greatly influenced by the goals and agenda of the civil rights leadership at the time of the survey. A finding that more Americans think that the civil rights leaders are moving too fast or too slowly may reflect not a change in attitude from past views about civil rights activism but a change in the civil rights agenda itself. In this case, follow-up questions designed to measure specific components of the civil rights agenda are needed to help define the trend.

And there are other difficulties in achieving comparability over time. For example, even if the wording of an item were to remain the same, its placement within the questionnaire could change, which in turn could alter the meaning of a question (see Chapter 3). Likewise, the definition of the sampling frame and the procedures used to achieve completed interviews could change. In short, comparability entails much more than simply wording questions identically. Unfortunately, consumers of poll results seldom receive the information that enables them to judge whether items are truly comparable over time.

Two studies demonstrate the advantages and disadvantages of using identical items over time. Abramson (1990) complained that the biennial National Election Studies (NES) conducted by the Survey Research Center at the University of Michigan, Ann Arbor, were losing their longitudinal comparability as new questions were added to the surveys and old ones removed. Baumgartner and Walker (1988), by contrast, complained that the use of the same standard question over time to assess the level of group membership in the United States had systematically underestimated the extent of such activity. They argued that new measures of group membership should be employed, which, of course, would make comparisons between past and present surveys more problematic. Although both the old and the new measures can be included in a survey, this becomes very costly if the survey must cover many other topics.

Two other studies show how variations in question wording can make the assessment of attitude change over time difficult. Borrelli and colleagues (1989) found that polls measuring Americans' political party loyalties in 1980 and in 1984 varied widely in their results. They attributed the different results in these polls to three factors: whether the poll sampled voters only; whether the poll emphasized "today" or the present in inquiring about citizens' partisanship; and whether the poll was conducted close to Election Day, which would tend to give the advantage to the party ahead in the presidential contest. The implications of this research for assessing change in party identification over time are evident—that is, to conclude that genuine partisan change occurred in either of the two polls, other possible sources of observed differences, such as modifications in the wording of questions, must be ruled out. In a study of support for aid to the Nicaraguan contras between 1983 and 1986, Lockerbie and Borrelli (1990) argue that much of the observed change in American public opinion was not genuine. Instead, it was attributable to changes in the wording of the questions used to measure support for the contras. Again, the point is that one must be able to eliminate other potential explanations for observed change before concluding that observed change is genuine change.

Smith's (1993) critique of three major national studies of anti-Semitism conducted in 1964, 1981, and 1992 is an informative case study of how longitudinal comparisons may be undermined by methodological differences across surveys. The 1981 and 1992 studies were ostensibly designed to build on the 1964 effort, thereby facilitating an analysis of trends in anti-Semitism. But, as Smith notes, longitudinal comparisons among the three studies were problematic because of differences in sample definition and interview mode, changes in question order and question wording, and insufficient information to evaluate the quality of the sample and the design execution. In examining an eleven-item anti-Semitism scale, he did find six items highly comparable over time that indicated a decline in anti-Semitic attitudes.

Despite the problems of sorting out true opinion change from change attributable to methodological factors, there are times when public opinion changes markedly and suddenly in response to a dramatic occurrence and the observed change is indeed genuine. Two examples from CBS News/ *New York Times* polls in 1991 about the Persian Gulf war illustrate dramatic and extensive attitude change. The first example concerns military action against Iraq. Just before the January 15 deadline imposed by the UN for the withdrawal of Iraq from Kuwait, a poll found that 47 percent of Americans favored initiating military action against Iraq if it did not withdraw; 46 percent were opposed. Two days after the deadline and after the beginning of the allied air campaign against Iraq, another poll found 79 percent of Americans agreeing that the United States had done the right thing in initiating military action against Iraq. The second example is related to people's attitudes toward a ground war in the Middle East. Before the allied ground offensive began, only 11 percent of Americans said the United States should begin fighting the ground war soon; 79 percent said bombing from the air should continue. But after the ground war began, the numbers shifted dramatically: 75 percent of Americans said the United States was right to begin the ground war, and only 19 percent said the nation should have waited longer. Clearly, the Persian Gulf crisis was a case in which American public opinion moved dramatically in the direction of supporting the president at each new stage.

Examining Subsets of Respondents

Although it is natural to want to know the results from an entire sample, often the most interesting information in a poll comes from examining the response patterns of subsets of respondents defined according to certain theoretically or substantively relevant characteristics. For example, a January 1986 CBS News/*New York Times* poll revealed that President Reagan was enjoying unprecedented popularity for a six-year incumbent: 65 percent approved of the president's performance, and only 24 percent disapproved. But these overall figures mask some analytically interesting variations. For example, among blacks only 37 percent approved of the president's performance; 49 percent disapproved. The sexes also differed in their views of the president, with men expressing a 72 percent approval rate compared with 58 percent for women. (As expected gories of party loyalists, 89 percent of Republicans, 66 per pendents, and only 47 percent of Democrats approved of the president's performance.) Why did blacks and whites—and men and women—differ in their views of the president?

There is no necessary reason for public opinion on an issue to be uniform across subgroups. Indeed, on many issues there are reasons to expect just the opposite. That is why a fuller understanding of American public opinion is gained by taking a closer look at the views of relevant subgroups of the sample. In doing so, however, one should note that dividing the sample into subsets increases the sampling error and lowers the reliability of the sample estimates. For example, a sample of 1,600 Americans might be queried about their attitudes on abortion. After the overall pattern is observed, the researcher might wish to break down the sample by religion— yielding 1,150 Protestant, 400 Catholic, and 50 Jewish respondents—to determine whether religious affiliation is associated with specific attitudes toward abortion. The researcher then might observe that Catholics on the whole are the most opposed to abortion. To find out which Catholics are most likely to oppose abortion, she might further divide the 400 Catholics into young and old Catholics or regular church attendees and nonregular attendees, or into four categories of young Catholic churchgoers, old Catholic churchgoers, young Catholic nonattenders, and old Catholic nonattenders. The more breakdowns done at the same time, the quicker the sample size in any particular category plummets, perhaps leaving insufficient cases in some categories to make solid conclusions.

Examples of the advantages of delving more deeply into poll data on subsets of respondents are plentiful. An ABC News/*Washington Post* poll conducted in February 1986 showed major differences in the attitudes of men and women toward pornography; an examination of only the total sample would have missed these important divergences. For example, in response to the question "Do you think laws against pornography in this country are too strict, not strict enough, or just about right?" 10 percent of the men said the laws were too strict, 41 percent said not strict enough, and 47 percent said about right. Among women, only 2 percent said the laws were too strict, a sizable 72 percent said they were not strict enough, and 23 percent thought they were about right (Sussman 1986c, 37).

A CBS News/*New York Times* poll of Americans conducted in April 1986 found widespread approval of the American bombing of Libya; 77 percent of the sample approved of the action, and only 14 percent disapproved. Despite the overall approval, differences among various subgroups are noteworthy. For example, 83 percent of men approved of the bombing compared with 71 percent of women. Of the white respondents, 80 percent approved in contrast to only 53 percent of the blacks (Clymer

1986c). Even though all of these demographically defined groups gave at least majority support to the bombing, the differences in levels of support are both statistically and substantively significant.

Polls showed dramatic differences by race in the O. J. Simpson case, with blacks more convinced of Simpson's innocence and more likely to believe that he could not get a fair trial. For example, a field poll of Californians (*U.S. News and World Report,* August 1, 1994) showed that only 35 percent of blacks believed that Simpson could get a fair trial compared with 55 percent of whites. Also, 62 percent of whites thought Simpson was "very likely or somewhat likely" to be guilty of murder compared with only 38 percent of blacks. Comparable results were found in a national *Time*/CNN poll (*Time,* August 1, 1994): 66 percent of whites thought Simpson got a fair preliminary hearing compared with only 31 percent of black respondents, and 77 percent of the white respondents thought the case against Simpson was "very strong" or "fairly strong" compared with 45 percent for blacks. A *Newsweek* poll (August 1, 1994) revealed that 60 percent of blacks believed that Simpson was set up (20 percent attributing the setup to the police); only 23 percent of whites believed in a setup conspiracy. When asked whether Simpson had been treated better or worse than the average white murder suspect, whites said better by an overwhelming 52 to 5 percent margin, while blacks said worse by a 30 to 19 percent margin. These reactions to the Simpson case startled many Americans who could not understand how their compatriots of another race could see the situation so differently.

School busing to achieve racial integration has been consistently opposed by substantial majorities in national public opinion polls. A Harris poll commissioned by *Newsweek* in 1978 found that 85 percent of whites opposed busing (Williams 1979, 48). An ABC News/*Washington Post* poll conducted in February 1986 showed 60 percent of whites against busing (Sussman 1986b). The difference between the two polls might reflect a genuine attitude change about busing in that eight-year period, or it might be a function of different question wording or different placement within the questionnaire. Whatever the reason, additional analysis of both polls shows that whites are not monolithic in their opposition to busing. For example, the 1978 poll showed that 56 percent of white parents whose children had been bused viewed the experience as "very satisfactory." The 1986 poll revealed sharp differences in busing attitudes among younger and older whites. Among whites age thirty and under, 47 percent supported busing and 50 percent opposed it, while among whites over age thirty, 32 percent supported busing and 65 percent opposed it. Moreover, among younger whites whose families had experienced busing firsthand,

54 percent approved of busing and 46 percent opposed it. (Of course, staunch opponents of busing may have moved to escape busing, thereby guaranteeing that the remaining population would be relatively more supportive of busing.)

Another example of the usefulness of examining poll results within age categories is provided by an ABC News/*Washington Post* poll conducted in May 1985 on citizens' views of how the federal budget deficit might be cut. One item read, "Do you think the government should give people a smaller Social Security cost-of-living increase than they are now scheduled to get as a way of reducing the budget deficit, or not?" Among the overall sample, 19 percent favored granting a smaller cost-of-living increase and 78 percent opposed. To test the widespread view that young workers lack confidence in the Social Security system and doubt they will ever get out of the system what they paid in, Sussman (1985d) investigated how different age groups responded to the preceding question. Basically, he found that all age groups strongly opposed a reduction in cost-of-living increases. Unlike the busing issue, this question showed no difference among age groups—an important substantive finding, particularly in light of the expectation that there would be divergent views among the old and young. Too often people mistakenly dismiss null (no difference) results as uninteresting and unexciting; a finding of no difference can be just as substantively significant as a finding of a major difference.

An example where age does make a difference in people's opinions is the topic of physician-assisted suicide. A *Washington Post* poll conducted in 1996 asked a national sample of Americans, "Should it be legal or illegal for a doctor to help a terminally ill patient commit suicide?" (Rosenbaum 1997). The attitudes of older citizens and younger citizens were markedly different on this question—the older the age group, the greater the opposition to doctor-assisted suicide. For example, 52 percent of respondents between ages eighteen and twenty-nine thought doctor-assisted suicide should be legal; 41 percent said it should be illegal. But for citizens over age seventy, the comparable figures were 35 and 58 percent. Even more striking were some of the racial and income differences on this question. Whites thought physician involvement in suicide should be legal by a 55 to 35 percent margin; blacks opposed it 70 to 20 percent. At the lowest income levels, doctor-assisted suicide was opposed by a 54 to 37 percent margin; at the highest income level it was supported by a 58 to 30 percent margin.

Two state-level polls on gun ownership and gun rights also demonstrate the importance of examining subsets of respondents. A 1999 Field poll queried Californians, "Which is more important—to protect the right of Americans to own guns, or to impose greater control on gun ownership?" Overall, 64 percent of Californians said it was more important to control gun ownership; 30 percent opted to protect the rights of gun owners. But an examination of responses by the respondent's party affiliation brought sharp differences to light. Democrats cited controlling gun ownership over protecting the right to own guns by a margin of 79 to 16 percent. But for Republicans, 49 percent thought protecting the right to own guns was more important, while 45 percent opted for greater regulation of gun ownership. Likewise, a 1999 poll conducted for the *Columbus Dispatch* (Rowland 1999) revealed sharp differences by gender in response to the question "Which one do you think is more important: To protect the right of Americans to own guns or to control gun ownership?" Men divided evenly on this item, while 70 percent of female respondents thought controlling gun ownership was more important, compared with only 21 percent who gave higher priority to protecting the right to own guns. The *Dispatch* survey also reinforces an earlier point: one cannot assume how respondents stand on particular issues based on their positions on other issues. Small to sizable majorities of Ohioans supported a variety of gun control and gun safety measures. Ninety percent favored a mandatory waiting period to allow background checks; 70 percent favored registering handguns with the government; 86 percent favored child safety locks; 85 percent favored requiring handgun owners to attend a course on gun safety; and 53 percent favored banning gun shows where guns are bought and sold without much supervision and regulation. But 53 percent would favor legislation (with various safeguards) that would enable adults to carry concealed weapons.

In many instances, the categories used for creating subgroups are already established or self-evident. For example, if one is interested in gender or racial differences, the categories of male and female or white and black are straightforward candidates for investigation. Other breakdowns require more thought. For example, what divisions might be used to examine the effects of age? Young, middle-aged, and old? If so, what actual ages correspond to these categories? Is middle age thirty-five to sixty-five, forty to sixty, or what? Or should more than three categories of age be defined? In samples selected to study the effects of religion, the typical breakdown is Protestant, Catholic, and Jewish. But this simple threefold division might overlook some interesting variations—that is, some Protestants are evangelical, some are fundamentalist, and others are in the so-called mainline denominations. Moreover, because most blacks are Protestants, comparisons of Catholics and Protestants that do not also control for race may be misleading.

Creating subsets by ideology is another common approach to analyzing public opinion. The ideological categories used most often are liberal, moderate, and conservative, and typically respondents are assigned to these categories based on their answers to this question: "Generally speaking, do you think of yourself as a liberal, moderate, or conservative?" But do people really assign common meanings to these terms? Do these terms oversimplify reality? Journalist Kevin Phillips (1981) has cited the work of political scientists Stuart A. Lilie and William S. Maddox, who argue that the traditional liberal-moderate-conservative breakdown is inadequate for analytical purposes. Instead, they propose a fourfold classification of liberal, conservative, populist, and libertarian, based on two underlying dimensions: whether one supports or opposes government intervention in the economy and whether one supports or opposes expansion of individual behavioral liberties and sexual equality. They define liberals as those who support both government intervention in the economy and expansion of personal liberties, conservatives as those who oppose both, libertarians as citizens who favor expanding personal liberties but oppose government intervention in the economy, and populists as persons who favor government economic intervention but oppose the expansion of personal liberties. According to one poll, populists make up 24 percent of the electorate, conservatives 18 percent, liberals 16 percent, and libertarians 13 percent. The rest of the electorate is not readily classifiable or unfamiliar with ideological terminology.

This more elaborate breakdown of ideology may be more helpful to those seeking to better understand public opinion, but the traditional categories still dominate political discourse. Even so, citizens who oppose government programs that affect the marketplace but support pro-choice court decisions on abortion and proposed gay rights statutes cannot be easily labeled liberals or conservatives, because they appear to be conservative on economic issues and liberal on lifestyle issues. Perhaps, then, they are best classified as libertarians.

Additional examples of how an examination of subsets of respondents can provide useful insights into the public's attitudes are provided by two CBS News/New York Times surveys conducted in 1991, one dealing with the Persian Gulf crisis and the other with attitudes toward police. Although the rapid and successful conclusion of the ground war against Iraq resulted in widespread approval of the enterprise, before the land assault began Americans differed in their opinions about a ground war. For example, in the February 12–13 CBS News/New York Times poll, Americans were asked: "Suppose several thousand American troops would lose their lives in a ground war against Iraq. Do you think a ground war against Iraq would be worth the cost or not?" A closer look at the percentage saying it would be worth the cost reveals the following results for different groups of Americans:

All respondents	45%	Independents	46%
Men	56%	Republicans	54%
Women	35%	Eighteen- to twenty-nine-year-olds	50%
Whites	47%	Thirty- to forty-four-year-olds	44%
Blacks	30%	Forty-five- to sixty-four-year-olds	51%
Democrats	36%	Sixty-five years and older	26%

Note that the youngest age group, the one most likely to suffer the casualties, is among the most supportive of a ground war. Note also the sizable differences between men and women, whites and blacks, and Democrats and Republicans.

Substantial racial differences in opinion also were expressed in an April 1–3, 1991, CBS News/*New York Times* poll on attitudes toward local police. Overall, 55 percent of the sample said they had substantial confidence in the local police; 44 percent said they had little confidence. But among whites the comparable percentages were 59 percent and 39 percent, while for blacks only 30 percent had substantial confidence and fully 70 percent expressed little confidence in the police. Even on issues in which the direction of white and black opinion was the same, there were still substantial racial differences in the responses. For example, 69 percent of whites said that the police in their own community treat blacks and whites the same, and only 16 percent said the police were tougher on blacks than on whites. Although a plurality—45 percent—of blacks agreed that the police treat blacks and whites equally, fully 42 percent of black respondents felt the police were tougher on blacks. Certainly if one were conducting a study to ascertain citizens' attitudes about police performance, it would be foolish not to examine the opinions of relevant subgroups.

Another example of the importance of examining subsets of respondents is provided by a January 1985 ABC News/*Washington Post* poll that queried Americans about their attitudes on a variety of issues and presented results not only for the entire sample but also for subsets of respondents defined by their attentiveness to public affairs (Sussman 1985b). Attentiveness to public affairs was measured by whether the respondents were aware of four news events: the subway shooting in New York City of four alleged assailants by their intended victim; the switch in jobs by two key Reagan administration officials, Donald Regan and James Baker; the Treasury Department's proposal to simplify the tax system; and protests against South African apartheid held in the United States. Respondents then were divided into four levels of awareness, with 27 percent in the highest category, 26 percent in the next highest, 25 percent in the next category, and 22 percent falling in the lowest. The next step in the analysis was to compare the policy preferences of the highest and lowest awareness subsets.

Some marked differences between these two groups emerged. For example, on the issue of support for the president's military buildup, 59 percent of the lowest-awareness respondents opposed any major cuts in military spending to lessen the budget deficit. By contrast, 57 percent of the highest-awareness group said that military spending should be limited to help with the budget deficit. On the issue of tax rates, a majority of both groups agreed with the president that taxes were too high, but the size of the majorities differed. Among the lowest-awareness respondents, 72 percent said taxes were too high and 24 percent said they were not; among the highest-awareness respondents, 52 percent said taxes were too high and 45 percent said they were not (Sussman 1985b).

Opinions about the future of Social Security and Medicare also are affected by citizens' knowledge about the two programs (Pianin and Brossard 1997). In one poll, the more people knew about Social Security and Medicare, the more likely they were to believe that these programs were in crisis and that major government action was needed. For example, among highly knowledgeable respondents, 88 percent believed that Social Security either was in crisis or had major problems; only 70 percent of respondents with little knowledge agreed. Likewise, 89 percent of the highly knowledgeable respondents believed Social Security would go bankrupt if Congress did nothing, compared with only 61 percent for the less-informed respondents.

All these findings raise some interesting normative issues about public opinion polls. As mentioned in Chapter 1, the methodology of public opinion polls is very democratic. All citizens have a nearly equal chance to be selected for a sample and have their views counted; all respondents are weighted equally (or nearly so) in the typical data analysis. Yet except in the voting booth all citizens do not have equal influence in shaping public policy. The distribution of political resources, whether financial or informational, is not uniform across the population. Polls themselves become a means to influence public policy, as various decision makers cite poll results to legitimize their policies. But should the views of all poll respondents be counted equally? An elitist critic would argue that the most informed segments of the population should be given the greatest weight. Therefore, in the preceding example of defense spending, more attention should be given to the views of the highest-awareness subset (assuming the validity of the levels of awareness), which was more supportive of reducing military spending. An egalitarian argument would assert that all respondents should be counted equally. We will return to the role of the polls in a democratic political system in the last chapter.

Interpreting Poll Results

An August 1986 Gallup poll on education showed that 67 percent of Americans would allow their children to attend class with a child suffering from AIDS; 24 percent would not. What reaction might there be to this finding? Some people might be shocked and depressed to discover that almost one-fourth of Americans could be so mean-spirited toward AIDS victims when the scientific evidence shows that AIDS is not a disease transmitted by casual contact. Others might be reassured and relieved that two-thirds of Americans are sufficiently enlightened or tolerant to allow their children to attend school with children who have AIDS. Some people might feel dismay: How could 67 percent of Americans foolishly allow their children to go to school with a child who has AIDS when there is no absolute guarantee that AIDS cannot be transmitted casually?

Consider this example from a 1983 poll by the National Opinion Research Center: "If your party nominated a black for President, would you vote for him if he were qualified for the job?" Eighty-five percent of the white respondents said yes. How might this response be interpreted? One might feel positive about how much racial attitudes have changed in the United States. A different perspective would decry the fact that in this supposedly tolerant and enlightened era, 15 percent of white survey respondents could not bring themselves to say they would vote for a qualified black candidate.

In neither example just given can a single correct meaning be assigned to the data. Instead, the interpretation favored will be a function of the interpreter's individual values and beliefs, as well as purposes in analyzing the survey. This observation is demonstrated in an analysis of two national surveys on gun control, one sponsored by the National Rifle Association (NRA) and conducted by Decision/Making/Information, Inc., and the other sponsored by the Center for the Study and Prevention of Handgun Violence and conducted by Cambridge Reports, Inc. (pollster Patrick Caddell's firm). Although the statistical results from both surveys were comparable, the two reports arrived at substantially different conclusions. The NRA's analysis concluded:

> Majorities of American voters believe that we do *not* need more laws governing the possession and use of firearms and that more firearms laws would *not* result in a decrease in the crime rate. (Wright 1981, 25)

Reprinted with special permission of King Features Syndicate.

By contrast, the center's report stated:

> It is clear that the vast majority of the public (both those who live with handguns and those who do not) want handgun licensing and registration. . . . The American public wants some form of handgun control legislation. (Wright 1981, 25)

Wright carefully analyzed the evidence cited in support of each conclusion and found that

> the major difference between the two reports is not in the findings, but in what is said about or concluded about the findings: what aspects of the evidence are emphasized or de-emphasized, what interpretation is given to a finding, and what implications are drawn from the findings about the need, or lack thereof, for stricter weapons controls. (Wright 1981, 38)

In essence, it was the interpretation of the data that generated the difference in the recommendations.

Two polls on tax reform provide another example of how poll data can be selectively interpreted and reported (Sussman 1985a). The first poll, sponsored by the insurance industry, was conducted by pollster Burns Roper. Its main conclusion, reported in a press conference announcing the poll results, was that 77 percent of the American public "said that workers should not be taxed on employee benefits" and that only 15 percent supported such a tax, a conclusion very reassuring to the insurance industry. However, Roper included other items in the poll that the insurance industry chose not to emphasize. As Sussman points out, the 77 percent opposed to the taxing of fringe benefits were then asked, "Would you still oppose counting the value of employee benefits as taxable income for employees if the additional tax revenues went directly to the reduction of federal budget deficits and not into new spending?" Twenty-six percent were no longer opposed to taxing fringe benefits under this condition, bringing the overall opposition down to 51 percent of the sample.

A second follow-up question asked, "Would you still oppose counting the value of employee benefits as taxable income for employees if the additional tax revenues permitted an overall reduction of tax rates for individuals?" (a feature that was part of the Treasury Department's initial tax proposals). Now only 33 percent of the sample was opposed to taxing fringes, 50 percent supported it, and 17 percent were undecided. Thus, depending on which results are used, anyone reporting this poll could show a majority of citizens supportive of or opposed to taxing fringe benefits.

The other poll that Sussman analyzed also tapped people's reactions to the Treasury Department's tax proposal. Several questions in the survey demonstrated public hostility to the Treasury proposal. One item read:

> The Treasury Department has proposed changing the tax system. Three tax brackets would be created, but most current deductions from income would be eliminated. Non-federal income taxes and property taxes would not be deductible, and many deductions would be limited. Do you favor or oppose this proposal? (Sussman 1985a)

Not surprisingly, 57 percent opposed the Treasury plan and only 27 percent supported it. But, as Sussman points out, the question is highly selective and leading, because it focuses on changes in the tax system that hurt the taxpayer. For example, nowhere does it inform the respondent that a key part of the Treasury plan was to reduce existing tax rates so that 80 percent of Americans would be paying either the same amount or less in taxes than they were paying before. Clearly, this survey was designed to obtain a set of results compatible with the sponsor's policy objectives.

Morin (1995d) describes a situation in which polling data were misinterpreted and misreported in the *Washington Post* because of faulty communication between a *Post* reporter and the local polling firm that was conducting an omnibus survey in the Washington, D.C., area. Interested in how worried federal employees were about their jobs given the budgetary battles between the Clinton White House and the Republican Congress in 1995, the reporter commissioned the polling firm to include the following questions in its survey: "Do you think your agency or company will probably be affected by federal budget cutbacks? Do you think your own job will be affected?" The poll discovered that 40 percent of the federal workers interviewed believed their own jobs might be affected. Unfortunately, when the polling outfit prepared a report for its client, the reporter, the report concluded that these federal workers felt their jobs were jeopardized. The reporter's story then stated, "Four out of every 10 federal employees fear losing their jobs because of budget reductions." As Morin points out, this conclusion does not follow from the polling questions asked. The belief that one's job will likely be affected is not equivalent to the fear of losing one's job. Instead, the effects might be lower salary increases, decreased job mobility, increased job responsibilities, and the like. A correction quickly appeared in the *Post* clarifying what the polling data had actually said. One lesson of this example is the responsibility that pollsters have to clients to communicate carefully and accurately what poll results mean. Another lesson is that no one should try to read too much into the responses to any single survey item. In this case, if the reporter wanted to know exactly how federal workers thought their jobs would be affected, a specific question eliciting this information should have been included in the survey.

When Polls Conflict: A Concluding Example

A variety of factors can influence poll results and their subsequent interpretation. Useful vehicles for a review of these factors are the polls that led up to the presidential elections between 1980 and 2000 — polls that were often highly inconsistent. For example, in the 1984 election, polls conducted at comparable times yielded highly dissimilar results. A Harris poll had Reagan leading Mondale by nine percentage points, an ABC News/ *Washington Post* poll had Reagan ahead by twelve points, a CBS News/ *New York Times* survey had Reagan leading by thirteen points, a *Los Angeles Times* poll gave Reagan a seventeen-point lead, and an NBC News poll had the president ahead by twenty-five points (Oreskes 1984). In September 1988 seven different polls on presidential preference were released within a three-day period with results ranging from Bush ahead by eight points to a Dukakis lead of six points (Morin 1988c). In 1992 ten national polls conducted in the latter part of August showed Clinton with leads over Bush ranging from five to nineteen percentage points (Elving 1992). In 1996 the final preelection polls showed Clinton leading Dole by margins ranging from seven to eighteen percentage points. And in 2000 six polls released on October 26 showed outcomes ranging from a Bush lead of thirteen percentage points to a Gore lead of two percentage points. How can polls on an ostensibly straightforward topic such as presidential vote preference differ so widely? Many reasons can be cited, some obvious and others more subtle in their effects.

Among the more subtle reasons are the method of interviewing and the number of callbacks that a pollster uses to contact respondents who initially were unavailable. According to Lewis and Schneider (1982, 43), Patrick Caddell and George Gallup in their 1980 polls found that President Reagan received less support from respondents interviewed personally than from those queried over the telephone. Their speculation about this finding was that weak Democrats who were going to desert Carter found it easier to admit this in a telephone interview than in a face-to-face situation.

As for callbacks, Dolnick (1984) reports that one reason a Harris poll was closer than others in predicting Reagan's sizable victory in 1980 was that it made repeated callbacks, which at each stage "turned up increasing numbers of well-paid, well-educated Republican-leaning voters." A similar situation occurred in 1984. Traugott (1987) found that persistence in callbacks resulted in a more Republican sample, speculating that Republicans were less likely to have been at home or available initially.

Some of the more obvious factors that help account for differences among compared polls are question wording and question placement. Some survey items mention the presidential and vice-presidential candidates; others mention only the presidential candidates. Some pollsters ask follow-up questions of undecided voters to ascertain whether they lean toward one candidate or another; others do not. And as noted in Chapter 3, question order can influence responses. Normally, incumbents and better-known candidates do better when the question on vote intention is asked at the beginning of the survey rather than later. If vote intention is measured after a series of issue and problem questions have been asked, respondents may have been reminded of shortcomings in the incumbent's record and may therefore be less willing to express support for the incumbent.

Comparable polls also can differ in how the sample is selected and how it is treated for analytical purposes. Some polls sample registered voters; others query adult Americans. There are differences as well in the methods used to identify likely voters, as discussed in Chapter 7. As Lipset (1980) points out, the greater the number of respondents who are screened out of the sample because they do not seem to be likely voters, the more probable it is that the remaining respondents will be relatively more Republican in their vote preferences. Finally, some samples are weighted to guarantee demographic representativeness; others are not.

It is also possible that discrepancies among polls do not stem from any of the above factors, but may simply reflect statistical fluctuations. For example, if one poll with a 4 percent sampling error shows Bush ahead of Gore by 52 to 43 percent, this result is statistically congruent with other polls that might have a very narrow Bush lead of 48 to 47 percent or other polls that show a landslide Bush lead of 56 to 39 percent.

Voss, Gelman, and King (1995) summarized and compared many of the methodological differences among polls conducted by eight polling organizations for the 1988 and 1992 presidential elections. Even though all eight organizations were studying the same phenomenon, there were enough differences in their approaches that polls conducted at the same time using identical questions might still get somewhat different results for reasons beyond sampling error. One feature Voss et al. examined was the sampling method—that is, how each organization generated a list of telephone numbers from which to sample. Once the sample was selected, polling organizations conducting telephone interviews still had to make choices about how to handle "busy signals, refusals, and calls answered by electronic devices, how to decide which household members are eligible to be interviewed, and how to select the respondent from among those eligible" (Voss, Gelman, and King 1995). The investigators also examined the various weighting schemes used by each survey operation to ensure a representative sample. Much of this methodological information is not readily available to the consumer of public opinion polls, and if it were many consumers would be overwhelmed by the volume of methodological detail. Yet these factors can make a difference. For example, the eight polling organizations analyzed by Voss et al. treated refusals quite differently. Some of the outfits did not call back after receiving a refusal from a potential respondent; other organizations did make callbacks. One organization generally tried to call back but with a different interviewer, but then gave up if a second refusal was obtained.

Thus conflicting poll results on the same topic may be less a matter of genuine substantive differences among the polls and more a function of differing methodological choices. This finding creates a challenge for the consumers of polls who are trying to bring some order to divergent results. Because poll consumers are likely unaware of the methodological and design differences among competing surveys, they often find it difficult to decide which poll results are the most compelling and how to reconcile conflicting results. When multiple polls on the same topic yield similar findings, citizens have greater confidence in the polls. But when polls disagree in their findings, citizens may find themselves perplexed about the sources of these differences. And when there is only one survey on a topic, citizens must hope that the substantive results obtained are genuine and not simply an artifact of the methodological choices made in the polling process. In short, because at times it is difficult to separate the substantive interpretation of the polling data from the methods and procedures that were used to collect the data in the first place, citizens will find it even more challenging to be informed consumers of polls.

9 Polling and Democracy

It's very clear
The polls are here to stay;
Not for a year,
But ever and a day.

The interviews and the questionnaires
And the pollsters that we know
Aren't just passing fancies—
Oh, my goodness, no!

The media
Love polls in every way.
It matters not
If polls have scant to say.

In time statistics may numb you,
Results may stun you.
Wait for another day,
For—the polls are here to stay.
—with apologies to George Gershwin

To death and taxes should be added public opinion polls, an integral and unavoidable part of American society today. Public opinion polling is a contemporary manifestation of classical democratic theory; it attests to the ability of the rational and wise citizen to make informed judgments on the major issues of the day. Polling makes it possible for political organizations to demonstrate that public opinion is on their side as they promote their ends. News organizations also are enamored of polling, in part because polls seem to elevate the citizen (and thus the media audience) into a more prominent political role; in effect, the polls transform the amorphous citizenry into a unified actor in the political process. Poll results that are not supportive of government actions provide the media with stories of conflict between the government and the people, just as points of contention between the president and the Congress or between the House and the Senate become a media focus.

As the technology of polling has been continually refined, upgraded, and made more available, many different kinds of groups, profit and nonprofit, public and private, have gained the ability to sponsor and conduct polls. These organizations can readily hire pollsters for surveys that will promote their aims, or, if they want to be absolutely sure that the poll results will be favorable, they can conduct their own surveys. Such self-serving polls are replete with loaded questions, skewed samples, and faulty interpretations similar to those associated with the surveys done by the Tobacco Institute and by the Michigan Tobacco and Candy Distributors and Vendors Association to try to head off higher cigarette taxes and antismoking legislation (Perlstadt and Holmes 1987; Morin 1989a).

Adding to the proliferation of surveys, the major news organizations have heavily invested in their own in-house polling operations. The resulting increase in the number of polls they conduct justifies their investment and enables them to keep up with the competition—that is, for certain news stories, such as presidential debates, a news organization that fails to conduct and report a poll on who wins is open to the criticism of incomplete news coverage. The unseemly contest among the media to be the first to "call" the outcome of particular elections illustrates how the pressures of competition and ratings promote the widespread use of polls. The media operate under the assumption that the public reactions to major news events are meaningful and that public opinion polls enhance the news value of a story.

How to Evaluate Polls: A Summary

Polls are a significant way for citizens to participate in society and to become informed about the relationship between the decisions of government and the opinions of the citizenry. As more organizations conduct polls and disseminate their results, whether to inform or to sway public opinion, citizens should become wary consumers, sensitive to the factors that can affect poll results. Gaining this sensitivity does not require familiarity with statistics or survey research experience. Consumers need only treat polls with a healthy skepticism and keep in mind the following questions as tools to evaluate poll results.

One basic question poll consumers should ask is whether a public opinion survey is measuring genuine opinions or nonattitudes. Are respondents likely to be informed and have genuine opinions about the topic? Or is the focus so esoteric that their responses reflect the social pressures of the interview situation, pressures that cause respondents to provide answers even when they have no real views on the subject at hand? The answers to questions about nonattitudes are not easy to find, for as Neuman (1986) argues, there is often not a clear demarcation between attitudes and nonattitudes. Indeed, Neuman coined the term *quasi-attitude* to designate something between an attitude and a nonattitude, and he points out that citizens' responses to survey questions are "a mixture of carefully thought-out, stable opinions, half-hearted opinions, misunderstandings, and purely random responses" (Neuman 1986, 184).

Another question to consider when evaluating polls concerns screening. Have the researchers made any effort to screen out respondents who lack genuine attitudes on the topic? Unfortunately, reports frequently omit information about screening questions and their effects—that is, often one cannot tell what proportion of the total sample answered a particular item and what proportion was screened out. To do a better job of reporting this information, news organizations should, at minimum, provide the number of respondents who answered a particular question. If this number is substantially smaller than the total sample size, they should explain the discrepancy.

When screening information is not presented, citizens are forced to form impressionistic judgments about whether the measurement of nonattitudes has been a problem in the survey. Of course, some issues of public policy that have been hotly debated and contested by political elites, even issues such as tax reform, may not be of much interest to many Americans and thus may be highly susceptible to the measurement of nonattitudes.

Citizens are in a better position to evaluate the potential effects of question wording than the presence of nonattitudes. Because the media usually provide the actual wording of questions, readers (or viewers) can judge whether any words or phrases in the questions are blatantly loaded, whether the alternatives are presented in a fair and balanced fashion, and whether a question accurately reflects the topic under study. If a report of a survey omits question wording, particularly on items dealing with controversial issues, the consumer should be wary and ask why.

Question wording is just one reason a complete questionnaire should be made available with a survey report. The questionnaire also is helpful when a survey contains many questions on a topic but reports the results for only one or two items. Without the complete questionnaire, a poll consumer is unable to assess whether the selective release of results has created any misleading impressions.

Another reason to examine the entire questionnaire is to assess the potential effects of question order. This is seldom possible, however, because press releases (other than those issued by news organizations) and news stories rarely include the complete survey form. Nevertheless, citizens should be aware that the way earlier questions are asked could affect responses to subsequent queries. This is a subtle phenomenon for which most citizens have little intuitive feel, yet the strategic placement of questions is one of the most effective ways to "doctor" a survey. While each individual question may be balanced and fair, the overall order of the questions could stimulate the specific responses preferred by the sponsor of the survey. One clue that this problem exists is the refusal of an organization, such as a political campaign team, to release the entire poll results.

The next question consumers should address is sampling. Although it is the most mysterious part of polling for most poll consumers, sampling is probably the least important for them to understand in detail. Sampling error is *not* where polls typically go astray. Reputable pollsters pick good samples and typically report sampling error and confidence levels so that citizens can form independent judgments about the significance of results. To make sure that a sample properly reflects the aims of a poll, a poll consumer should pay close attention to how the sample is defined. And certainly the consumer should confirm that the sample is a scientifically selected probability sample rather than a purposive one that an investigator selected for reasons of convenience.

One aspect of sampling that citizens should not overlook is the proportion of the total sample to which a particular finding applies. For a variety of reasons, such as the use of screening questions or the need to study analytically interesting subsets of the original sample, the proportion of respondents on which a result is based may be substantially smaller than the overall sample. Thus one should know not only the sampling error of the total sample but also the sampling error of the subsets.

Interviewers and interviewing are aspects of polling that can influence outcomes, but they are aspects not easily questioned. It is almost impossible for citizens to evaluate the effects of interviewing on poll results, because reports usually provide too little information about the interviewing process beyond the method of interviewing (for example, telephone or personal) and the dates of the interviews. The poll consumer normally assumes that an interview was performed competently, undoubtedly a safe assumption with reputable polling firms. But consumers should note that an interviewer bent on generating biased responses has many opportunities to achieve that end while asking questions. The best way for the poll consumer to gain some sense of potential interviewer effects is to be a poll respondent who carefully observes the performance of the interviewer—an opportunity that may or may not come one's way.

The final questions to ask when evaluating a poll relate to the end products, analyses and interpretation. Most citizens do not have access to raw poll data; instead they must rely on the analyses and interpretations provided by the media and other sources. But do these sources of information have a vested interest in a particular poll outcome? If so, poll consumers should scrutinize poll results even more carefully. For example, a poll sponsored by the insurance industry purporting to demonstrate that the liability insurance crisis is due to the rapacious behavior of trial lawyers should be viewed with greater skepticism than a similar poll sponsored by an organization with a less direct interest in the outcome. Likewise, election poll results released by a candidate should be viewed more cautiously than those released by a respected news organization.

After evaluating the source of a poll, the consumer then faces the more difficult task of ascertaining whether the pollster's conclusions follow from the data. This task is problematical, because often, as noted earlier, only a portion of the relevant evidence is presented in a news story or press release. Or a poll may have included many items on a particular topic, yet the report may present only a subset of those items. Without knowledge of the total questionnaire, one can only hope that the analyst has reported a representative set of results, or speculate on how different items on the same topic might have yielded different results. Likewise, reports might include results from the entire sample but not important variations in the responses of subsets of the sample. Lacking direct access to the data, the citizen is left to ponder how the overall results might differ within subsets of respondents.

Interpretation of a poll is not an objective enterprise; different analysts examining the same polling data may come to different conclusions. Although this outcome may occur for a variety of reasons, an obvious one is that analysts bring different values and perspectives to the interpretation of polls. Often there are no objective standards on what constitutes a high or low level of support on an issue; it may indeed be partly cloudy or partly sunny depending on one's perspective. Thus poll consumers should ask themselves whether they would necessarily come to the same conclusions on the basis of the data presented. Just because a poll is sponsored by a prestigious organization and conducted by a reputable firm does not mean that consumers have to defer automatically to the substantive conclusions of the sponsors. If a poll is conducted by an organization with an obvious vested interest in the results, then the poll consumer is certainly warranted in making an independent judgment.

Polls and Their Effect on the Political System

Do polls promote or hinder citizens' influence in their society? Is the overall effect of polls on the political system positive or negative? These questions continue to be vigorously debated. Writing in 1940, Cherington argued that polls enhanced the public's influence, because they provided a way for the voices of a representative cross-section of Americans to be heard; no longer would the views of a tiny segment of the population be the only ones to gain prominence. Meyer (1940) further argued that polls provided political decision makers with accurate information about the preferences of the citizenry, thereby enabling political leaders to resist the pressures of narrow groups pushing their own special agenda in the name of the broader public.

These arguments are still true today, yet the limitations inherent in polls as a mode of citizen influence must be recognized. First, as discussed in Chapter 1, the United States is a representative democracy that includes, in addition to elected representatives, a wide variety of organized groups trying to promote their own interests. Any assumption that the results of public opinion polls can be translated directly into public policy is naive. Moreover, it might not be desirable for public opinion polls to be routinely translated into public policy. After all, polls at times may tap only the most ephemeral and transitory of opinions. Little deliberation and thought may have gone into the responses offered by the public. And certainly the rich complexities of issues can never be captured in a public opinion poll as effectively as they are in a legislative debate or a committee hearing.

Second, even if the public's views as reflected in the polls are well formed, the implementation of those views might be objectionable. Polling often demonstrates that there is no majority view on an issue; opinion may be split in many different ways. The problem then becomes one of determining which subset of public opinion merits adoption. But automatically opting for the majority or plurality position would call into question such cherished values as the protection of minority rights. One can envisage situations in which the unqualified use of public opinion polls might threaten rather than enhance representative democracy and related values.

Third, a focus on poll results ignores the processes by which the public's opinions are formed and modified. For example, one factor that shapes popular opinion is the behavior of political elites. Thus when the White House orchestrates a massive public relations campaign laden with a nationally televised presidential address, subsequent highly publicized presidential travels, and the submission of a legislative package to Congress, it is not surprising to see public opinion shift in the direction intended by the White House. Public opinion is not always an independent expression of the public's views; it can be an opinion that has been formed, at least in part, from manipulation by elites.

Sometimes the behavior of political elites initiates a shift in opinion, and sometimes the behavior is the result of a shift. For example, the presi-

ROB ROGERS reprinted by permission of United Feature Syndicate, Inc.

dent may take the lead on an unpopular issue, as typically occurs during an international crisis. After the president delivers a major address to the nation, public opinion polls usually indicate an upsurge of support for the president's actions emerging from feelings of patriotism and a desire for national unity in times of crisis. Such was the case with the Persian Gulf crisis that arose in 1990.

Or the president may scramble to catch up with and then shape public opinion. This happened in the summer and fall of 1986 in response to Americans' heightened concern about the drug abuse problem. In response to the tragic deaths of famous athletes and increased media coverage of the drug crisis, a plurality of Americans cited drugs as the nation's most important problem in a CBS News/*New York Times* poll conducted in August 1986 (Clymer 1986d). Congress, particularly House Democrats, trying to get out in front on this issue, proposed a major antidrug offensive. The White House responded by taking the initiative from Congress: President Ronald Reagan offered his own proposals, and he and the first lady gave an unprecedented joint address on national television. Major new legislation was passed to address the drug problem. Then, in 1989 President George Bush declared a war on drugs and named a drug "czar" to coordinate federal initiatives. The president announced many antidrug proposals, which, according to the polls, were supported overwhelmingly by Americans even though they felt strongly that Bush's plan did not go far enough.

What do these examples have to say about citizen influence? Certainly, the drug example suggests the potency of popular opinion on issues that arouse the public. But even there the salience of the issue was very much a function of the behavior of media and political elites who brought it to the fore; the public responded to the issue but did not create it. The adoption of antidrug measures into law suggests that public opinion, once aroused, spurs government policy initiatives. But when the media and political leaders stop talking about drugs, the issue becomes less salient and recedes from popular consciousness, and citizens may have a misguided feeling that somehow the problem has been resolved.

The Persian Gulf example raises a different problem—namely, elites' misinterpretation (deliberate or unintentional) of what the polls are actually saying. Unfortunately, political leaders sometimes fail to recognize the limitations and circumstances of poll responses and automatically construe supportive poll results as ringing endorsements of a broad policy agenda. The tendency of Americans to rally around the leadership of the president during an international crisis should not be blindly interpreted as a popular mandate for particular policies, even though in the case of the Persian Gulf crisis citizen support for the president's policies at each stage of the crisis was genuine.

Ginsberg (1986) has argued that polling weakens the influence of public opinion in a democratic society. He asserts that there are many ways besides participating in a poll for citizens to express their opinions, such as demonstrations and protests, letter-writing campaigns, and interest group activities. But because polling is deemed to be scientific and representative of the broad public, it has dominated these other types of expression.

According to Ginsberg, four basic changes in the nature of public opinion are attributable to the increased frequency of polling. First, responding to a public opinion survey is an easier form of expression than writing a letter or participating in a protest—activities usually undertaken by citizens who are intensely committed to their positions. Anyone can respond to a poll question, whether or not the feelings about an issue are strong. Thus in a public opinion poll the intense opinions of a small minority can be submerged by the indifferent views of the sizable majority. Indeed, government leaders may try to dismiss the views of dissidents by citing polls that indicate that most Americans do not support the dissidents' position.

Second, polling changes public opinion from a *behavior,* such as letter writing or demonstrating, to an *attitude,* as revealed in a verbal response to a poll question. Ginsberg argues that public opinion expressed through polls is less threatening to political elites than are opinions expressed through behavioral mechanisms. Moreover, polls can inform leaders about dissidents' attitudes before they become behaviors. The information on attitudes gives government a kind of early warning as well as an opportunity to change attitudes either by seeking remedies to problems or by relying on public relations techniques to manipulate opinions.

Third, polls convert public opinion from a characteristic of groups to an attribute of individuals. This factor enables public officials to ignore group leaders and instead attend directly to the opinions of citizens. Unfortunately, this attention may effectively weaken individuals' political power, because organized activity, not individual activity, is the key to citizen influence in the United States. If government leaders are able to use the polls as an excuse to ignore group preferences, then citizen influence will be lessened.

Finally, polling reduces citizens' opportunities to set the political agenda. The topics of public opinion polls are those selected by the polls' sponsors rather than by the citizenry. Therefore, citizens lose control over the agenda of issues, and the agenda as revealed through the polls may differ in major ways from the issues that really matter to people.

Ginsberg's fundamental conclusion is that polling makes public opinion safer and less threatening for government. Opinions expressed through the polls place fewer demands and constraints on decision makers and provide political leaders with an enhanced ability "to anticipate, regulate, and manipulate popular attitudes" (Ginsberg 1986, 85). In short, Ginsberg's thesis is that the advent and growth of public opinion polling have been detrimental to citizen influence.

Ginsberg has raised some important issues about the dangers inherent in the proliferation of public opinion polling, even if one does not agree with all of his conclusions. Clearly, citizens must be on guard against allowing public opinion to become synonymous with the results of public opinion polls. Public opinion manifests itself in many ways, including those Ginsberg mentioned—protests, letter-writing campaigns, direct personal contact with decision makers, and many others. Political elites recognize the potential costs of ignoring these alternative forms of political expression, but it is critical that the media also recognize that polls are not the only legitimate expression of public opinion. Citizens too must avoid allowing a passive activity such as responding to a poll to replace more active modes of political participation.

Although there is evidence that direct electoral participation has declined in the United States, other group-based activities are on the rise. And if groups have the resources, they can use polls to promote their agenda when it differs from that of the political elites. Contrary to Ginsberg's assertion, polls need not make public opinion a property of individuals rather than groups. Polls can identify clusters of citizens (often defined by demographic characteristics) who do not share the prevailing views of the citizenry at large. For example, public opinion polls on the ultimate outcome of the 2000 presidential election campaign showed sharp differences between white and black Americans on the perceived legitimacy of the Bush victory and the overall fairness of the legal and election process. Whether Ginsberg's concerns are overstated or not, the polls are playing a growing role in American political life, in campaigns, in governance, and in popular discourse.

Observers have been concerned about the effect of polls not only on citizens' political clout but also on the performance of elected officeholders. More than fifty-five years ago Bernays (1945) warned that polls would dominate the political leadership and that decision makers would slavishly follow the polls in order to please the people and maintain popularity. The polls might even paralyze political leaders, preventing them from taking unpopular positions and from trying to educate the public on controversial issues. Political observers like Bernays still contemptuously deride politicians who run around with polls in their pockets, lacking the courage to act on their own convictions no matter what the polls say.

Some officeholders do blindly follow the polls, but today the greater concern is over those who use, abuse, manipulate, and misinterpret polls. In particular, presidents have increasingly tried to manage and manipulate public opinion. For example, Altschuler (1986) describes how President Lyndon Johnson tried to take the offensive when his poll ratings began to decline. To convince key elites that he was still strong, Johnson attacked the public polls, selectively leaked private polls, and tried to influence poll results and poll reporting by cultivating the acquaintance of the pollsters. Likewise, the Nixon administration tried to manipulate the Gallup and Harris polling organizations by influencing how they carried out and reported their national polls (Jacobs and Shapiro 1995–1996).

In-house polling was a central part of the skillful public relations efforts of the Reagan presidency (Blumenthal 1981). Writing about the Reagan administration, Beal and Hinckley (1984) argued that polls became more important after the presidential election than before it; indeed, polls were a much more important tool of governing than was commonly recognized. Likewise, polling was central to the operation of the Clinton White House. And if the presidency of George W. Bush at all resembles the Bush presidential campaign, polling and focus groups will be used extensively to test political messages and themes. Jacobs and Shapiro (1995) have shown how the polling operations of the Kennedy, Johnson, and especially the Nixon presidencies served as precursors for the contemporary White House use of polls. Certainly, no one would deny the president and other elected officials their pollsters. But the measure of an incumbent's performance should not simply be the degree of success achieved in shaping public opinion in particular ways.

One final effect of polls on the political system merits consideration: the contribution of polls to political discourse. Whether as topics of conversation or more structured exchange, the polls contribute to political debate. And because they often are cited as evidence in support of particular positions, they have become a central part of political discussion. But polls have more subtle effects; in particular, Americans' awareness of the attitudes of their fellow citizens as learned through the polls may alter their opinions and subsequent behaviors. This phenomenon has been explained in terms of the theories of the spiral of silence and pluralistic ignorance.

The spiral of silence thesis, developed by Noelle-Neumann (1974, 1977), argues that individuals desire to be respected and popular. To accomplish this, they become sensitive to prevailing opinions and how they are changing. If, on the one hand, individuals observe that their opinions seem to be in the minority and are losing support, they are less likely to express them publicly. Consequently, such opinions will seem to the individuals to be weaker than they actually are. On the other hand, if people perceive that their views are popular and on the ascendance, they are more likely to discuss them openly. Such opinions then gain more adherents and seem stronger than they actually are. Thus one opinion becomes established as dominant, while the other recedes to the background. Pluralistic ignorance refers to people's misperception of what other individuals and groups believe (O'Gorman 1975; O'Gorman and Garry 1976–1977). This, in turn, affects their own views and their willingness to express them. Lang and Lang (1984, 141) link the notions of pluralistic ignorance and the spiral of silence in a discussion of American racial attitudes:

> Typical of pluralistic ignorance has been the unwillingness of many whites to acknowledge their own antiblack prejudice, which they believe to contradict an accepted cultural ideal. As a way of justifying their own behavior, these whites often attribute such prejudice to other whites by saying "I wouldn't mind having a black neighbor except that my neighbors wouldn't stand for it."
>
> But what if such fears about their neighbors' reactions proved unjustified? What if polls showed an expressed readiness for a range of desegregation measures that these whites do not believe others are prepared to accept? Such a finding contrary to prevailing belief would be controversial. Where the real opinion lies may be less important than the change in perception of the climate of opinion. A definitive poll finding can destroy the premise that underlies the justification for behavior clearly at variance with professed ideals. In these circumstances a spiral of silence about the real opinion fosters a climate inhospitable to segregationist sentiment and drives it underground.

PEANUTS reprinted by permission of United Feature Syndicate, Inc.

As this example illustrates, public opinion polls provide citizens with a mechanism for knowing what their fellow citizens think and believe. This is especially important for those citizens who interact mostly with like-minded individuals and therefore may have little sense of the diversity of opinions that may exist on an issue. If the polls can accurately measure the underlying beliefs and values of the citizenry, then all citizens no longer have to be at the mercy of unrepresentative views that mistakenly are thought of as the majority voice. The polls can tell them a lot about themselves as part of American society, and this self-knowledge may foster a healthier and more open political debate. This being said, it also is possible that what they learn from polls about the views of their fellow citizens may surprise, shock, offend, and even divide them.

Conclusion

As the "Peanuts" cartoon makes clear, Americans have ambivalent feelings about the polls. Citizens resent the polls when surveys become too intrusive and seem to be telling citizens what they will be doing even before they do it. Yet Americans are also fascinated by what the polls tell them about themselves. They are suspicious because they seldom are respondents in a poll, yet they readily cite the surveys conducted by reputable and even disreputable pollsters. They complain about the pervasiveness of polls, yet they are apt to raise questions that can be answered only by polls.

Perhaps this ambivalence arises out of their uncertainty about just what goes into a poll. Polls are called scientific, yet citizens know that the polls are sometimes wrong. Politicians on one day swear by the polls; the next day they swear at them. Clearly, Americans are in a better position to evaluate polls if they understand the factors that can affect poll results. Thus the aim of this book has been to remove the mystery of public opinion research and to help the consumer come to terms with polls. Only then can citizens master the polls rather than be mastered by them.

References

Abrams, Floyd. 1985. "Press Practices, Polling Restrictions, Public Opinion and First Amendment Guarantees." *Public Opinion Quarterly* 49 (spring): 15–18.

Abramson, Paul R., Brian D. Silver, and Barbara Anderson. 1987. "The Effects of Question Order in Attitude Surveys: The Case of the SRC/CPS Citizen Duty Items." *American Journal of Political Science* 31 (November): 900–908.

———. 1990. "The Decline of Overtime Comparability in the National Election Studies." *Public Opinion Quarterly* 54 (summer): 177–190.

Akron Beacon Journal. 1994. "Foreign Poll-icy" (editorial), 8 May, A14.

Aldrich, John H., Richard Niemi, George Rabinowitz, and David Rohde. 1982. "The Measurement of Public Opinion about Public Policy: A Report on Some New Issue Question Formats." *American Journal of Political Science* 26 (May): 391–414.

Alpern, David M. 1986. "A *Newsweek* Poll: Sex Laws." *Newsweek,* 14 July, 38.

Altschuler, Bruce E. 1986. "Lyndon Johnson and the Public Polls." *Public Opinion Quarterly* 50 (fall): 285–299.

Alvarez, Lizette. 1998. "After Polling, G.O.P. Offers a Patients' Bill." *New York Times*, 16 July, A1, A20.

American Association for Public Opinion Research (AAPOR). 1986. "The Code."

———. 1997. *Best Practices for Survey and Public Opinion Research and Survey Practices AAPOR Condemns.*

———. 2000. "Standard Definitions: Final Disposition of Case Codes and Outcome Rates for Surveys."

Anderson, Barbara A., Brian D. Silver, and Paul R. Abramson. 1988. "The Effects of the Race of the Interviewer on Race-Related Attitudes of Black Respondents in SRC/CPS National Election Studies." *Public Opinion Quarterly* 52 (fall): 289–324.

Apple, R. W., Jr. 1986. "President Highly Popular in Poll; No Ideological Shift Is Discerned." *New York Times,* 28 January, A1, A14.

Aquilino, William S. 1994. "Interview Mode Effects in Surveys of Drug and Alcohol Use." *Public Opinion Quarterly* 58 (summer): 210–240.

Aquilino, William S., and Leonard A. Losciuto. 1990. "Effects of Interview Mode on Self-reported Drug Use." *Public Opinion Quarterly* 54 (fall): 362–395.

Asher, Herbert B. 1974a. "The Reliability of the Political Efficacy Items." *Political Methodology* 1 (May): 45–72.

————. 1974b. "Some Consequences of Measurement Error in Survey Data." *American Journal of Political Science* 18 (May): 469–485.

————. 1974c. "Some Problems in the Use of Multiple Indicators." Paper presented at the Conference on Design and Measurement Standards for Research in Political Science, Delevan, Wis., 13–15 May.

————. 1992. *Presidential Elections and American Politics.* 5th ed. Pacific Grove, Calif.: Brooks/Cole.

Baker, Russell. 1988. "Nearing Rope's End." *New York Times,* 9 November, 31.

————. 1990. "Paralyzing Polls." *New York Times,* 4 April, A15.

Balz, Dan. 1989. "About Those Predictions We Made Last Tuesday . . ." *Washington Post* National Weekly Edition, 13–19 November, 38.

Barnes, James A. 1993. "Polls Apart." *National Journal* 25 (10 July): 1750–1754.

Bauman, Sandra, and Susan Herbst. 1994. "Managing Perceptions of Public Opinion: Candidates' and Journalists' Reactions to the 1992 Polls." *Political Communication* 11: 133–144.

Baumgartner, Frank R., and Jack L. Walker. 1988. "Survey Research and Membership in Voluntary Associations." *American Journal of Political Science* 32 (November): 908–928.

Beal, Richard S., and Ronald H. Hinckley. 1984. "Presidential Decision Making and Opinion Polls." *Annals of the American Academy of Political and Social Science* 472 (March): 72–84.

Belden, Nancy. 2000. "Response Rate by Size of Place." E-mail communication, 8 May.

Berke, Richard L. 1996. "As Dole Weighs Tougher Image, Poll Finds He Already Has One." *New York Times,* 16 October, A1, A14.

Berke, Richard L., and Janet Elder. 2000. "Candidates Given High Marks in Poll on Fitness to Lead." *New York Times,* 3 October, A1, A18.

Bernays, Edward L. 1945. "Attitude Polls—Servants or Masters?" *Public Opinion Quarterly* 9 (fall): 264–268b.

Bernick, E. Lee, and David J. Pratto. 1994. "Improving the Quality of Information in Mail Surveys: Use of Special Mailings." *Social Science Quarterly* 75 (March): 212–219.

Bishop, George F. 1987. "Experiments with the Middle Response Alternative in Survey Questions." *Public Opinion Quarterly* 51 (summer): 220–232.

————. 1990. "Issue Involvement and Response Effects in Public Opinion Surveys." *Public Opinion Quarterly* 54 (summer): 209–218.

Bishop, George F., Robert W. Oldendick, and Alfred J. Tuchfarber. 1980. "Pseudo-Opinions on Public Affairs." *Public Opinion Quarterly* 44 (summer): 198–209.

————. 1982. "Political Information Processing: Question Order and Context Effects." *Political Behavior* 4: 177–200.

————. 1984. "What Must My Interest in Politics Be If I Just Told You 'I Don't Know'?" *Public Opinion Quarterly* 48 (summer): 510–519.

Black, Joan S. 1991. "Presidential Address: Trashing the Polls." *Public Opinion Quarterly* 55 (fall): 474–481.

Blumenthal, Sidney. 1981. "Marketing the President." *New York Times Magazine,* 13 September, 110–118.

Borrelli, Stephen, Brad Lockerbie, and Richard G. Niemi. 1989. "Why the Democrat-

Republican Partisan Gap Varies from Poll to Poll." *Public Opinion Quarterly* 51 (spring): 115–119.

Broder, David S. 1984. "The Needless Exit-Polls Battle." *Washington Post* National Weekly Edition, 2 January, 4.

Broh, C. Anthony. 1980. "Horse-Race Journalism: Reporting the Polls in the 1976 Presidential Election." *Public Opinion Quarterly* 44 (winter): 514–529.

Buchwald, Art. 1987. "The Poll Watcher's Compendium." *Washington Post,* 20 August, C1.

Budiansky, Stephen. 1995. "Consulting the Oracle." *U.S. News and World Report,* 4 December, 52, 53, 55, 58.

Busch, Ronald J., and Joel A. Lieske. 1985. "Does Time of Voting Affect Exit Poll Results?" *Public Opinion Quarterly* 49 (spring): 94–104.

Campbell, Bruce A. 1981. "Race-of-Interviewer Effects Among Southern Adolescents." *Public Opinion Quarterly* 45 (summer): 231–244.

Carter, Bill. 1996. "3 Networks Admit Error in Arizona Race Reports." *New York Times,* 29 February, A9.

Cherington, Paul T. 1940. "Opinion Polls as the Voice of Democracy." *Public Opinion Quarterly* 4 (June): 236–238.

Church, Allan H. 1993. "Estimating the Effect of Incentives on Mail Survey Response Rates: A Meta-Analysis." *Public Opinion Quarterly* 57 (spring): 62–79.

Clymer, Adam. 1985. "Pollsters Cite Surveys Indicating Confidence in Their Work." *New York Times,* 20 May, B7.

———. 1986a. "Most Blacks Back Reagan, Poll Finds." *New York Times,* 5 January, 20.

———. 1986b. "One Issue That Seems to Defy a Yes or No." *New York Times,* 23 February, 22-E.

———. 1986c. "A Poll Finds 77% in U.S. Approve Raid on Libya." *New York Times,* 17 April, A23.

———. 1986d. "Public Found Ready to Sacrifice in Drug Fight." *New York Times,* 2 September, D16.

———. 1996. "Phony Polls That Sling Mud Raise Questions over Ethics." *New York Times,* A1, A11.

Columbus Dispatch. 1994a. "This Is How Dispatch Poll Was Conducted." 11 September, 5B.

———. 1994b. "Random Sampling of Voters Used to Create Gallup Survey." 25 September, 2C.

Converse, Jean M. 1976–1977. "Predicting No Opinion in the Polls." *Public Opinion Quarterly* 40 (winter): 515–530.

Converse, Philip E. 1970. "Attitudes and Nonattitudes: Continuation of a Dialogue." In *The Quantitative Analysis of Social Problems,* edited by Edward Tufte. Reading, Mass.: Addison-Wesley, 168–189.

Coombs, Clyde H., and Lolagene C. Coombs. 1976–1977. "'Don't Know': Item Ambiguity or Respondent Uncertainty?" *Public Opinion Quarterly* 40 (winter): 497–514.

Cotter, Patrick R., Jeffrey Cohen, and Philip B. Coulter. 1982. "Race-of-Interviewer Effects on Telephone Interviews." *Public Opinion Quarterly* 46 (summer): 278–284.

Crespi, Irving. 1980. "Polls as Journalism." *Public Opinion Quarterly* 44 (winter): 462–476.

———. 1988. *Pre-election Polling: Sources of Accuracy and Error.* New York: Russell Sage Foundation.

Crossley, Archibald M., and Helen M. Crossley. 1969. "Polling in 1968." *Public Opinion Quarterly* 33 (spring): 1–16.

Curtin, Michael. 1986a. "Celeste Leading Rhodes 48% to 43%, with Kucinich Trailing." *Columbus Dispatch,* 10 August, 1-A.

———. 1986b. "Here Is How Poll Was Taken." *Columbus Dispatch,* 10 August, 8-E.

Davis, Darren W. 1997. "The Direction of Race of Interviewer Effects among African-Americans: Donning the Black Mask." *American Journal of Political Science* 41 (January): 309–322.

Day, Richard, and Kurt M. Becker. 1984. "Preelection Polling in the 1982 Illinois Gubernatorial Contest." *Public Opinion Quarterly* 48 (fall): 606–614.

de Bock, Harold. 1976. "Influence of In-State Election Poll Reports on Candidate Preference in 1972." *Journalism Quarterly* 53 (autumn): 457–462.

Delli Carpini, Michael X. 1984. "Scooping the Voters? The Consequences of the Networks' Early Call of the 1980 Presidential Race." *Journal of Politics* 46 (August): 866–885.

Delli Carpini, Michael X., and Scott Keeter. 1991. "Stability and Change in the U.S. Public's Knowledge of Politics." *Public Opinion Quarterly* 55 (winter): 583–612.

Dionne, E. J., Jr. 1980. "The Debate Decision Put Polls and Pollsters on the Firing Line." *New York Times,* 14 September, E3.

Dolnick, Edward. 1984. "Pollsters Are Asking: What's Wrong." *Columbus Dispatch,* 19 August, C1.

Dran, Ellen M., and Anne Hildreth. 1995. "What the Public Thinks about How We Know What It Is Thinking." *International Journal of Public Opinion Research* 7, no. 2: 128–144.

Elving, Ronald D. 1989. "Proliferation of Opinion Data Sparks Debate over Use." *Congressional Quarterly Weekly Report,* 19 August, 2187–2192.

———. 1992. "Polls Confound and Confuse in This Topsy-Turvy Year." *Congressional Quarterly Weekly Report,* 12 September, 2725–2727.

Epstein, Laurily, and Gerald Strom. 1984. "Survey Research and Election Night Projections." *Public Opinion* 7 (February/March): 48–50.

Erikson, Robert S. 1976. "The Relationship between Public Opinion and State Policy: A New Look Based on Some Forgotten Data." *American Journal of Political Science* 20 (February): 25–36.

Eubank, Robert B., and David John Gow. 1983. "The Pro-incumbent Bias in the 1978 and 1980 National Election Studies." *American Journal of Political Science* 27 (February): 122–139.

Faulkenberry, G. David, and Robert Mason. 1978. "Characteristics of Nonopinion and No Opinion Response Groups." *Public Opinion Quarterly* 42 (winter): 533–543.

Felson, Marcus, and Seymour Sudman. 1975. "The Accuracy of Presidential Preference Primary Polls." *Public Opinion Quarterly* 39 (summer): 232–236.

Finkel, Steven E., Thomas M. Guterbock, and Marian J. Borg. 1991. "Race-of-Interviewer Effects in a Preelection Poll: Virginia 1989." *Public Opinion Quarterly* 55 (fall): 313–330.

Fishkin, James. 1992. "A Response to Traugott." *Public Perspective* 3 (May/June): 29–30.

———. 1996. "Bringing Deliberation to Democracy." *Public Perspective* 7 (December/January): 1–4.

Fitzgerald, Michael R., Patra Rule, and Claudia Bryant. 1998. "Polls, Politics and the TV News: A Longitudinal Study of the Uses of Public Opinion Polling on the Evening News Broadcasts." Paper presented at the annual meeting of the American Political Science Association, Boston.

Fowler, Floyd Jackson, Jr. 1992. "How Unclear Terms Affect Survey Data." *Public Opinion Quarterly* 56 (summer): 218–231.

Fox, Richard J., Melvin R. Crask, and Jonghoon Kim. 1988. "Mail Survey Response Rate: A Metaanalysis of Selected Techniques for Inducing Response." *Public Opinion Quarterly* 52 (winter): 467–491.

Frey, James H. 1983. *Survey Research by Telephone.* Beverly Hills, Calif.: Sage Publications.

Gallup, George. 1947. "The Quintamensional Plan of Question Design." *Public Opinion Quarterly* 11 (fall): 385–393.

———. 1965–1966. "Polls and the Political Process—Past, Present, and Future." *Public Opinion Quarterly* 29 (winter): 544–549.

Galtung, Johan. 1969. *Theory and Methods of Social Research.* New York: Columbia University Press.

Gawiser, Sheldon R., and G. Evans Witt. *Twenty Questions a Journalist Should Ask About Poll Results.* 2d ed. National Council on Public Polls. <http://www.ncpp.org/qajsa.htm> (6 August 2000).

Genesys News. 1996. "Unlisted Numbers: What's *Really* Important?" (spring): 1–2.

Genesys Q & A. 1997. "Number Portability." January.

Gilljam, Mikael, and Donald Granberg. 1993. "Should We Take Don't Know for an Answer?" *Public Opinion Quarterly* 57 (fall): 348–357.

Ginsberg, Benjamin. 1986. *The Captive Public: How Mass Opinion Promotes State Power.* New York: Basic Books.

Glanz, James. 2000. "Poll Finds That Support Is Strong for Teaching 2 Origin Theories." *New York Times.* <http://www.nytimes.com/library/national/science/031100sci-evolution-poll.html> (13 March 2000).

Goldhaber, Gerald M. 1984. "A Pollster's Sampler." *Public Opinion* 7 (June/July): 47–50, 53.

Goldman, Ari L. 1991. "Portrait of Religion in U.S. Holds Dozens of Surprises." *New York Times,* 10 April, A1.

Gow, David John, and Robert B. Eubank. 1984. "The Pro-Incumbent Bias in the 1982 National Election Study." *American Journal of Political Science* 27 (February): 224–230.

Goyder, John. 1985. "Face-to-Face Interviews and Mailed Questionnaires: The Net Difference in Response Rate." *Public Opinion Quarterly* 49 (summer): 234–252.

Greenberg, Daniel S. 1980. "The Plague of Polling." *Washington Post,* 16 September, A17.

Grove, Lloyd. 1988a. "New Hampshire Confounded Most Pollsters." *Washington Post,* 18 February, A1.

————. 1988b. "Focus Groups: Politicians' Version of Taste-Testing." *Washington Post,* 6 July, A5.

Harker, Kathryn. 1998. "Asking About Income: A Preliminary Experiment." *National Network of State Polls Newsletter* 33 (summer).

Harmon, Amy. 1998. "Underreporting Found On Male Teen-Ager Sex." *New York Times,* 8 May, A14.

Harwood Group. 1993. "Meaningful Chaos: How People Form Relationships with Public Concerns." A report prepared for the Kettering Foundation, Dayton, Ohio.

Harwood, Richard. 1992. "The 'Bumps' and the Reality Are Polls Apart." *Cleveland Plain Dealer,* 29 August, 4C.

Hatchett, S., and H. Schuman. 1975–1976. "White Respondents and Race-of-Interviewer Effects." *Public Opinion Quarterly* 39 (winter): 523–528.

Herbers, John. 1982. "Polls Find Conflict in Views on Aid and Public Welfare." *New York Times,* 14 February, 19.

Hernandez, Debra Gersh. 1995. "Formats Recommended for Presidential Debates." Abridged from *Editor and Publisher,* 18 November.

Herrmann, Robert O., Arthur Sterngold, and Rex H. Warland. 1998. "Comparing Alternative Question Forms for Assessing Consumer Concerns." *Journal of Consumer Affairs* 32 (summer): 1329.

Huddy, Leonie, and John Bracciodieta. 1992. "The Effects of Interviewer Gender on the Survey Response." Paper presented at the annual meeting of the American Political Science Association, Chicago.

Hyman, Herbert H., and Paul B. Sheatsley. 1950. "The Current Status of American Public Opinion." In *The Teaching of Contemporary Affairs,* edited by J. C. Payne. Twenty-First Yearbook of the National Council of Social Studies. Washington, D.C.: National Council of Social Studies, National Education Association, 11–34.

Jackson, John. 1983. "Election Night Reporting and Voter Turnout." *American Journal of Political Science* 27 (November): 615–635.

Jackson, John, and William McGee. 1981. "Election Reporting and Voter Turnout." Report of the Center for Political Studies, University of Michigan, Ann Arbor.

Jacobs, Lawrence R., and Robert Y. Shapiro. 1995. "The Rise of Presidential Polling: The Nixon White House in Historical Perspective." *Public Opinion Quarterly* 59 (summer): 163–195.

————. 1995–1996. "Presidential Manipulation of Polls and Public Opinion: The Nixon Administration and the Pollsters." *Political Science Quarterly* 110 (winter).

James, Jeannine M., and Richard Bolstein. 1990. "The Effect of Monetary Incentives and Follow-Up Mailings on the Response Rate Quality in Mail Surveys." *Public Opinion Quarterly* 54 (fall): 346–361.

Johnson, Timothy P. 1989. "Obtaining Reports of Sensitive Behavior: A Comparison of Substance Use Reports from Telephone and Face-to-Face Interviews." *Social Science Quarterly* 70 (March): 174–183.

Kagay, Michael. 1998. "Stalking the Elusive Likely Voter." *New York Times,* 18 October, 5.

————. 1999. "A Sample of a Sample." *New York Times.* <http://www.nytimes.com/library/national/110499poll-watch.html> (9 November 1999).

Kagay, Michael R., with Janet Elder. 1992. "Numbers Are No Problem for Pollsters. Words Are." *New York Times,* 9 August.

Kane, Emily W., and Laura J. Macaulay. 1993. "Interview Gender and Gender Attitudes." *Public Opinion Quarterly* 57 (spring): 1–28.

Keene, Karyln H., and Victoria A. Sackett. 1981. "An Editors' Report on the Yankelovich, Skelly and White 'Mushiness Index.'" *Public Opinion* 4 (April/ May): 5051.

Kifner, John. 1994. "Pollster Finds Error on Holocaust Doubts." *New York Times,* 20 May, A6.

Kinder, Donald R., and Lynn M. Sanders. 1986. "Survey Questions and Political Culture: The Case of Whites' Response to Affirmative Action for Blacks." Paper presented at the annual meeting of the American Political Science Association, Washington, D.C., 28–31 August.

Knap, Ted. 1980. "League Weighs Anderson's Standing for Debates." *Columbus Citizen Journal,* 9 September, 7.

Koch, Nadine S. 1985. "Perceptions of Public Opinion Polls." Ph.D. diss., Ohio State University.

Kohut, Andrew. 1983. "Illinois Politics Confound the Polls." *Public Opinion* 5 (December/January): 42–43.

———. 1993. "The Vocal Minority in American Politics." *Times Mirror* Center for the People and the Press, Washington, D.C., 16 July.

Kolbert, Elizabeth. 1995. "Public Opinion Polls Swerve with the Turns of a Phrase." *New York Times,* 5 June, A1, C11.

Kostrzewa, John. 1986a. "Rhodes Has Solid Edge over Primary Rivals." *Akron Beacon Journal,* 23 March, A5.

Krosnick, Jon A. 1989. "Question Wording and Reports of Survey Results: The Case of Louis Harris and Associates and Aetna Life and Casualty." *Public Opinion Quarterly* 53 (spring): 107–113.

Krosnick, Jon A., and Duane F. Alwin. 1987. "An Evaluation of a Cognitive Theory of Response-Order Effects in Survey Measurement." *Public Opinion Quarterly* 51 (summer): 201–219.

Krosnick, Jon A., and Matthew K. Berent. 1993. "Comparisons of Party Identification and Policy Preferences: The Impact of Survey Question Format." *American Journal of Political Science* 37 (August): 941–964.

Krysan, Maria, Howard Schuman, Lesli Jo Scott, and Paul Beatty. 1994. "Response Rates and Response Content in Mail Surveys versus Face-to-Face Surveys." *Public Opinion Quarterly* 58 (fall): 410–430.

Ladd, Everett Carll. 1980. "Polling and the Press: The Clash of Institutional Imperatives." *Public Opinion Quarterly* 44 (winter): 574–584.

———. 1994. "The Holocaust Poll Error: A Modern Cautionary Tale." *Public Perspective* 5 (July/August): 3–5.

———. 1996. "The Election Polls: An American Waterloo." *Chronicle of Higher Education,* 22 November, A52.

Lang, Kurt, and Gladys Engel Lang. 1984. "The Impact of Polls on Public Opinion." *Annals of the American Academy of Political and Social Science* 472 (March): 130–142.

Lardner, George, Jr. 1985. "A Majority of the People Are Against the 'Star Wars' Defense Plan." *Washington Post* National Weekly Edition, 9 September, 37.

Lau, Richard R. 1994. "An Analysis of the Accuracy of 'Trial Heat' Polls during the 1992 Presidential Election." *Public Opinion Quarterly* 58 (spring): 2–20.

Laumann, Edward O., et al. 1994. *The Social Organization of Sexuality: Sexual Practices in the United States.* Chicago: University of Chicago Press.

Lavrakas, Paul J. 1986. "Surveying the Survey Differences." *Chicago Tribune,* 17 June, 12.

———. 1987. *Telephone Survey Methods: Sampling, Selection, and Supervision.* Newberry Park, Calif.: Sage Publications.

Lever, Janet. 1994. "Sexual Revelations." *The Advocate,* 23 August, 15–24.

Levy, Mark R. 1983. "The Methodology and Performance of Election Day Polls." *Public Opinion Quarterly* 47 (spring): 54–67.

Lewis, I. A., and William Schneider. 1982. "Is the Public Lying to the Pollsters?" *Public Opinion* 5 (April/May): 42–47.

Lipset, Seymour Martin. 1980. "Different Polls, Different Results in 1980 Politics." *Public Opinion* 3 (August/September): 19–20, 60.

Lockerbie, Brad, and Stephen A. Borrelli. 1990. "Question Wording and Public Support for Contra Aid, 1983–1986." *Public Opinion Quarterly* 54 (summer): 195–208.

Margolis, Michael. 1984. "Public Opinion, Polling, and Political Behavior." *Annals of the American Academy of Political and Social Science* 472 (March): 61–71.

Marsh, Catherine. 1984. "Do Polls Affect What People Think?" In *Surveying Subjective Phenomena,* edited by Charles F. Turner and Elizabeth Martin. New York: Russell Sage Foundation, 565–591.

Martin, Elizabeth. 1999. "Who Knows Who Lives Here? Within-Household Disagreements as a Source of Survey Coverage Error." *Public Opinion Quarterly* 63 (summer): 220–236.

Meislin, Richard J. 1987. "Racial Divisions Seen in Poll on Howard Beach Attack." *New York Times,* 8 January, 16.

Merkle, Daniel M. 1996. "The National Issues Convention Deliberative Poll." *Public Opinion Quarterly* 60 (winter): 588–619.

Meyer, Eugene. 1940. "A Newspaper Publisher Looks at the Polls." *Public Opinion Quarterly* 4 (June): 238–240.

Michael, Robert T., John H. Gagnon, Edward O. Laumann, and Gina Kolata. 1994. *Sex in America: A Definitive Survey.* Boston: Little, Brown.

Michaels, Stuart, and Alain Giami. 1999. "The Polls—Review: Sexual Acts and Sexual Relationships: Asking about Sex in Surveys." *Public Opinion Quarterly* 63 (fall): 401–420.

Miller, M. Mark, and Robert Hurd. 1982. "Conformity to AAPOR Standards in Newspaper Reporting of Public Opinion Polls." *Public Opinion Quarterly* 46 (summer): 243–249.

Miller, Tim. 1986. "Statewide Poll Has Rhodes Far Ahead in GOP." *Dayton Daily News,* 23 March, 1.

Mills, Kim I. 1993. "Cheers' Fans Wanted to See Sam Malone Single." *Akron Beacon Journal,* 2 May, A13.

Mitofsky, Warren J. 1992. "What Went Wrong with Exit Polling in New Hampshire." *Public Perspective* 3 (March/April): 17.

———. 1996. "It's Not Deliberative and It's Not a Poll." *Public Perspective* 7 (December/January): 4–6.

———. 1999. "Pollsters.com." *Public Perspective* 10 (June/July): 24–26.

Moore, David W., and Frank Newport. 1994. "Misreading the Public: The Case of the Holocaust Poll." *Public Perspective* 5 (March/April): 28–29.

Morin, Richard. 1987. "Pay Your Taxes and You, Too, Can Give a Useless Opinion." *Washington Post* National Weekly Edition, 7 December, 38.

———. 1988a. "What Went Wrong?" *Washington Post* National Weekly Edition, 22–28 February, 37.

———. 1988b. "Tracking a Formula for Success." *Washington Post* National Weekly Edition, 25 April–1 May, 37.

———. 1988c. "Behind the Numbers: Confessions of a Pollster." *Washington Post,* 16 October, C1, C4.

———. 1989a. "Where There's a Smoking Poll, There's Smoke." *Washington Post* National Weekly Edition, 30 January–5 February, 37.

———. 1989b. "The Answer May Depend on Who Asked the Question." *Washington Post* National Weekly Edition, 6–21 November, 38.

———. 1990. "Women Asking Women about Men Asking Women About Men." *Washington Post* National Weekly Edition, 15–21 January, 37.

———. 1991. "2 Ways of Reading the Public's Lips on Gulf Policy." *Washington Post,* 14 January, A9.

———. 1992a. "Another Contribution to SLOPpy Journalism." *Washington Post* National Weekly Edition, 10–16 February, 37.

———. 1992b. "This Time in New Hampshire, A Somewhat More Graceful Exit." *Washington Post* National Weekly Edition, 24 February–1 March, 37.

———. 1992c. "Surveying the Surveyors." *Washington Post* National Weekly Edition, 2–8 March, 37.

———. 1992d. "Polling '92: Who's on First." *Washington Post,* 6 June, A1.

———. 1992e. "Putting the Focus on Presidents and Peanut Butter." *Washington Post* National Weekly Edition, 19–25 October, 37.

———. 1993a. "Getting a Handle on the Religious Right." *Washington Post* National Weekly Edition, 5–11 April, 37.

———. 1993b. "Economics: A Puzzle to Many." *Washington Post* National Weekly Edition, 31 May–6 June, 37.

———. 1993c. "Wrong About the Religious Right." *Washington Post* National Weekly Edition, 1–7 November, 37.

———. 1993d. "Ask and You Might Deceive." *Washington Post* National Weekly Edition, 6–12 December, 37.

———. 1994a. "Public Enemy No. 1: Crime." *Washington Post* National Weekly Edition, 24–30 January, 37.

———. 1994b. "Don't Know Much About Health Care Reform." *Washington Post* National Weekly Edition, 14–20 March, 37.

———. 1994c. "The Answer Depends on the Question." *Washington Post* National Weekly Edition, 21–27 March, 37.

———. 1994d. "From Confusing Questions, Confusing Answers." *Washington Post* National Weekly Edition, 18–24 July, 37.

———. 1994e. "When the Data Tell Shockingly Different Stories." *Washington Post* National Weekly Edition, 8–14 August, 37.

———. 1995a. "What Informed Public Opinion?" *Washington Post* National Weekly Edition, 26 June–2 July, 34.

————. 1995b. "How Perceptions of Race Can Affect Poll Results." *Washington Post* National Weekly Edition, 26 June–2 July, 34.

————. 1995c. "Medicare Changes Get a Jaundiced Look." *Washington Post* National Weekly Edition, 10–16 July, 37.

————. 1995d. "Reading between the Numbers." *Washington Post* National Weekly Edition, 4–10 September, 30.

————. 1995e. "How Do People Really Feel about Bosnia?" *Washington Post* National Weekly Edition, 4–10 December, 32.

————. 1996a. "What Nature Never Intended." *Washington Post* National Weekly Edition, 8–14 July, 34.

————. 1996b. "Taking the Pulse on Pulse-Takers," *Washington Post* National Weekly Edition, 23–29 September, 37.

————. 1997a. "Right on the Money." *Washington Post* National Weekly Edition, 3 March, 3.

————. 1997b. "Getting Behind a Bigger NATO." *Washington Post* National Weekly Edition, 24 March, 35.

————. 1997c. "Warts and All." *Washington Post* National Weekly Edition, 13 October, 34.

————. 1997d. "Public Policy Surveys: Lite and Less Filling." *Washington Post* National Weekly Edition, 10 November, 35.

————. 1998a. "The Pollsters' Greatest Enemy: Themselves." *Washington Post* National Weekly Edition, 23 February, 35.

————. 1998b. "Missing the Story on Bosnia." *Washington Post* National Weekly Edition, 27 April, 35.

————. 1999a. "It's All in the Wording." *Washington Post* National Weekly Edition, 18 January, 21.

————. 1999b. "Believe Them, or Not." *Washington Post* National Weekly Edition, 12 July, 34.

————. 2000a. "Flaming the Messenger." *Washington Post* National Weekly Edition, 28 February, 34.

————. 2000b. "Will Traditional Polls Go the Way of the Dinosaur?" *Washington Post* National Weekly Edition, 15 May, 34.

Morin, Richard, and John M. Berry. 1996. "Economic Anxieties." *Washington Post* National Weekly Edition, 4–10 November, 6–7.

Morin, Richard, and Claudia Deane. 2000. "What's Up With Gallup?" *Washington Post* National Weekly Edition, 16 October, 34.

Munro, Ralph, and Curtis B. Gans. 1988. "Let's Say No to Exit Polls." *New York Times,* 4 November, 27.

Nagourney, Adam. 2000. "Sound Bites Over Jerusalem." *New York Times Magazine,* 25 April, 42–61,70.

National Council on Public Polls (NCPP). Undated. "Statement About Internet Polls." <http://www.ncpp.org/internet.htm> (6 August 2000).

————. 1995. "A Press Warning from the National Council on Public Polls." Press release, 22 May.

————. 2000. "Errors Associated with 'Instant' and Overnight Polls." Polling Review Board, 14 August.

Neuman, W. Russell. 1986. *The Paradox of Mass Politics: Knowledge and Opinion in the American Electorate.* Cambridge: Harvard University Press.

Newport, Frank. 1997. "The Pre-election Polls Performed Well in '96." *Public Perspective* 8 (December/January): 50–51.

Noelle-Neumann, Elisabeth. 1974. "The Spiral of Silence: A Theory of Public Opinion." *Journal of Communication* 24 (spring): 43–51.

———. 1977. "Turbulence in the Climate of Opinion: Methodological Applications of the Spiral of Silence Theory." *Public Opinion Quarterly* 41 (summer): 143–158.

Norpoth, Helmut, and Milton Lodge. 1985. "The Difference between Attitudes and Non-attitudes in the Mass Public: Just Measurement?" *American Journal of Political Science* 29 (May): 291–307.

O'Gorman, Hubert J. 1975. "Pluralistic Ignorance and White Estimates of White Support for Racial Segregation." *Public Opinion Quarterly* 39 (fall): 313–330.

O'Gorman, Hubert J., and Stephen L. Garry. 1976–1977. "Pluralistic Ignorance—A Replication and Extension." *Public Opinion Quarterly* 40 (winter): 449–458.

O'Neill, Harry W. 1997. "An Honorable Profession, Warts and All." Comments delivered on the occasion of receiving the 1997 Award for Outstanding Achievement, New York Chapter, American Association for Public Opinion Research, June 18, 1997. <http://www.mediastudies.org/ho.html> (6 August 2000).

Oreskes, Michael. 1984. "Pollsters Offer Reasons for Disparity in Results." *New York Times,* 20 October, A8.

———. 1990. "Drug War Underlines Fickleness of Public." *New York Times,* 6 September, A22.

Orton, Barry. 1982. "Phony Polls: The Pollster's Nemesis." *Public Opinion* 5 (June/July): 56–60.

Page, Benjamin I., and Robert Y. Shapiro. 1983. "Effects of Public Opinion on Policy." *American Political Science Review* 77 (March): 175–190.

———. 1992. *The Rational Public: Fifty Years of Trends in Americans' Policy Preferences.* Chicago: University of Chicago Press.

Paletz, David L., Jonathan Y. Short, Helen Baker, Barbara Cookman Campbell, Richard J. Cooper, and Rochelle M. Oeslander. 1980. "Polls in the Media: Content, Credibility, and Consequences." *Public Opinion Quarterly* 44 (winter): 495–513.

Payne, Stanley L. 1951. *The Art of Asking Questions.* Princeton: Princeton University Press.

Perlstadt, Harry, and Russell E. Holmes. 1987. "The Role of Public Opinion Polling in Health Legislation." *American Journal of Public Health* 77 (May): 612–614.

Perry, Paul. 1979. "Certain Problems in Election Survey Methodology." *Public Opinion Quarterly* 43 (fall): 312–325.

Peterson, Robert A. 1984. "Asking the Age Question: A Research Note." *Public Opinion Quarterly* 48 (spring): 379–383.

Pew Research Center for the People and the Press. 1998. "Conservative Opinions Not Underestimated, But Racial Hostility Missed." <http://www.people-press.org/resprpt.htm> (14 August 2000).

Phillips, Kevin P. 1976. "Polls Used to Reflect Electability." *Columbus Dispatch,* 19 July, B2.

———. 1981. "Polls Are Too Broad in Analysis Divisions." *Columbus Dispatch,* 8 September, B3.

Pianin, Eric, and Mario Brossard. 1997. "Hands Off Social Security and Medicare." *Washington Post* National Weekly Edition, 7 April, 35.

Piekarski, Linda B. 1989. "Choosing between Directory Listed and Random Digit Dialing in Light of New Demographic Findings." Paper presented at the AAPOR Conference, St. Petersburg, Fla.

Piekarski, Linda, Gwen Kaplan, and Jessica Prestgaard. 1999. "Telephony and Telephone Sampling: The Dynamics of Change." <http://www.worldopinion.com/latenews.taf?f=d&news=3966> (26 December 1999).

Presser, Stanley, and Howard Schuman. 1980. "The Measurement of a Middle Position in Attitude Surveys." *Public Opinion Quarterly* 44 (spring): 70–85.

Public Opinion Quarterly. 1987. Fiftieth Anniversary Issue. 51, supplement (winter): S1–S191.

Reese, Stephen D., Wayne A. Danielson, Pamela J. Shoemaker, Tsan-Kuo Chang, and Huei-Ling Hsu. 1986. "Ethnicity-of-Interviewer Effects among Mexican-Americans and Anglos." *Public Opinion Quarterly* 50 (winter): 563–572.

Rivlin, Allan. 1999. "First, Kill All the Pollsters." *National Journal*, 9 November, 2572–2573.

Robinson, Michael J., and Margaret A. Sheehan. 1983. *Over the Wire and on TV: CBS and UPI in Campaign '80.* New York: Russell Sage Foundation.

Roper, Burns W. 1985. "Early Election Calls: The Larger Dangers." *Public Opinion Quarterly* 49 (spring): 5–9.

Rosenbaum, David E. 1997. "Americans Want a Right to Die. Or So They Think." *New York Times,* 8 June, E3.

Rothenberg, Stuart, ed. 1983. *Political Report* 6 (5 August).

———. 1985. *Political Report* 8 (25 October).

Rowland, Darrel. 1998. "Abortion Poll: Government Should Have No Say in Decision." *Columbus Dispatch.* 22 May, 1E–2E.

———. 1999. "Poll Indicates Support for Concealed-Gun Bill." *Columbus Dispatch.* 7 November, 4A.

Rubin, Alissa J. 2000. "Americans Narrowing Support for Abortion." *Los Angeles Times.* 18 June.

Salwen, Michael B. 1985a. "Does Poll Coverage Improve as Presidential Vote Nears?" *Journalism Quarterly* 62 (winter): 887–891.

———. 1985b. "The Reporting of Public Opinion Polls During Presidential Years, 1968–1984." *Journalism Quarterly* 62 (summer): 272–277.

Schneider, William. 1989. "One Poll May Be Worse than None." *National Journal* 2 (December): 2970.

———. 1996. "How to Read a Trial Heat Poll." Transcript, CNN, "Inside Politics Extra," 12 May. <http://www.cnn.com/ALLPOLITICS/>.

Schuman, Howard, and Jean M. Converse. 1971. "The Effects of Black and White Interviewers on Black Responses in 1968." *Public Opinion Quarterly* 35 (spring): 44–68.

Schuman, Howard, and Stanley Presser. 1977. "Question Wording as an Independent Variable in Survey Analysis." *Sociological Methods and Research* 6 (November): 151–170.

———. 1981. *Questions and Answers in Attitude Surveys: Experiments on Question Form, Wording, and Context.* New York: Academic Press.

Schuman, Howard, Graham Kalton, and Jacob Ludwig. 1983. "Context and Contiguity in Survey Questionnaires." *Public Opinion Quarterly* 47 (spring): 112–115.

Schuman, Howard, Stanley Presser, and Jacob Ludwig. 1981. "Context Effects on Survey Responses to Questions About Abortion." *Public Opinion Quarterly* 45 (summer): 216–223.

Schwarz, Norbert, and Hans J. Hippler. 1995. "Subsequent Questions May Influence Answers to Preceding Questions in Mail Surveys." *Public Opinion Quarterly* 59 (spring): 93–97.

Sheler, Jeffrey L. 2000. "Hell Hath No Fury." *U.S. News and World Report,* 31 January, 45–50.

Shipler, David K. 1986. "Public Is Confused on Contra Aid Issue, Poll Indicates." *New York Times,* 15 April, 4.

Shlapentokh, Vladmir. 1994. "The 1993 Russian Election Polls." *Public Opinion Quarterly* 58 (winter): 579–602.

Sigel, Roberta S. 1996. *Ambition and Accommodation: How Women View Gender Relations.* Chicago: University of Chicago Press.

Sigelman, Lee. 1981. "Question-Order Effects on Presidential Popularity." *Public Opinion Quarterly* 45 (summer): 199–207.

Smith, Andrew E., and Clark Hubbard. 2000. "First in the Nation: Lessons Learned from New Hampshire." *Public Perspective* (May/June): 46–49.

Smith, Ted. J., III, and J. Michael Hogan. 1987. "Public Opinion and the Panama Canal Treaties of 1977." *Public Opinion Quarterly* 51 (spring): 5–30.

Smith, Ted J., III, and Derek O. Verrall. 1985. "A Critical Analysis of Australian Television Coverage of Election Opinion Polls." *Public Opinion Quarterly* 49 (spring): 58–79.

Smith, Tom W. 1984. "Nonattitudes: A Review and Evaluation." In *Surveying Subjective Phenomena,* vol. 2. Edited by Charles F. Turner and Elizabeth Martin. New York: Russell Sage Foundation, 215–255.

———. 1987. "How Comics and Cartoons View Public Opinion Surveys." *Journalism Quarterly* 64: 208–211.

———. 1988. "Speaking Out: Hite vs. Abby in Methodological Messes." *AAPOR News* (spring): 3–4.

———. 1993. "Actual Trends or Measurement Artifacts? A Review of Three Studies of Anti-Semitism." *Public Opinion Quarterly* 57 (fall): 380–393.

Sniderman, Paul, Edward Carmines, Philip Tetlock, and Anthony Tyler. 1993. In Richard Morin, "Racism Knows No Party Lines." *Washington Post* National Weekly Edition, 20–26 September, 37.

Specter, Michael. 1996. "Russian Pollsters Are Seldom Right." *New York Times,* 15 May, A1, A4.

Spolar, Christine. 1997. "Not Everyone Is Hot to Trot for NATO." *Washington Post* National Weekly Edition, 30 June, 8–9.

Squire, Peverill. 1988. "Why the 1936 *Literary Digest* Poll Failed." *Public Opinion Quarterly* 52 (spring): 125–133.

Squires, Sally, and Richard Morin. 1987. "What Is This Thing Called Love?" *Washington Post* National Weekly Edition, 16 November, 37.

Stevenson, Richard W. 2000. "Tuesday's Big Test: How Deep in the Heart of Taxes." *New York Times,* 30 January, 3.

Sudman, Seymour. 1986. "Do Exit Polls Influence Voting Behavior?" *Public Opinion Quarterly* 50 (fall): 331–339.

Survey Sampling Inc. 1997. "Sacramento Is Most Unlisted." *The Frame* (March): 1, 3.

Sussman, Barry. 1984a. "Why Both Parties Are Courting 50 Million Opinion-Switchers." *Washington Post* National Weekly Edition, 16 January, 37.

———. 1984b. "Do-It-Yourself Tax Reform: Many Think Cheating Is Okay." *Washington Post* National Weekly Edition, 28 May, 36.

———. 1985a. "To Understand These Polls, You Have to Read the Fine Print." *Washington Post* National Weekly Edition, 4 March, 37.

———. 1985b. "Reagan's Support on Issues Relies Heavily on the Uninformed." *Washington Post* National Weekly Edition, 1 April, 37.

———. 1985c. "Americans Prefer Tax Cheating to Being Paid to Inform the IRS." *Washington Post* National Weekly Edition, 13 May, 37.

———. 1985d. "Social Security and the Young." *Washington Post* National Weekly Edition, 27 May, 37.

———. 1985e. "Pollsters Cheer Up about Public's Opinions of Polls." *Washington Post* National Weekly Edition, 3 June, 37.

———. 1985f. "Do Pre-election Polls Influence People to Switch Their Votes?" *Washington Post* National Weekly Edition, 10 June, 37.

———. 1985g. "These Polls Are Part Public Opinion, Part Public Relations." *Washington Post* National Weekly Edition, 4 November, 37.

———. 1986a. "Do Blacks Approve of Reagan? It Depends on Who's Asking." *Washington Post* National Weekly Edition, 10 February, 37.

———. 1986b. "It's Wrong to Assume that School Busing Is Wildly Unpopular." *Washington Post* National Weekly Edition, 10 March, 37.

———. 1986c. "With Pornography, It All Depends on Who's Doing the Looking." *Washington Post* National Weekly Edition, 24 March, 37.

Swift, Al. 1985. "The Congressional Concern About Early Calls." *Public Opinion Quarterly* 49 (spring): 2–5.

Tanur, Judith M. 1994. "The Trustworthiness of Survey Research." *Chronicle of Higher Education,* 25 May, B1–B3.

Taylor, Humphrey, and George Terhanian. 1999. "Head Days Are Here Again: Online Polling Is Rapidly Coming of Age." *Public Perspective* (June/July): 2023.

Taylor, Marylee C. 1983. "The Black-and-White Model of Attitude Stability: A Latent Class Examination of Opinion and Nonopinion in the American Public." *American Journal of Sociology* 89 (September): 373–401.

Tourangeau, Roger, and Tom W. Smith. 1996. "Asking Sensitive Questions: The Impact of Data Collection Mode, Question Format, and Question Context." *Public Opinion Quarterly* 60 (summer): 181–227.

Traugott, Michael W. 1987. "The Importance of Persistence in Respondent Selection for Preelection Surveys." *Public Opinion Quarterly* 51 (spring): 48–57.

———. 1992. "A General Good Showing, But Much Work Remains to Be Done." *Public Perspective* 4 (November/December): 14–16.

Traugott, Michael W., and Vincent Price. 1992. "Exit Polls in the 1989 Virginia Gubernatorial Race: Where Did They Go Wrong?" *Public Opinion Quarterly* 56 (summer): 245–253.

Visser, Penny S., Jon A Krosnick, Jesse Marquette, and Michael Curtin. 1996. "Mail Surveys for Election Forecasting: An Evaluation of the *Columbus Dispatch* Poll." *Public Opinion Quarterly* 59 (spring): 98–132.

Voss, D. Stephen, Andrew Gelman, and Gary King. 1995. "Preelection Survey Methodology: Details from Eight Polling Organizations, 1988 and 1992." *Public Opinion Quarterly* 59 (spring): 98–132.

Wanke, Michaela. 1996. "Comparative Judgements as a Function of the Direction of Comparison versus Word Order." *Public Opinion Quarterly* 60 (fall): 400–409.

Wanke, Michaela, Norbert Schwarz, and Elisabeth Noelle-Neumann. 1995. "Asking Comparative Questions: The Impact of the Direction of the Comparison." *Public Opinion Quarterly* 59 (fall): 347–352.

Washington Post. 1985. "A Grain of Salt Please" (editorial). 17 June.

Weeks, Michael F., and R. Paul Moore. 1981. "Ethnicity-of-Interviewer Effects on Ethnic Respondents." *Public Opinion Quarterly* 45 (summer): 245–249.

Werner, Jan. 2000. "Misleading Survey Reporting by NY Times." E-mail communication, 11 March.

Wiese, Cheryl J. 1998. "Refusal Conversion: What Is Gained?" *National Network of State Polls Newsletter* 32 (spring).

Williams, Dennis A. 1979. "A New Racial Poll." *Newsweek,* 26 February, 48, 53.

Winkler, Karen J. 1996. "Organizer Hails Results of Political-Science Experiment." *Chronicle of Higher Education,* 2 February, A13.

Wright, Debra L., William S. Aquilino, and Andrew J. Supple. 1998. "A Comparison of Computer-Assisted and Paper-and-Pencil Self-Administered Questionnaires in a Survey on Smoking, Alcohol, and Drug Use." *Public Opinion Quarterly* 62 (fall): 331–353.

Wright, James D. 1981. "Public Opinion and Gun Control: A Comparison of Results from Two Recent National Surveys." *Annals of the American Academy of Political and Social Science* 455 (May): 24–39.

Yammarino, Francis J., Steven J. Skinner, and Terry L. Childers. 1991. "Understanding Mail Survey Response Behavior: A Meta-Analysis." *Public Opinion Quarterly* 55 (winter): 613–639.

Zaller, John, and Stanley Feldman. 1992. "A Simple Theory of the Survey Response: Answering Questions versus Revealing Preferences." *American Journal of Political Science* 36 (August): 579–616.

Web Sites

Media

www.abc.com	ABC
www.cbs.com	CBS
www.nbc.com	NBC
www.cnn.com	CNN
www.msnbc.com	MSNBC
www.nytimes.com	*New York Times*
www.washingtonpost.com	*Washington Post*
www.latimes.com	*Los Angeles Times*
www.usatoday.com	*USA Today*
www.nationaljournal.com	*National Journal*
www.wire.ap.org	Associated Press

Organizations

www.census.gov	U.S. Census Bureau
www.gallup.com	Gallup Organization
www.louisharris.com	Harris Interactive
www.zogby.com	Zogby International
www.ropercenter.uconn.edu	Roper Center
www.pollingreport.com	The Polling Report
www.aapor.org	American Association for Public Opinion Research
www.ncpp.org	National Council on Public Polls
www.people-press.org	Pew Research Center for the People and the Press
www.umich.edu/~nes	National Election Studies
www.epinet.org/pulse/pulse/html	Economic Policy Institute—The Pulse
www.ama.org	American Marketing Association
www.casro.org	Council of American Survey Organizations
www.irss.unc.edu/nnsp	National Network of State Polls
www.cmor.org	Council for Marketing and Opinion Research
www.worldopinion.com	World Opinion

Miscellaneous

www.voter.com	Voter.com
www.vanishingvoter.org	The Vanishing Voter Project
www.votesmart.com	VoteSmart

Index

ABC News polls: Bosnia, 52–53; exit polls, 129–130; methodology reports, 74; pseudo-types, 11, 108–109, 137; *Washington Post* relationship, 3

ABC News/Station WLS poll, 74

ABC News/*Washington Post* polls: military strength, 35; Persian Gulf crisis, 154, 155, 157; pornography, 166; presidential popularity, 57; public affairs attentiveness, 171–172; race-related, 91; Reagan approval, 72, 73; Reagan's health, 4; Reagan versus Mondale, 176; school busing, 167–168; Social Security, 168; Strategic Defense Initiative, 75–76; voter choice and polls, 147–148; voter turnout estimation methods, 145

Abortion polls, 59, 89–90, 104–105, 161

Abrams, Floyd, 128

Abramson, Paul R., 59–60, 91, 164

Accuracy in predicting vote results: economic/political climate and, 146–147; failure overview, 70–71, 125–126, 139–142; timing influences, 141–142; turnout estimation and, 144–146; undecided voter treatment and, 142–144

Action on Smoking and Health, 10

Adultery survey, 12–13

Advisory Commission on Intergovernmental Relations, 48

The Advocate, 13, 162

Aetna Life and Casualty, 107

Affirmative action question, 60

AFL-CIO meeting story, 62

African Americans. *See* Race-related polls; Subgroups and poll analysis

Age measurement questions, 47

AIDS in children poll, 173

Akron Beacon Journal, 23

Alcohol abuse polls, 83, 85–86, 94

Aldrich, John H., 30

Alexander, Lamar, 16

Alpern, David M., 152–153

Altschuler, Bruce E., 188

Alvarez, Lizette, 23

Alwin, Matthew K., 37

Ambiguity in questions, 47–48

American Association for Public Opinion Research (AAPOR): disclosure standards, 19, 96–98, 99; push polling, 19, 130; rebuke of Luntz, 19; response rate information, 77

American Association of Political Consultants, 131

American Farmland Trust, 7, 10

American Foundation for AIDS Research, 46

American Immigration Council, 10

American Jewish Committee on the Holocaust, 48–49

American National Election Studies (ANES), 29–34, 58, 89

Analysis of polls: interpreting the data, 173–176, 183; selection of topics/questions, 151–163; sources of conflicting results, 176–178; subgroup patterns, 165–173; subjective nature, 150, 182–183; trend examination, 163–165